Kevin Trudeau's
Mega Memory™

Kevin Trudeau's Mega Memory™

How to Release Your

Superpower Memory in

30 Minutes or Less a Day

Kevin Trudeau

William Morrow and Company, Inc.
New York

This book is not intended to replace the services of a trained health professional. All matters regarding your health require medical supervision. You should consult your physician before adopting the procedures in this book. Any applications of the treatments set forth in this book are at the reader's discretion.

Library of Congress Cataloging-in-Publication Data

Trudeau, Kevin.
   [Mega Memory]
   Kevin Trudeau's Mega Memory : how to release your superpower
memory in 30 minutes or less a day / Kevin Trudeau.
      p.   cm.
   ISBN 0-688-13582-X
   1. Mnemonics.   I. Title.
BF385.T78   1995
153.1'4—dc20
                                                                    95-16470
                                                                    CIP

Printed in the United States of America
FIRST EDITION
1   2   3   4   5   6   7   8   9   10
BOOK DESIGN BY LAURA HOUGH

This book is dedicated to all of the "memory masters" I have had the pleasure and honor of being associated with over the last fifteen years:

Michael Van Masters
J. Mark Dufner
Fred Van Liew
Blaine Athorn
Jeremy Haworth
Dave Coffill
Matthew Goerke

It was their sharing and willingness to learn that helped me become better!

Acknowledgments

First, thanks go to Michael Van Masters for his determination and courage in the pursuit of Teaching Memory Training across the nation. To J. Mark Dufner, the man with the best natural memory I have ever seen: His personal power has always been awe-inspiring. To Blaine Athorn, whose brilliance keeps amazing me day after day. Thanks also to Peter Tocci, whose work on this text was invaluable, Matthew Goerke, Andy Ambraziejus, and Kathy Niemeyer: Thank you all for touching my life and making a lasting impact.

To Ed Foreman, the first motivational speaker I ever heard, whose words have helped me motivate toward action every day.

And finally to Dexter Yager, the dream builder. If you didn't plant seeds of greatness in me, you certainly unearthed them! God bless you.

Contents

Part II: Advanced Mega Memory

1 | How to Use This Book

We are not given the world: we make our world through incessant experience, categorization, memory, reconnection.
—Oliver Sacks, *An Anthropologist on Mars*

How would you like to make more money, increase your intelligence, and impress everyone you meet? All this is possible, and much more, when you have a Mega Memory.

Imagine meeting over fifty brand-new people at a party, and a few hours later being able to say good-bye using the first and last name of every single person you met! Imagine making a speech without notes, or instantaneously recalling dates, appointments, things to do, directions, phone numbers, playing cards, verses of the Bible, lines of a play, poetry, facts, figures. Imagine being a student studying for exams and being able to recall instantly everything needed to earn great marks, and even more important, studying about one third the normal time to get those tremendous results. Imagine feeling totally confident in your own natural abilities because of your powerful memory.

You can have all of the above with a Mega Memory. Sound

just like another sales pitch? It isn't—because you already have a perfect, instant-recall, better-than-photographic memory just waiting to be released. When you apply the techniques taught in *Kevin Trudeau's Mega Memory*™, you will do just that—release this natural ability to recall things you have heard, things you have seen, and even things you have thought about briefly and then forgotten—or thought you had forgotten. The only problem is, you may not know you have a great memory, a memory that has the capacity and flexibility of a high-powered computer. With the twenty-eight lessons in this book, you will be tapping that power.

The Mega Memory program will teach you how to organize and process new information. You will be taught to take things that you see, hear, and experience and put them in a certain order so that this information will be available in your mind for recall in the future. The key word is "order"—the cornerstone of the Mega Memory program. Your brain operates just like a file cabinet. The more you place memos, letters, reports, notes, and documents into their proper files—the more organized you are—the easier it is to retrieve things when you need them. It's a simple, powerful, and ultimately very practical concept.

Like so many schoolchildren, I had some problems with my studies, especially with remembering things. The situation became so bad in high school, several teachers told me I might have a learning disability. This warning pushed me to educate myself about memory and the way the mind works. And what I discovered was that I didn't have a learning disability, I just had an untrained memory.

In showing you how to "file" away information, I'm going to be teaching you to train your memory. We won't spend a tremendous amount of time on the theories of how the brain and memory work. The actual process of reading this book will constitute training because Mega Memory is a technique that *you learn as you read*. Learning to use your memory is just like learning how to ride a bike or jog or swim properly—you have to actually participate in the sport to achieve the best results. But it's also important that you be well prepared before you hop on that bike, run a marathon, or swim long distances. That's why Mega Memory consists of both exercises and techniques. The exercises will limber up your brain and prepare it for the techniques you will be applying in real-life situations. If you follow the instructions for the exercises precisely as given, you will reap the benefits and gain your desired results.

The Ground Rules

In order to get the most out of the Mega Memory program, it is very important that you follow these ground rules for using the book:

1. *You must go through the lessons in order.* Each chapter builds upon previous chapters, so that you use what you have learned in new and exciting ways. But just like the jogger who risks injury if she hasn't done some exercises to loosen her muscles, or the swimmer who can't quite get his strokes together because he hasn't learned to feel comfortable in the water, you won't be able to release that Mega Memory if you haven't built the right foundation of skills. So don't skim the table of contents to find a chapter that may be of interest to you. That approach won't work. You must start at the beginning and complete one lesson after the other, mastering each one before you continue.

2. *Each chapter in this book should be completed in about twenty to thirty minutes.* Every lesson is designed to present a certain amount of material that does not take a large amount of time to absorb. If you read along and do the exercises and apply the techniques as they are presented, you will not be spending more than a half hour on each chapter. I've organized the book this way for a reason. People can concentrate on something only for so long before their attention starts to flag. (Just look at the short attention span required for television programs these days!) So don't overdo it. Many people find that working on one chapter a day is ideal.

3. *If you read more than one lesson per day, take a ten- or fifteen-minute break between lessons.* Not everybody processes infor-

mation at the same rate. If you find yourself absorbing this information at a fast pace and want to keep going, that's okay, too. You can study more than one lesson per day. But take a break after each lesson. That allows the mind to relax and subconsciously review the material you have just learned. After that, you can go on to the next lesson. Otherwise, you will begin to feel overloaded and burn out.

4. *Do your studying when there is no distraction.* This book is intended to be fun to use, but you do need to pay full attention to what you're doing and be directly "tuned in" to the material. Unlike other courses, in which you must review repeatedly to have the material sink in, you'll only have to read this book once. But you must make sure that you're focused during study time. So find a place where you can sit down and not be interrupted. Relax and be comfortable—and go to it.

5. *Set aside a time and a specific place to study.* Each lesson is short enough to fit into various parts of your day. Whatever works for you—the morning, after school or work, the evenings—is fine. And the only additional material needed to apply the lessons is a piece of paper and pencil. But once you've decided where and when you will study, try to stick with it. When you work out a routine for yourself, it is much easier to follow through and not find excuses to put things off.

6. *Before you do a lesson, refrain from eating a big meal.* If you must eat, have something light. I recommend that you wait a few hours after eating before you work on the program. Why? If you eat a lot of food or have just finished a meal, your body will rush blood to your stomach for digestion. That deprives the brain of the blood it needs to do its work most efficiently; therefore, your thinking and concentration are not sharp.

There are some foods in particular you should stay away from. First of all, of course, no drugs or alcohol before your lessons. Also, nothing heavy or greasy. And—this may surprise some of you—you should especially stay away from sugar and white flour for at least a couple of hours before you begin a lesson. We will learn more about certain foods and their effect on your memory in a later chapter, but as you begin the book you should know that sugar and white flour dull the senses. They make you foggy, unable to concentrate well. Stay away from them if you are serious about improving your memory. Remember that this includes sodas and tonics as well. A lot of people drink such things as they are reading. It's one of the worst things you can do. All that sugar and gook and syrup are going to negatively affect your concentration.

7. *Do not take any notes while you are reading.* We've been taught that if you really want to learn something, write it down. Nothing could be further from the truth. As you read through this book, you will see that when you write something down, you create the opposite effect. Writing something down frequently signals to the unconscious that it doesn't have to be remembered—after all, it's already written down. You should write only if I specifically ask you to do so or give an excercise that involves writing. Otherwise, don't even have a pen or pencil in your hand while reading.

Your Teachability Index

There are several other things we need to consider in preparation for reading this book. The first is these involves the spirit, or attitude, with which you approach these lessons. It's what I call your teachability index.

We all have an index, a rating, which determines how easily we can be taught anything. That index has two variables:

1. willingness to learn
2. willingness to accept change

You can measure each of these variables on a scale of 0 to 10. To find your overall index, you multiply these two variables together. Your score can be anywhere from 0 to 100.

As far as the first variable is concerned, I believe that when people invest time and money in books, cassettes, and other self-improvement programs, they have a very high willingness to learn. If you weren't motivated to learn these memory techniques, you wouldn't have invested your money in this book, and you certainly wouldn't be investing your valuable time reading it. So on a scale of 1 to 10, give yourself a 10.

But what is your willingness to accept change? Some people are very set in their ways and have a very hard time changing anything they do. A perfect example involves the current computer revolution. Computers are taking over in many areas of life and have been shown to be very efficient and effective. Yet many people still say no to computers, not wanting to have anything to do with them either out of fear of something new or because they don't want to be bothered with the initial difficulty of learning how to use this new tool.

If you're similar to the people described above, rate yourself 0 on the willingness-to-accept-change scale. If your rating is 0, think what it means for your teachability index. Even if your willingness-to-learn rating is a 10, what is 10 times 0? A big fat 0. Your teachability index will be a 0 if you're unwilling to change.

Now, what if you're one of those people who have said yes to computers. Even though you may have had some fear initially or had to go through a period of frustration while learning how to use an IBM or a Mac, you were willing to do so. Perhaps initially you felt as though you had to take a few steps backward in order to go forward; but now that you've completed this process, how do you feel about it? Would you ever go back to using typewriters? Your willingness to change is a 10, and your teachability index is closer to 100.

I use the analogy of computers because the same thing happens in acquiring a Mega Memory. This book is going to be exposing you to different ways of thinking. Though they'll always be fun, the exercises might not make much sense in the beginning. At first glance some of the techniques might also seem difficult or complicated. I'm not saying that there won't be any learning curve at all, but believe me, it will be painless as far as learning curves go. You might be scratching your head for the first few days, but then you'll get more and more excited as you see your memory power increasing dramatically.

I can't stress enough this matter of having a positive attitude. As I've already said, because of the rather unique format of this book, it's important to do the lessons in precise order, because each lesson builds on the last. You have to have a good grasp of the material in one chapter before going on to the next. I will emphasize this over and over, because I want to make sure you have an appreciation for how important the fundamentals are in acquiring a Mega Memory.

Keep in mind that in the early lessons we are mainly going to be doing exercises, building a foundation. Consider this: As you walk past any construction site, you can estimate how high the building is going to be by seeing how deep the hole in the ground is. The same principle applies to the Mega Memory technique. We're going to work on building a solid foundation for your memory. The firmer it is, the more dramatic your memory improvement will be.

Some of the exercises we do will make you laugh. Some will seem intriguing, others crazy, and even foolish. Just like a baseball player in spring training, who has to start with push-ups and sit-ups before he can take the field, you will be doing mental calisthenics to expand and focus your mind. If you learn to accept change, allow yourself to be fully open to these exercises, and follow the instructions carefully, you will be preparing your unconscious in the best way possible to release the amazing memory that it is capable of.

Motivation and Technique

I would like to say a few words about what I call a "training balance scale." In any type of training program or course of learning, there must be a balance between two primary things:

1. motivation
2. technique

If the two aren't in balance, those who designed the program should take another look at it because something's wrong. If the students are given an overdose of motivation and very little substance, then one ends up with excited fools. Such people may think they know a lot, but in fact they have learned very little, which becomes apparent in the long run. Salespeople are sometimes like that—very excited about their product or service, but having little knowledge of it, a fact that very quickly becomes apparent to any buyer. Sometimes the situation is reversed. A program that overdoses on technique and provides little motivation results in very poor graduates as well—if people are bored and unmotivated, they won't learn no matter how valuable the material is.

I have structured the Mega Memory program with this very much in mind. Each chapter provides information in small bits and shows you how to work through each exercise and apply each technique every step of the way. Thus you will learn and gain confidence in equal measure. And as that happens, as each exercise becomes easier and the applications more exciting, your motivation will increase as well, propelling you to the following chapters and further exercises and techniques.

The Four Steps to a Mega Memory

There are four steps you will see yourself advancing through as you study Mega Memory.

Level 1: unconscious incompetence
Level 2: conscious incompetence
Level 3: conscious competence
Level 4: unconscious competence

The first level is the one that you were at before you knew Mega Memory existed. What that means is that you simply didn't know that you didn't know. Perhaps you weren't too happy with your memory, or perhaps you thought your memory was pretty good, but in any case, you were willing to accept the status quo.

You didn't know you had a memory with amazing capability that was just waiting to be released. You had no appreciation of how much that status quo could really be changed, so you were unconsciously incompetent.

But because you have started reading this book and are beginning to get an inkling of what can be done to release the power of one's memory, you're quickly approaching level two, conscious incompetence. You're very quickly becoming aware of what you can or cannot do regarding memory. You are searching for some help because you recognize there's room for improvement. Perhaps you know someone else who has read this book or taken one of my seminars. Or maybe you've seen a demonstration of someone's Mega Memory, and you're thinking, "Boy, if he can do it, I can, too!" And how right you are!

Within about a week of starting to work with this book, you'll reach level three, conscious competence. Now things will become more exciting because you will know that you know. Mega Memory will have begun working for you. You will be doing the exercises with me and will begin to apply some of the techniques to real-life situations. Things may not be happening smoothly yet, but they will be happening. A good analogy for this stage is that of someone learning to drive a car with a manual transmission. After you're taught the basics, you're at the conscious competence level because you still have to think through each step of the process. "Let's see ... I push in the clutch, put it into first, ease out on the clutch, give it a little gas—" And perhaps you stall the car. But you keep going.

Within three or four weeks, you will be at level four—the unconscious competence stage. At this point, the techniques that you've been working at will be second nature. You will be applying them every day with hardly any effort, just like tying your shoe, breathing, walking, or, in the case of our driver, zooming around using a stick shift. You're shifting gears unconsciously, not thinking about it anymore.

This is the most exciting part of the book. These techniques will take you to the point where they are used unconsciously. I call it automatic pilot. Since I began teaching Mega Memory in 1981, I have received many, many letters from around the country. For so many people, being at level four is a revelation. It's like opening floodgates—knowledge and recall come to the fore, and people find themselves automatically recalling things they had no idea they had stored in their memory. If you do the lessons as they are presented, I guarantee that you will be at level four within a few short weeks as well.

One final thing. I mentioned that I'm flooded with letters from people who have benefited from the techniques they've learned in the Mega Memory program. It's exciting for me to receive those letters, and I hope that after you, the reader, have completed the book, following its instructions, you will write me and tell me your success story. I want to hear how Mega Memory has affected your life.

Maybe you won a job promotion. Maybe your self-esteem has increased. Perhaps the book gave you a better outlook on life. Perhaps you now draw the admiration of people because of your super-power memory. I want to hear these success stories. I'm waiting to see the letters, and someday, I hope to be in your city doing a Mega Memory seminar. I'll be looking forward to meeting you then.

This is the end of lesson one. I hope with all my heart this book will be everything you want it to be, and I know it will. It may be different from other books you've read because we're going to be interacting, in a sense. I'd like you to feel that I'm right there talking to you, and teaching you this breakthrough technology. I know you will benefit from the book beyond your wildest expectations. Apply the techniques, do the exercises with vigor, and enjoy this Mega Memory program.

Chapter 1—Review

Ground Rules for the Mega Memory Home Study Course
1. You must study the lessons in order.
2. Each chapter in this book should be completed in about twenty to thirty minutes.

3. If you work on more than one lesson per day, take a ten- to fifteen-minute break between lessons.
4. Do your studying when there is no distraction.
5. Set aside a time and a specific place to study.
6. Before you work on a lesson, refrain from eating a big meal.
7. Do not take any notes while you are reading.

Your Teachability Index
Willingness to learn *times* willingness to accept change.

Charting Your Progress: The Four Steps to a Mega Memory
Level 1: unconscious incompetence. You don't know what you don't know.

Level 2: conscious incompetence. You know what can be done, but you can't do it.

Level 3: conscious competence. You consciously think your way through any Mega Memory technique or exercise.

Level 4: unconscious competence. You apply the techniques automatically.

Part I

Mega Memory

2　Learning Basic Association

The first thing we're going to do on our way to a Mega Memory is a little memory test. I'm going to give you a list of words, and I want you to try to remember the words in order. That's all I want you to do. Once you've read the list, you're going to close the book, attempt to write down the words, and see how many you recalled. You may not do very well, but that's okay because in just about fifteen minutes, you are going to improve your memory dramatically. You'll be astounded by your rapid progress.

Have a pencil and paper handy. Sit back and relax. Now read through the list below *once* and try to remember it as best you can. When you have finished, close the book, number from 1 through 20 down on the left-hand side of a sheet of paper, and try to write the words in the order in which they appeared. Give yourself about five minutes, then open the book and check yourself. Here's the list:

tree

light switch

stool

car

glove

gun

dice

skate

cat

bowling ball

goalpost

eggs

witch

ring

paycheck

candy

magazine

voting booth

golf club

cigarettes

Now close the book and write down the words.◆

Compare your list with the one in the book. Put a check mark next to any correct answer. Remember, your words have to be in the same order as those in the book, so if you have "cigarettes" as the first word on your list, that doesn't count. Check the ones that you had in the *correct* order. That point is very important because I don't believe in reinforcing people's weaknesses but rather in building up their strengths. In other words, I want you to be concerned with what you did right, not what you did wrong. (Unlike school, where so many children are told what they did badly, as I was, instead of what they did well.) That doesn't help build confidence, which is one of the hallmarks of the Mega Memory program.

Tally the number of correct answers, put the total at the top of your paper, and circle it. Most people, about 90 percent, have fewer than five words in the correct order. So if you had less than five, you're among the vast majority of people. If you had more than five, you should be proud of your memory. It's in the top 10 percent. Either way, however, by the end of this chapter you'll see how fast you can improve your performance.

Basic Association

Before starting our first exercise, we need to discuss basic association a bit. This memory technique is emphasized by virtually every memory expert and is the foundation of many memory improvement programs. When you use basic association, you take something you know, like a letter of the alphabet, and associate it with something you're trying to remember, like a name. Think of HOMES, the tried-and-true acronym for remembering the Great Lakes (Huron, Ontario, Michigan, Erie, Superior).

Many people in my workshops have a negative response when I mention basic association. They feel it's awkward, ineffective, a tired old way of doing things. And they're right—up to a point. I feel that basic association has both positive and negative aspects to it. It works well enough in certain cases, like remembering the Great Lakes. But in many fast-paced real-life situations, like a party or a business meeting, when it's simply too cumbersome to create acronyms, basic association isn't practical. There's just no time for it.

For all of you basic-association haters, the good news is that Mega Memory is not a program of basic association. Although we do some exercises using this technique, we will be going way beyond what basic association can do for us. "Then why am I discussing it in the first place?" is another question I am asked very often at this point. There are three main reasons:

1. Understanding basic association will help you to stop a bad habit from the very beginning.
2. It will increase your mind's speed.
3. It will also help you understand a fundamental concept of how the minds works.

First, because basic association is so universal, I'm assuming that's how you understand memory improvement techniques, too. Banish that thought right now. As I said earlier, basic association is too limiting. This book is not about limiting the mind, but expanding it.

Second, even though basic association is limiting, it is useful as a tool for mental gymnastics. And mental gymnastics increase the flexibility of the mind, which makes memory recall faster. So even though it's not a big part of the Mega Memory program, you will see it occasionally as an exercise.

Third, and most important, I am going to use basic association to explain a very important concept of how the mind works.

What do all the words on the list above—tree, light switch, stool, car, glove, and so on—have in common? How do you associate them? If you said they are all objects that you can picture, you are 100 percent correct. Every word creates a picture in your mind. Every one (as long as the word is familiar to you). Why is that important? It is important because the most fundamental concept in the Mega Memory program that you must completely understand is this: *Your mind thinks in pictures.*

Your mind thinks in pictures. Pictures are its vocabulary, what it understands best. It's like an instant camera, clicking away, taking pictures and reproducing them in all of sorts of combinations.

You may be asking, as many of my workshop participants do: Are you sure, Kevin? Are you sure I don't think in words? Are you sure I don't think in abstracts or thoughts or concepts? No. You think in pictures.

Let me give you an example. As you are reading along here, do not—do not—think of an elephant. Let me ask you what's the first thing that popped into your mind? It was a picture of a big, gray beast with a trunk, wasn't it? It wasn't the letters *E-L-E-P-H-A-N-T* spelling the word. It was a picture of an elephant because on seeing the word "elephant," you simply created a picture of an actual elephant in your mind.

Let me give you another example. If I were to ask you right now to describe your couch to me, you might start by telling me, "It's blue with stripes and has a rip in the left corner." As you are describing that couch to me, do the words "couch," "blue, with rip in corner" appear in your mind? Or does the picture of the couch appear in your mind? Of course, it's the picture.

And consider this. Apple Computer produces the very popular

Macintosh machine. Now the IBM computers have begun using the same feature that the "Mac" started with—the icon. What are icons? Icons are pictures on the screen that help the user choose various functions. For exmaple, there's a picture of a trash can on the screen. If you want to delete a file from the Mac, you simply put the file (which is, by the way, indicated by a picture of a file folder), in the trash can. Putting something in the trash can means you've thrown it away, doesn't it? This method of operating is called being user-friendly, because people understand pictures. Apple Computer's genius was first in recognizing this.

As children, we were taught by pictures. Our mother or father, would look at us, hold a glass in their hand, and say, "Glass." We'd look at the glass and repeat the word, learning to associate the sound "glass" with the picture of the object. The sound produced the picture in our minds. Imagine if our parents had tried to teach us what a glass was by describing it only and not showing us the object?

That's why HOMES is such a popular memory technique. Every schoolchild knows his or her home. When they are taught to associate HOMES with the Great Lakes, they are actually being taught to create a picture of their home in their mind's eye. It's an easy picture to remember, and then they can sound out each letter and come up with the five Great Lakes.

Let me ask you, do you dream at night in words? You're probably laughing, "Kevin, of course, I don't dream in words; I dream in pictures." Exactly right. You dream in pictures. That's how your unconscious mind communicates to you. Basic-association techniques make use of these pictures in the unconscious. But they only skim the surface of its vast power.

The Tree List

Now that you understand the importance of visual images, it's time to start releasing some of their power. For your first exercise, you will learn how to replace the numbers 1 through 20 with pictures that represent those numbers. The pictures that I'm going to use for this exercise will be the list of twenty words you just tested yourselves on. I will show you why I chose to link each picture with each number, why there's an association between the two in my mind. As you begin reading, I hope that you too will begin thinking of similar associations.

I chose "tree" for number 1. If you picture a tree in your mind, the trunk looks like the shape of the number 1, doesn't it? That's an association that helps us remember that "tree" is 1.

I decided on "light switch" for number 2 because there are several associations that can help us remember that light switch is 2. It might be the two words. Or the fact that those two words are also two syllables, or that a light switch has two positions—on/off, up/down. Or it might be because there are two screws attaching the plate housing of a light switch to the wall. Also, current flows in two directions through a light switch. All these things come to my mind when I think of a light switch. They all remind me that the number 2 and "light switch" go together.

How about "stool" and the number 3? How do you think I decided on that one? Three legs. When I picture three legs, that reminds me of a stool.

Here's an easy one. The number 4 and "car." How do you think I arrived at 4 for "car"? Try to think of some ideas of your own right now. Maybe you're thinking four wheels, four doors, four cylinders, four speeds, four passengers, four-barrel carburetor, four on the floor, four-wheel drive. There are a whole bunch of associations that will help you remember that "car" goes with 4.

I'm going to repeat the images now, and I want you to think of what number is associated with each. Tree is what number? Why? Because the trunk of a tree looks like the number 1. Light switch is what number? Why? Because we think of two words, two syllables, up/down, on/off, light/dark. Stool is what number? Why? Three legs. Car is what number? Why? Four wheels, four doors, four-cylinder, four-barrel carburetor, for sale. (When I hear the words "for sale," I always think of cars!)

Here are more numbers. Five goes with "glove." Why? Five fingers, of course. Six goes with "gun." Why? Six-cylinder, six-shooter, six-inch barrel, six bullets, six chambers, six-gun. Someone once said, "Six feet under if you get shot by one." A lot of associations help us remember that 6 goes with "gun."

How about 7 and "dice"? Lucky number seven or "seven come eleven." How about 8 and "skate"? They rhyme. How about a figure eight? Maybe eight wheels.

Let's go back. What number is glove? Why? Five fingers. What number is gun? Why? Six-gun, six-shooter, six cylinder, six-inch barrel, six feet under. Dice is what number? Seven come eleven, lucky number seven. What number is skate? Why? Because they rhyme, eight wheels, figure eight.

Now 9. That's easy: 9 goes with "cat." Why? Nine lives. Or maybe cat-o'-nine-tails. How about 10 and "bowling ball"? Ten frames, ten-pound ball, a strike, tenpins.

Let's review again. What number is tree? Why? The trunk of a tree looks like the number 1. What number is light switch? Why? Two words, two syllables, on/off, light/dark, up/down. What number is stool? Why? Three legs. What number is gun? Why? Six-gun, six-shooter, six bullets, six cylinders, six-inch barrel, six feet under? What number is car? Why? Four-door, four-cylinder, four-speed. What number is glove? Why? Five fingers. What number is skate? Eight. Why? Figure eight, eight wheels, they rhyme.

What number is bowling ball? Why? Ten frames, ten-pound ball, a strike, tenpins. What number is cat? Why? Nine lives, cat-o'-nine-tails. What number is dice? Seven come eleven, lucky number seven.

I hope at this point you are coming up with associations of your own. Can you see what we are doing here? These associations are the link that holds what you want to remember (the list of twenty words) with something you already know (the numbers 1 through 20). It's the associations that will allow you to remember these words.

Let's continue. For 11, I selected "goalpost." Why? A goalpost looks like the number 11. Someone else may be thinking of eleven men on a football field. Twelve goes with "eggs." Why? One dozen.

Thirteen goes with "witch." Why? I'm reminded of something unlucky, Friday the thirteenth. Fourteen is "ring." Why? Maybe 14-carat, or how about Valentine's Day, February fourteenth.

Let's review once more. What number is "bowling ball"? Why? Ten frames, tenpins, ten-pound ball, strike. What number is eggs? Why? A dozen eggs, a dozen equals twelve. What number is goalpost? Why? A goalpost looks like an 11. What number is ring? Why? Fourteen-carat. What number is cat? Why? Nine lives. What number is glove? Why? Five fingers. What number is car? Why? Four-door, four-cylinder.

Okay, let's go on. Fifteen is "paycheck." Why do you think we can link "paycheck" with 15? Many people are paid on the fifteenth of the month. Some people say April fifteenth because that's when you have to pay taxes and give away part of your paycheck. How about 16 and "candy"? Sixteen ounces to a pound, sweet sixteen, or sixteen candles. We put "magazine" with 17. Why? *Seventeen* is the name of a magazine. How about 18 and "voting booth." That's obvious—at eighteen years old you can vote. How about 19 and "golf club"? The nineteenth hole. And how about 20 and "cigarettes"? Twenty are in a pack.

Let's review once again. What number is paycheck? Why? The fifteenth of the month when you get a paycheck or April fifteenth when you give away part of your paycheck in taxes. What number is cigarettes? Why? Twenty in a pack. What number is voting booth? Why? At eighteen years old you can vote. What number is golf club? Why? Nineteenth hole. What number is witch? Why? Friday the thirteenth, something unlucky. What number is ring? Why? February fourteenth, 14-carat. What number is magazine? Why? *Seventeen* is the name of a magazine. What number is candy? Why? Sweet sixteen or sixteen ounces to a pound.

Now I'm going to give the associations, and you are going to think of the number and the word. When I mention the association, you'll notice that your mind instantly throws out the number and the word. Here we go. The association is legs. Instantly, you should have thought of 3 and "stool." The association is doors, wheels, or carburetor or "on the floor." Obviously, you know it's 4 and "car."

The association is the number in a pack. That gives you 20 and "cigarettes." How about the age to vote? That gives you 18 and "voting booth." How about ounces to a pound, or sweet? That gives "candy" and 16. How about up/down, on/off, light/dark? You've got it, 2 and "light switch." How about the trunk? One and "tree." How about fingers? Five and "glove." How about the figure eight, eight wheels, or what rhymes with "skate?" How about lives or tails? That's 9 and "cat." How about pins or frames? That's right, 10 and "bowling ball." How about the numbers of players on a field? "Goalpost" and 11. How about one dozen? Twelve and "eggs." How about something unlucky or Friday? "Witch" and 13. How about a certain carat or Valentine's Day? "Ring" and 14. How about the time of the month you get paid? Fifteen and "paycheck." How about the name of a magazine? *Seventeen* is the name of a "magazine." How about the number of the hole? That's right, the nineteenth hole, which gives you nineteen and "golf club." How about one number that's a name? *Seventeen* and "magazine" again. How about a lucky number or something come eleven? Seven come eleven. Seven goes with "dice." How about chambers, bullets? They call this number that many feet under. That's right, 6 and "gun." Do you see how these associations help you remember what number goes with what word?

I will next ask you to go to the Tree List below and read the associations out loud. Saying things out loud is another important part of the Mega Memory program. Why? Research shows that the body has what it called neuromuscular memory. When you say something out loud, you are using your vocal chords in addition to just thinking about something. You're reinforcing your memory in a new way because now the brain not only has to think about the words, but also has to instruct your vocal chords to say them out loud. I will be asking you to say things out loud often. Better yet, if you can get a friend or colleague to work with you on these drills, one of you can read the instructions while the other does the drills, and then you can switch roles. Whether you do these exercises with someone or alone, however, the important thing is saying things out loud.

Now go to the Tree List. Read each number, the association, and each word out loud. Then close your eyes and create a picture in your mind of each item, each word, and review in your mind the associations. Do this exercise now.◆

Tree List

Number	Association	Word
1	looks like the trunk of a tree	tree
2	two words, two positions, up/down, on/off, light/dark	light switch
3	three legs	stool
4	four doors, four-speed, four-wheel drive	car
5	five fingers	glove
6	six-shooter, six feet under	gun
7	lucky number seven, seven come eleven	dice
8	figure eight, eight wheels, rhymes with eight	skate
9	nine lives, cat-o'-nine-tails	cat
10	tenpins, ten frames, ten-pound ball, a strike	bowling ball
11	looks like an 11, eleven players on a football team	goalpost
12	one dozen	eggs
13	unlucky, Friday the thirteenth	witch
14	14-carat, February fourteenth (Valentine's Day)	ring
15	get paid on the fifteenth of every month, April fifteenth is when you pay taxes	paycheck
16	sweet sixteen, sixteen ounces to a pound	candy
17	*Seventeen* is the name of one of these	magazine
18	old enough to do this at eighteen	voting booth
19	nineteenth hole	golf club
20	twenty in a pack	cigarettes

I want to review an important concept in the exercise you just completed. *The most important thing you need to remember is not the word but the association.* If you're going over number five, for example, you aren't trying to focus on "glove." The only thing you want the number 5 to give you is fingers. What you want your brain to picture when you read 5 is fingers. Five gives you fingers, because they are associated, they go together. And then fingers will give you what? "Glove." When you see the number 13, I don't want you to remember "witch." All I want you to remember is unlucky or Friday the thirteenth, because 13 goes with unlucky or Friday. And what do unlucky and Friday the thirteenth give you? "Witch."

These associations are an important link between what you know and what you don't know. You know numbers 1 through 20 already. You don't know "tree," "light switch," "stool," etc. How do you remember them? By the association—it links the number and the word together. If the associations are still hazy in your mind, do the above exercise a few more times until the associations are clear to you.

Now I'm going to drill you one more time. I'm going to give you the numbers, and you are to say the word out loud. Make sure you can do it without hesitation. Number 3. Number 5. Number 20. Number 19. Number 10. Number 11.

Now for some words, and you call out the numbers. How about witch? Cigarettes. Goalpost. Paycheck. Light switch. Tree. Stool. Car. Cat. Bowling ball. Glove. Gun. Dice. Skate. Eggs. Witch. Magazine. Voting Booth. Golf Club. Cigarettes.

Next I want you to close the book and again review the Tree List. In your mind, repeat this list. Say, "One is tree, two is light switch, three is stool, four is car, five is glove," and so on. Go through the entire list. If you get stuck on one, ask yourself the right question: "What is my association?" For example, if you are on number 6 and you don't remember the word, ask yourself, "What does six give me? What's the association?" It should pop into your mind. Six-gun, six-shooter, six feet under . . . which will give you, what? Gun. So think about the association if you feel the word doesn't come into your mind quickly.

If you become stuck on a particular number, keep reviewing it. I have found in my seminars that some of these are easier than others to remember depending on people's backgrounds and interests. An important thing to keep in mind, too, is that I'm the one who made up the associations. You may have chosen something else for each word. Keep reviewing the associations if you feel stuck and you will soon see that they do really "lock in" the words. Now close the book and review the Tree List out loud, saying the number, the association, and the word.◆

Next I want you to take a piece of paper, number 1 through 20 down the left-hand side, and write the words associated with each number. Close the book and do it now.◆

We're back again. Check your sheet against the Tree List and see how well you did. This is your first test. If you didn't get twenty out of twenty, that means you need a little work on the assocations. Keep reviewing them. You need to get twenty out of twenty before you go on to the next lesson. And you should know this list backward and forward. Every number should spring the association in your mind, which will give you the word, and every word should spring the assocation that will give you the number.

Chapter 2—Review

Word Association
Linking together in logical fashion something you know and something you don't know.

Three Reasons for Studying Word Assocation
1. Stop a bad habit from the beginning.
2. Increase your mind's speed with a form of mental gymnastics.
3. Understand a fundamental concept of how the mind works.

Your Mind Thinks in Pictures

Tree List

Number	Association	Word
1	looks like the trunk of a tree	tree
2	two words, two positions, up/down, on/off, light/dark	light switch
3	three legs	stool
4	four doors, four-speed, four-wheel drive	car
5	five fingers	glove
6	six-shooter, six feet under	gun
7	lucky number seven, seven come eleven	dice
8	figure eight, eight wheels, rhymes with eight	skate
9	nine lives, cat-o'-nine-tails	cat
10	tenpins, ten frames, ten-pound ball, a strike	bowling ball
11	looks like an 11, eleven players on a football team	goalpost
12	one dozen	eggs
13	unlucky, Friday the thirteenth	witch
14	14-carat, February fourteenth (Valentine's Day)	ring
15	get paid on the fifteenth of every month, April fifteenth is when you pay taxes	paycheck
16	sweet sixteen, sixteen ounces to a pound	candy
17	*Seventeen* is the name of one of these	magazine
18	old enough to do this at eighteen	voting booth
19	nineteenth hole	golf club
20	twenty in a pack	cigarettes

Chapter 2—Required Mental Exercise

Exercise

If you're completing the course alone, review the Tree List in your mind—while you are doing something else: listening to music, cooking, as you drive.

Say to yourself, for example, "One looks like the trunk of a tree. A six-shooter, which puts me six feet under, gives me a gun. Tenpins, ten frames, and a ten-pound ball remind me of a bowling ball." You must know why the number and the word go together. Focus on the association.

If you're completing this course with a partner, quiz one another by having one person call out numbers and the other call out items from the Tree List throughout the day.

3 Chaining: Putting the Power of Vivid Images to Work

In this chapter, we are going to learn a technique called chaining or linking. I will explain it first, and then we'll do a fun exercise that will show you how it works. If you can find a partner for this exercise, it will be helpful.

But first I want to repeat how important it is that you have the Tree List from Chapter 2 memorized before you go on to chaining. If you think of a number between 1 and 20, the word associated with it should pop into your mind immediately. If you think of the word first, its corresponding number should come to your mind. As you do more exercises in the book, your mind will work more and more quickly and smoothly. In order to get there, though, you have to do the work that has come before.

And now on to chaining, which is simply creating a picture in your mind of one thing, then a second thing, and putting both pictures together in some crazy way. For example, a mountain lion is one picture, and a fur coat is another. Put both of those pictures together, and maybe you have a mountain lion wearing a fur coat. What you've done is put two very dissimilar pictures together in a ludicrous way. This is slightly different from the basic-association exercises in Chapter 2, in which we were putting together one thing we knew (a number) with something we didn't know (a word). In chaining, both things we are putting together are new to us.

When you are chaining, the pictures you create must be very vivid. And when I say vivid, I mean crystal clear and as detailed as possible. If you're picturing a car, you must know whether it's a Cadillac, a Lincoln limousine, or a Honda. You need to be able to "see" whether the windows are blacked out. You have to be able to tell whether it has an antenna at the back, what the wheels look like, and how the car company name is written on the body.

If you're picturing an envelope, you need to know the color of the paper. Is it stamped or metered? Is the address printed or written? Is the return address on the front or the back? The more details you have, the more vivid your picture is. And the more vivid your picture, the better exercise it is for your memory.

To demonstrate the power of vivid images, let me give you an example. Read the following description of a lemon, and as you're reading, picture it in your mind. Even better, if you have a partner, close your eyes and picture what is being read to you.

I want you to vividly imagine a lemon in your right hand. The lemon is bright yellow. You can feel the hard, slightly nubby texture, and the harder knobs at either end. Now, in your mind's eye, put that lemon down on a table in front of you, and pick up a black, shiny knife. Picture the handle of the knife, how the lemon is lying on the table, where your hands are. Now begin to slice that lemon slowly with the shiny knife. As you do, watch the knife penetrate the skin and cut the lemon in two halves. Pick up one of those lemon halves in your right hand and squeeze lightly. Feel the juices ooze through and down your fingers and into your hand. Feel the texture of the skin and the juices. Is it sticky or slippery? Hold that lemon up to your nose. Smell that lemon aroma. Now I want you to open your mouth and bite into that lemon.

You probably have a locked jaw right about now. When I do this exercise in a large group, it's funny to see the expressions on all the faces of the participants. Everyone is grimacing, swallowing a mouthful of saliva in an effort to wash away the sour taste. Vivid images are very powerful. If you create a vivid picture, the body does not know the difference between what is imagined and what's real. That imagined lemon made you salivate as if you had bitten into a real lemon. Your body reacted to an imagined picture as if it were real.

Why is this important? It's another way of reinforcing your memory. Everything that you have seen with your "real" eyes has been photographed and stored in your mind. That's why I said at the very beginning of the book that you already have a photographic memory. When you re-create some of those pictures in your mind, it's as if you are seeing them again for real. When you call back—or recall—what's already in your memory, you're giving it a great workout!

Picturing a Story

Now it's time for an exercise to help you practice chaining. You will read a story. After you read each sentence of the passage below, I'd like you to sit back, close your eyes, and spend about five or ten seconds vividly seeing the action in your mind's eye. If you're having trouble visualizing a particular image, go on to the next one. If you have a partner, let him or her read the story while you remain with eyes closed, creating the vivid images. If your partner is also going through the Mega Memory program, take turns with the reading.

A final reminder: As you re-create the images, be as vivid and as detailed as you can. At one point, I'll mention a padlock. You need to have a picture so clear, so vivid (just like that lemon) that you can see the color of the padlock. You must know if it's a Master or a Yale lock, if it's a combination or a key lock. Is it old and rusty or new and shiny? How big is it? How heavy? In another part of the story, I'm going to mention a house trailer. You'll have to know the color of the house trailer. How it's shaped, how large it is. You need to see all these things in that powerful mind's eye that you have.

Okay, let's begin:

Imagine the Statue of Liberty with its torch and its book. On top of the Statue of Liberty is a big fat man. In his right hand is an electric power drill. In his left hand is a bar of soap. He drills into the soap, and out of the soap come tumbling purple pennies. They fall into a padlock on the back of a long house trailer being pulled by a big black limousine. The limousine is being driven by John Travolta, who is wearing a black Stetson hat, a black vest, and black leather boots. Sitting next to John Travolta is Cathy Lee Crosby. She's wearing a pink polka-dot bikini. On her lap is a letter to her agent.

In the backseat of the limousine is a big Saint Bernard who is wearing a big fur coat and a diamond collar. In his mouth is a ham bone. A mountain lion jumps into the backseat, grabs the ham bone, jumps out the other side, runs up a palm tree, and the palm tree falls on the Statue of Liberty.

Let me ask you some questions to make sure you are doing this exercise correctly. Are your mental pictures in color? They should be. Are they descriptive? For example, what type of soap did you picture? Is it a very clear picture? Do you know exactly how big the bar is? What did Travolta have on his feet? What do the black leather boots look like? The reason I ask these questions is this: When you picture something vividly, you know exactly what it is. When you're not sure, you see it in a rather half-baked way, sort of fuzzy or foggy. In answering what John Travolta had on his feet, you may have said black *shoes*. If you said black shoes or anything except black leather boots, it means one thing. Your picture wasn't vivid enough.

If you had some trouble with your pictures (maybe you had difficulty picturing purple pennies because you haven't seen them in real life; or maybe you feel you know very little about house trailers, so you couldn't develop a vivid picture of one), that's okay. We're going to read the story again, and this time you'll see that your mind will work a little faster. The pictures will come more easily, and they will also be a little more detailed, more colorful. And if you are doing this exercise with a partner, you may find that you actually get ahead of him or her. You will recall the picture of the next scene before it is read to you. Watch for this phenomenon; it means your brain is already picking up speed.

Now sit back, relax, and vividly see the images from the story in as much detail as possible. And don't forget to get all your senses involved, feeling the feelings, smelling smells, and hearing any sounds. Make believe you are really there.

> Imagine the Statue of Liberty with its torch and its book. On top of the Statue of Liberty is a big fat man. In his right hand is an electric power drill. In his left hand is a bar of soap. He drills into the soap, and out of the soap come tumbling purple pennies. They fall into a padlock on the back of a long house trailer being pulled by a big black limousine. The limousine is being driven by John Travolta, who is wearing a black Stetson hat, a black vest, and black leather boots. Sitting next to John Travolta is Cathy Lee Crosby. She's wearing a pink polka-dot bikini. On her lap is a letter to her agent.
>
> In the backseat of the limousine is a big Saint Bernard who is wearing a big fur coat and a diamond collar. In his mouth is a ham bone. A mountain lion jumps into the backseat, grabs the ham bone, jumps out the other side, runs up a palm tree, and the palm tree falls on the Statue of Liberty.

How did you do this time? Did the images come a little more easily? Did you get ahead of the story, as some people do? Your memory is being strengthened pretty quickly, isn't it? We're going to review the story one more time. This time, try to go even faster. And again, close your eyes to help you focus on the images.

Let's begin:

Imagine the Statue of Liberty with its torch and its book. On top of the Statue of Liberty is a big fat man. In his right hand is an electric power drill. In his left hand is a bar of soap. He drills into the soap, and out of the soap come tumbling purple pennies. They fall into a padlock on the back of a long house trailer being pulled by a big black limousine. The limousine is being driven by John Travolta, who is wearing a black Stetson hat, a black vest, and black leather boots. Sitting next to John Travolta is Cathy Lee Crosby. She's wearing a pink polka-dot bikini. On her lap is a letter to her agent.

In the backseat of the limousine is a big Saint Bernard who is wearing a big fur coat and a diamond collar. In his mouth is a ham bone. A mountain lion jumps into the backseat, grabs the ham bone, jumps out the other side, and runs up a cherry tree.

Was it a cherry tree? No. It was what, a palm tree? When you read "cherry tree," I bet you realized that was wrong. And that's good because you knew that it was a palm tree. Why? Two separate pictures. Did I make any other mistakes during that story? Of course, I didn't finish it. What happens to the palm tree? It falls on the Statue of Liberty.

Focusing

We're going to do something a little different now. Remember, early in this chapter we mentioned that when we put two pictures together in chaining, this has to be done in a crazy, illogical way? When you have to create something that doesn't really make any sense, a scene that couldn't happen in "real" life, you have to think about it a little harder, a little longer. You have to *focus* on it. The ability to focus on something is another important part not only of chaining but of all memory work. Have you ever searched for your house keys frantically because you couldn't remember where you put them the night before? Most of us have been in that predicament, and it happens because we weren't paying attention when we took those keys out of our pocket or handbag and put them down someplace. We weren't focusing on them. With a Mega Memory you will be focusing better without even trying to do so.

I will ask you to stand up in a minute. You will be reading the Statue of Liberty story again, this time out loud and standing up. Doing that makes your brain perceive things a bit differently. It forces you to focus a little more. Before, you were just picturing the pictures. Now you are going to be picturing the pictures, repeating the entire story, and doing both of these things standing up, which is adding yet another dimension to the exercise.

Stand up now. If you are alone, read the first line silently, then repeat the italicized line. If you are doing this exercise with someone, have your partner read the first line aloud, and then both of you repeat the italicized line. And always, remember to picture the story vividly in your mind's eye.

Imagine the Statue of Liberty with its torch and its book. *Imagine the Statue of Liberty with its torch and its book.* On top of the Statue of Liberty is a big fat man. *On top of the Statue of Liberty is a big fat man.* In his right hand is an electric power drill. *In his right hand is an electric power drill.* In his left hand is a bar of soap. *In his left hand is a bar of soap.* He drills into the soap, and out of the soap come tumbling purple pennies. *He drills into the soap, and out of the soap come tumbling purple pennies.* They fall into a padlock on the back of a long house trailer being pulled by a big black limousine. *They fall into a padlock on the back of a long house trailer being pulled by a big black limousine.* The limousine is being driven by John Travolta, who is wearing a black Stetson hat, a black vest, and black leather boots. *The limousine is being driven by John Travolta, who is wearing a black Stetson hat, a black vest, and black leather boots.* Sitting next to John Travolta is Cathy Lee Crosby. She is wearing a pink polka-dot bikini. On her lap is a letter to her agent. *Sitting next to*

John Travolta is Cathy Lee Crosby. She is wearing a pink polka-dot bikini. On her lap is a letter to her agent.

In the backseat of the limousine is a big Saint Bernard who is wearing a fur coat and a diamond collar. In his mouth is a ham bone. *In the backseat is a big Saint Bernard who is wearing a fur coat and a diamond collar. In his mouth is a ham bone.* A mountain lion jumps into the backseat, grabs the ham bone, jumps out the other side, runs up a palm tree, and the palm tree falls on the Statue of Liberty. *A mountain lion jumps into the backseat, grabs the ham bone, jumps out the other side, runs up a palm tree, and the palm tree falls on the Statue of Liberty.*

During my seminars, most people tell me that when you're vocalizing the words the pictures don't come as quickly. For some people it's also tougher to make the pictures vivid. Did you find this to be true? It is, don't worry. Your brain is just learning to do more things at the same time, just like that driver who's learning to drive a stick shift. When you had your eyes closed in the earlier exercise, you were able to completely focus on the visual aspects of the story. Now, however, you are verbalizing the story and trying to picture it at the same time, and you are standing up. It all is a little more difficult.

Remain standing. We're going to do the exercise again, but this time you're going to read the story entirely out loud, with or without a partner. Say the words and vividly see the pictures in your mind's eye. Remember, the key to vivid pictures is color and detail.

Imagine the Statue of Liberty with its torch and its book. On top of the Statue of Liberty is a big fat man. In his right hand is an electric power drill. In his left hand is a bar of soap. He drills into the soap, and out of the soap come tumbling purple pennies. They fall into a padlock on the back of a long house trailer being pulled by a big black limousine. The limousine is being driven by John Travolta, who is wearing a black Stetson hat, a black vest, and black leather boots. Sitting next to John Travolta is Cathy Lee Crosby. She's wearing a pink polka-dot bikini. On her lap is a letter to her agent.

In the backseat of the limousine is a big Saint Bernard who is wearing a big fur coat and a diamond collar. In his mouth is a ham bone. A mountain lion jumps into the backseat, grabs the ham bone, jumps out the other side, runs up a palm tree, and the palm tree falls on the Statue of Liberty.

You can sit now. We are going to do this exercise once more, but this time really try to get a partner if you've been doing it alone. If you can't, you'll have to skip it. This time, your partner should read the story very fast, as fast as possible, while you sit back and visualize everything. You'll notice something extraordinary: that you are able to keep pace with your partner easily, and may go ahead of him or her. As I mentioned earlier, this could have been happening to you already. Think about the ramifications of this. You can think faster than you speak. You can think faster than you write. That's why training your memory is so important—you can remember things faster and more efficiently than you can ever write them down. Are you beginning to appreciate that your brain is the powerful, superefficient computer I've been telling you it is?

Okay, sit back, relax, and close your eyes. Create vivid, detailed pictures in crystal clear colors as the story is read.

Imagine the Statue of Liberty with its torch and its book. On top of the Statue of Liberty is a big fat man. In his right hand is an electric power drill. In his left hand is a bar of soap. He drills into the soap, and out of the soap come tumbling purple pennies. They fall into a padlock on the back of a long house trailer being pulled by a big black limousine. The limousine is being driven by John Travolta, who is wearing a black Stetson hat, a black vest, and black leather boots. Sitting next to John

Travolta is Cathy Lee Crosby. She's wearing a pink polka-dot bikini. On her lap is a letter to her agent.

In the backseat of the limousine is a big Saint Bernard who is wearing a big fur coat and a diamond collar. In his mouth is a ham bone. A mountain lion jumps into the backseat, grabs the ham bone, jumps out the other side, runs up a palm tree, and the palm tree falls on the Statue of Liberty.

Now I'd like you to write the Statue of Liberty story on paper, jotting down only the key pictures. Your list should go something like this: "Statue of Liberty, torch, book, fat man, power drill, bar of soap, purple pennies, padlock, long house trailer, limousine, John Travolta, black Stetson hat, black vest, black leather boots, etc." You should make it from memory only. I'm sure you'll have no problem completing it in about five or ten minutes, and probably much more quickly. You'll be amazed at how rapidly you can recall these pictures. Close the book and do it now.

Okay. You may be thinking, this is incredible. I remembered all of those things. Well, the fact is, you can remember five hundred things doing what we've just done. Reviewing the story six times took only about ten or fifteen minutes. And keep in mind, we only began to do the exercises. I hope you're starting to see how fast your mind and memory actually can work.

Before you go on to the next lesson, make sure you can vividly create the pictures from the Statue of Liberty story, and make sure you can remember all of them without a problem. If you're still feeling a little stuck, review the story a few more times, reading it out loud and then testing yourself again by writing it down.

Chapter 3—Review

Chaining or Linking
Putting together in illogical or nonsensical fashion vivid pictures for two new things you are trying to remember.

Three Differences Between Basic Word Association and Chaining

1. In word association, using pictures, or visualizing, is not emphasized.
2. In word association, the link is logical; in chaining, the link is illogical.
3. In word association, the link is between two things you already know—both are in your memory; in chaining, the link is between two things you do not know.

The Pictures from the Statue of Liberty Story

Statue of Liberty   torch   book   big fat man   electric power drill   bar of soap   purple pennies   padlock   house trailer   black limousine   John Travolta   black Stetson hat   black vest   black boots   Cathy Lee Crosby   pink polka-dot bikini   letter to her agent   a big Saint Bernard   fur coat   diamond collar   ham bone   mountain lion   palm tree   Statue of Liberty

Chapter 3—Required Mental Exercises

Exercise 1

1. Close your eyes.
2. Silently go through the entire Statue of Liberty story by memory, creating vivid images.
3. As you are doing this, call out loud all the major elements of the story above.

Exercise 2

Let's do it again! But this time vividly describe out loud *everything* you see. Create as detailed, colorful, and crystal clear images as you can—the more details you describe the better. This exercise will get you thinking in pictures while simultaneously verbalizing.

4 Creating Peg Lists: Mental File Folders

In this chapter, we are going to learn an exercise that will develop our ability to store information in a particular way so we can retrieve it more easily at a later date. This information is stored on what I call pegs.

Earlier, I used the image of a file cabinet as a way of describing how your brain stores information. Think of pegs as the tabs on the file folders, where you label each folder so that you know at a glance what's inside it. Some people also think of pegs as hooks in a closet or on a wall, where you might hang a jacket or a coat. Except this is a mental hook where one hangs information.

To understand how we work with pegs, it is important to know a little bit about short-term and long-term memory. When we store information in our brains for recall later, we do it either for a short or long period of time. When we hear a name or a telephone number, for example, we may remember it for thirty seconds or perhaps a minute, and then it's gone, forgotten. We say that that information was in short-term memory only. When someone tells us something or we read a piece of news that makes a deep impression on us, that information has entered our long-term memory. It is there for good, something we can retrieve a day, a month, or a year later.

When they talk about improving their memories, most people are really talking about improving their short-term memory, or more specifically, making sure that information from short-term memory gets into long-term memory. That is, if you hear that name or phone number at a party or business meeting, you want to be able to remember it for more than just thirty seconds or a minute. You don't want to have to say five minutes later, "I'm sorry. I've forgotten your name."

I want to emphasize an important point about long-term memory. When information is in long-term memory—I call it the knowledge bank—that information cannot be forgotten. Now think about that. If you have information in your knowledge bank, you can't forget it. For example, try to forget your own name. You can't. You can't forget your name because at some point early in your life it entered long-term memory. And you'll always know it (except in the extreme case of amnesia or another illness). Even if you tried, you could not forget your name. Why? Because the name is in the knowledge bank. It's in long-term memory.

Since a lot of useful information is already in the knowledge bank of the mind, and since that information cannot be forgotten, we're going to use that to our advantage in Mega Memory. We are going to take information that we want to remember and peg it to information that cannot be forgotten. When we need to recall the new information later on, it will be easier to do so because we have *pegged* it to information that's readily available to us.

Think of pegs, then, as simply bits of information that have already been committed to memory. The pegs are already part of your knowledge bank and therefore cannot be forgotten. And on these pegs we will put new information to be recalled at a later date. We're taking something you know (the peg) and something you don't know (the new information) and we'll be putting them together. And we'll be using the power of vivid images that we learned about in the previous chapter to make our pegs strong.

The Body List

Before we can use pegs, we have to create them. We're going to develop two peg lists. The first one is the Body List. We are going to establish ten pegs, or parts of your body. Obviously, you can't forget parts of your body. If I ask you where your elbow is, for example, you know where it's located. If I ask you to locate your toes and knees, head and nose, you can tell me where they are instantly. The only thing you'll need to remember is the sequence of these body parts.

I'd like you to stand up and follow my instructions carefully.

Number 1 is toes. Wiggle your toes and repeat out loud, "Number 1, toes." Number 2 is knees. Pat your knees and repeat, "Number 2, knees." Number 3 is going to be your thigh muscle, and we're going to call it just muscle. Pat your muscle and repeat, "Number 3, muscle." Number 4 is your rear. Pat your rear and repeat, "Number 4, rear." Number 5 is your love handles. Grab your love handles and repeat, "Number 5, loves handles." Number 6 is your shoulders. Tap your shoulders and repeat, "Number 6, shoulders." Number 7 is your collar. Touch your collar and repeat, "Number 7, collar." Number 8 is your face. Touch your face, and repeat, "Number 8, face." Number 9 is your point. That is, it's the top of your head. I call it your point because you point to it. Point to your point, tap it, and repeat, "Number 9, point." Number 10 is actually off the body; it's the ceiling. Point to the ceiling and repeat, "Number 10, ceiling."

Now let's do this exercise again. Reamin standing and repeat each peg out loud. And make sure that you repeat the action from the previous exercise, too.

"Number 1, toes." Wiggle your toes. "Number 2, knees." Pat your knees. "Number 3, muscle." Pat your muscle. "Number 4, rear." Pat your rear. "Number 5, love handles." Grab your love handles. "Number 6, shoulders." Tap your shoulders. "Number 7, collar." Touch your collar. "Number 8, face." Touch your face. "Number 9, point." Point to your head. "Number 10, ceiling." Point to the ceiling.

Let's do it a third time.

"Number 1, toes. Number 2, knees. Number 3, muscle. Number 4, rear. Number 5, love handles. Number 6 shoulders. Number 7 collar. Number 8, face. Number 9, point. Number 10, ceiling."

One more time, very quickly.

"Number 1, toes. Number 2, knees. Number 3, muscle. Number 4, rear. Number 5, love handles. Number 6, shoulders. Number 7, collar. Number 8, face. Number 9, point. Number 10, ceiling."

Make sure that when you did this exercise each time you repeated each peg out loud, and carried out the action I had specified for each body part. If you forgot to do both together, go back and go through the three repetitions again.

Let's do it all one last time.

"Number 1, toes. Number 2, knees. Number 3, muscle. Number 4, rear. Number 5, love handles. Number 6, shoulders. Number 7, collar. Number 8, face. Number 9, point. Number 10, ceiling."

You may sit down now to continue reading.

These ten parts of your body have become pegs. Notice that it didn't take us more than a few minutes to commit to memory the pegs on our Body List. In fact, we didn't have to commit them to memory at all because they already were in our knowledge bank. We were only learning the sequence. That's why we went in a nice, orderly flow, from toes to the ceiling.

I want you to be aware of a few other things, too. We did not use basic association linking the numbers to the pegs. Remember, basic association is a logical linking of two things. There's no logical reason why number 5 on this Body List, for example, is our love handles. It's 5 only because we made it 5. In the Tree List we created in Chapter 2, we associated the number 5 with glove because glove reminded us of five fingers. There was a reason for it. When you peg, there is no logical association. You're only creating a sequence.

Being able to create peg lists will help you in real-life situations because the world around us is ordered in a particular sequence as well. When you can remember things in order (and when I say "remember" I am using it in an active sense—the act of putting the information into your brain), you can later retrieve that information more easily. This process works just like retrieving a memo from the right file at the office. If you have a good filing system, you'll be able to do it quickly.

Now you will write down the Body List from memory. Number from 1 through 10 on the left-side of a piece of paper, and beside each number write the appropriate term of the Body List. Close the book and do it now.◆

We're back. If for some reason, you dropped one or two, stand up and review the exercise once or twice. It usually takes people about two minutes to have the Body List committed to memory. Even if you remembered the entire list, stand up and repeat it again to make sure those pegs are really solid.

Let's go.

"Number 1, toes. Number 2, knees. Number 3, muscle. Number 4, rear. Number 5, love handles. Number 6, shoulders. Number 7, collar. Number 8, face. Number 9, point. Number 10, ceiling."

Now close the book and take a break.

The House List

Before we establish the second peg list, I want to quickly review what we just did. In creating a Body List, we made up a specific sequence, or order. This was different from the Tree List we developed in Chapter 2, which was an example of basic association. You now have two ways of creating lists for later use, and have also exercised your memory in two different ways.

Now I'd like to develop another peg list that you will commit to memory for future use. This next list is called a House List. There are three things you are going to do in creating this list:

1. Pick four rooms in your house.
2. Mentally go into each room and choose five items in that room.
3. Write each item in sequence on a piece of paper. That is, you should write them down in the same order they are placed in the room.

Pick any four rooms in your house (or four distinct areas if you live in a small apartment). The rooms themselves should go in order, too, as if you were walking through your home. For example, when I walk into my house, the first room I enter is the kitchen. That would be room 1. Then there is the dining room, the living room, and the bedroom. Those would be rooms 2, 3, and 4, respectively.

Now that you have chosen four rooms in your house, in your mind's eye go to the first room and pick out five items in that room. It's better if the items are large, having some mass and weight to them. Each item should be different from the next. (Don't choose two chairs in a room, for example.) The items should not be placed close to one another. And most important, they should be in the order in which they are placed in the room, either clockwise or counterclockwise. Keep this sequence the same in all four rooms.

If the first room you've chosen is your kitchen, for example, your items may be countertop, microwave, sink, refrigerator, trash can. Those go clockwise in my kitchen.

Now take a piece of paper, number 1 through 5, and write

down the items you've chosen. When you're finished with the first room, mentally visit the other three rooms and do same thing, so that you have twenty items listed on your piece of paper. Don't repeat any items. And remember, you are doing this in your mind's eye. You shouldn't be walking through the house physically.

Your list may look something like this:

Example of a House List

ROOM 1
   1. refrigerator
   2. stove
   3. sink
   4. coffeepot
   5. trash can

ROOM 2
   6. organ
   7. chair
   8. lamp
   9. fireplace
   10. couch

ROOM 3
   11. shower head
   12. tub
   13. towels
   14. toilet
   15. medicine cabinet

ROOM 4
   16. dresser
   17. mirror
   18. bed
   19. vanity
   20. closet

It should have taken about ten minutes to write down those pegs. Remember, they're pegs because they are in your knowledge bank already and you will be using them as reference points later on. Just as with the Body List, they are places on which we can put new information. All you have to do now is remember the sequence in which you chose them.

Now listen to my instructions carefully. First, check your list and make sure that none of the twenty pegs that you have chosen is repeated. Also, make sure each peg flows in a nice orderly fashion, in whatever direction you have chosen for the entire exercise.

I will now ask you to look at your paper, read the first peg out loud, then close your eyes and, as vividly as you can, see that peg in your mind's eye. Then go to the next peg. Read it out loud, close your eyes, and vividly see it in your mind's eye. Do that with all twenty pegs. It should take five to ten minutes. Do it now.◆

We're going to do it again, but this time you don't have to call the peg out loud. I still want you to read the name of the peg, but this time repeat it silently. Then close your eyes and vividly see the peg in your mind's eye. Proceed in sequence through all the pegs. The key here is not speed, but making sure you silently repeat each one by name, and vividly see the peg in your mind's eye. Do that now.◆

We're going to do it one more time. But this time, start with peg 20 and go backward through your list. Look at each item in sequence, close your eyes, call it by name silently, and vividly see it in your mind's eye. Be deliberate, and make sure the images are crystal clear—as if you were really there, looking at each object. Do that now.◆

Now stand up and hold your paper in your hand. This time I want you to work on a little speed. You're going to do exactly the same thing. Take a mental journey through your house, read the name of each peg out loud, and as you do, see it vividly in your mind's eye. Proceed through all the pages, and try to keep a more brisk pace. Do it now.◆

Now turn the paper over and remain standing. Do it again, calling out every peg by name and vividly seeing it. But there's one big difference this time—you're not going to read the list off your paper because the pegs are now committed to memory. Go through the list now.◆

Remain standing. You're going to do this again without reading from the paper, only now you will be going backward. Start with peg 20 and go all the way to peg 1. Close your eyes and take that mental journey through your four rooms. You will be seeing each peg and calling it by name out loud. When you are through, have a seat. Do that now.◆

Please sit down now. We're going to do it one more time, with another small difference. You do not have to call the name of the peg out loud. Take the mental journey through your house, from peg 1 to 20. Seeing each peg as vividly as you can, call it by name, but call it by name silently. Do that now.◆

Now we're going to add yet another little twist. You are going to do exactly the same thing, starting with the first peg, ending with the last. You will vividly see each peg as before, but this time you won't have to call it by name at all. You will notice that your speed dramatically increases. Why? Because, as I've said previously, you can think faster than you can write or talk. If we could communicate with thoughts, communication would go 10,000 times faster than it is today, perhaps even 100,000 times faster.

Vividly see each peg in your mind's eye. Don't call it by name. Just visualize each peg, then go to the next. Do it now.◆

Do this exercise again without calling out each peg. Just visualize it, starting with the first peg, ending with the last. Do it now.◆

We're going to do this two more times, but with a little twist again. Start with the first peg, end with the last, but this time try to visualize the pegs in groups rather than individually. Use the four groups you created. You'll be able to do that easily because of that photographic memory you have been training. Do it now.◆

Isn't it dramatic how fast you're getting? You can go through all twenty pegs in just a few seconds, because now you're seeing them in groups. Do it one more time, seeing the pegs in groups, starting with the first peg, ending with the last. Do it now.◆

Now take a sheet of paper. Number 1 through 20 down the

left side and write down by memory your House List pegs. Do it now.◆

We're back. Take out another sheet of paper and number 1 through 10 and write down by memory the pegs of your Body List. We created these at the beginning of the chapter, and you'll notice they are still committed to memory. Write them down now.◆

I hope you're pretty excited by now. You know the Body List. You know your House List, too. They are both reference points, parts of your knowledge bank, which is long-term memory. The items on both lists didn't have to be recalled. All we did was put them in a particular sequence. It all took about a half hour, and now you can start using these pegs.

Chapter 4—Review

How Your Memory Works

Short-term memory—recalls things you hear, see, and think about for a few seconds to several hours.

Long-term memory—accessible long-term information (your knowledge bank). It is information you couldn't forget if you tried: your name, address, and so forth.

Inaccessible long-term memory—all other experiences recorded by the human tape recorder (the ear), the human camera (the eyes), and all other senses.

Your Mind Is Like a File Cabinet.

When you have a trained memory, your mind is organized. Things you hear, see, or think go into mental files for easy recall in the future.

With an untrained memory, the files are literally jumbled together, like actual files, thrown onto the floor.

Body List Pegs

A list in long-term memory—so it can't be forgotten.

1. toes
2. knees
3. muscle
4. rear
5. love handles
6. shoulders
7. collar
8. face
9. point
10. ceiling

Creating House-List Pegs
1. Pick out four rooms.
2. Pick out five pegs in each room, in a sequential order.
3. Each peg should be completely different from every other peg.

A Typical House List
ROOM 1
1. refrigerator
2. stove
3. sink
4. coffeepot
5. trash can

ROOM 2
6. organ
7. chair
8. lamp
9. fireplace
10. couch

ROOM 3
11. shower head
12. tub
13. towels

14. toilet
15. medicine cabinet

ROOM 4
16. dresser
17. mirror
18. bed
19. vanity
20. closet

Chapter 4—Required Mental Exercises

Exercise 1
1. From memory, review the Body List and the House List. See each peg vividly in your mind.
2. Once you are sure you know them in order, review them again, calling each one out loud by name.

Exercise 2
From memory, review the Body List and the House List—while you drive, eat dinner, watch TV.

5 Using Your Peg Lists

Now that we have pegs established, the question arises: What do we do with them? Let's go back to our image of pegs as tabs on file folders. For example, you may have a mental file folder with the heading "Today's Errands." If you want to remember "What do I have to do today?" you look in that folder to see what, if anything, has been put there. You may have another folder titled "Bills to Pay," and when you look inside, you see which bills need attention.

When you have a Mega Memory and something in your experience brings you to a peg, whatever information you have put in the folder represented by that peg will be accessible to you. And even more important, after you have been exercising your memory for a while, the information will pop back instantly.

To explain how this might work in real life, think of the furniture in your house again, any piece of furniture, not necessarily one of the pieces you used for your House List. What if I blindfolded you, led you into one of the rooms, and spun you around. You wouldn't know exactly where you were. You'd begin to grope and look and feel to try to find something that you recognized. But when you touched the television set, you would know immediately where everything else was in the room. Why? The television set is a reference point, one of many that you have created over time in your house. That is, over time you have learned the arrangement of furniture in your house, and it's in your memory in that order. Each piece of furniture has become a peg and allows you to orient yourself instantly.

Pegging works the same way. Just like knowing where the furniture is in your living room, it's a way of ordering information in your mind so that you can recall it later quickly and easily.

When pegging:

1. You take a preestablished peg (remember, it's always a vivid picture, as vivid as you can make it!);
2. You create another vivid picture of something you want to put into your knowledge bank; and
3. You link the two pictures in a ludicrous, nonsensical fashion using action.

This is different from chaining, remember, which is linking two totally new things, like the different images in the Statue of Liberty story. In pegging, you are linking one new piece of information with something that's already in your knowledge bank.

Let's say, for example, we decide to use our toes as our preestablished peg. In our mind's eye, we would get a crystal clear picture of our toes. Then, we would create a vivid picture of something that we want to peg to it, let's say our computer. And then we link the two together with nonsensical action, let's say by imagining ourselves kicking the computer around the room like a beach ball. We have just pegged the computer to our toes.

The kind of action you use in pegging is important. I define action as being of two kinds, passive or active. Passive action is walking, sauntering, balancing, holding. There's not a lot of movement or activity there. It's rather slow and uninspired. Active action is what we want in pegging. It's animated, dynamic, the crazier the better, like a music video on MTV or the Saturday morning cartoons in which anything can happen. Running, throwing, jumping, smashing, hitting—lots of movement, lots of dynamism, that's what we want.

There's an acronym I've created that should help you in pegging—VIA, which stands for vivid visualization, imagination, and action. It's the process you go through in pegging. First of all, vividly creating pictures is the most important thing. Second, use your imagination to create pictures that are interesting and unique. And third, use active action to really give those pictures punch, a sense of dynamic movement. If you think of VIA as you're pegging, you will be building a very solid foundation for your Mega Memory.

At about this point in my seminars, I get a lot of questions. "Kevin, why are we doing this?" "Kevin, all the exercises are getting confusing. Can you explain the difference between them again?" "Can't we just use one peg list for everything?" I want to reassure you if you're starting to feel the same way. I have been throwing a lot of concepts at you. If you can't remember everything—the reasons for doing this exercise or that one, the differences among all the exercises—that's okay. As I've said before, you don't have to explain the exercises or understand how they work. Your part is *doing* the exercises. It's as if we were getting ready to jog, and I was teaching you stretching exercises. If you know the names of all the muscles that you are stretching and the reasons for stretching them, that's fine. But it's not necessary. What's important is that you are doing the stretching, and doing it correctly.

We're doing the same thing for your mind right now. We're exercising it so it can think and order information properly, information that it will want to recall in the future. And if some of these exercises seem nonsensical, have fun with them, as much crazy fun as you possibly can. Remember, the willingness to accept change is the hallmark of learning.

Before we go on to some actual exercises, I want to make one important point, perhaps the most exciting point in this book. To remember virtually anything, you will only need three things. The three things are:

1. a place to put the information (peg)
2. a vivid picture of the information you are pegging
3. mental glue to hold the picture on the peg

The place to put the information, as we've just learned, is a peg, a reference point. You can think of it as a cubbyhole, mental filing folder, mental mailbox, whatever term you want to use. We've also learned the importance of vivid images, just like that lemon in Chapter 3. And we've talked about mental glue, which is—what do you think?—action. Active action. As we practice pegging, you will be repeating these three steps, and when you get into real-life situations, it will work the same way.

Pegging to the Body List

We're now going to do some pegging exercises. We'll take it slowly, and I'll give you some tips on what to do and what not to do. Don't get discouraged if you think you are progressing too slowly. We're just getting started. In Part II of this book, when you start applying pegging to real-life situations, you'll be performing this process very fast and without consciously thinking about it. You'll be amazed at how much more efficient this pegging method is than writing things down.

For our first exercise, we're going to peg things to our bodies. We are going to put the first thing we want to remember on our toes, which is the first peg on our Body List. The second thing we want to remember will go to our second peg, which is the knees. The third thing will go to the third peg, which is the muscle, and so on, through to our tenth peg, which is the ceiling.

The first thing we want to remember is eggs. Using animation and movement, vividly link eggs to your toes somehow.

In trying this for the first time, many people reason as follows: "Well, let's see. Kevin said we need to get a vivid picture of our toes and a vivid picture of an egg, and put both together using action. Okay, I'll make a picture in my mind of an egg, and I'll put it on my toe." That's not very good. Why? The action is very passive—you're just putting an egg on your toes and then it just stays there. The picture has very little life.

Remember, we want *active* action: something dynamic and with a lot of movement, like running, jumping, throwing, smashing. And most important, with the power of your imagination, make the action impossible—something that could never happen in real life. In other words, make it crazy, nonsensical. The crazier, the better. If it's illogical, it's good. Keep VIA in mind: vivid visualization, imagination, and action. Those three factors must always be present for a peg to be effective.

Here's a tip for good pegging: *If you think it's boring, it's bad.* Keep that in mind whenever you are pegging. Boring things are forgotten. Crazy, animated, ridiculous, nonsensical things are remembered. Why? As I've said before, your mind automatically locks onto something that could not or would not happen in real life, precisely because it's so different and unique. The crazier, the better. Use your imagination as much as possible.

This is an example of a good peg for toes and an egg. "Well, Kevin said to exaggerate the picture, so maybe instead of just visualizing an egg, I'll see a giant egg, or maybe thousands of eggs." The picture is exaggerated, which is much better. "Kevin also said to animate the picture. Well, maybe the egg has legs and arms and it's pink. He said use lots of action. Okay, maybe that egg is in front of me, and I'm kicking the egg with my toe." This person gave his picture a lot of life and made it something that is absolutely ridiculous.

Here's a tip for an even better peg: *More is always better than less.* That is, use more action rather than less. Keep the scene going; keep the action happening.

For example, if we say, "I see a giant egg with legs and arms, and I kick him," that's an acceptable action. If you apply more-is-better-than-less, maybe you'll be kicking the egg several times. Maybe the egg is biting your toe or kicking you back. Maybe you kick him so hard that he breaks open and yolk spreads all over your toes. Maybe you scoop up the egg, put it in a big bowl, and begin to mix it up with your toes.

Ready? Now stand up.

Peg an egg to your toes. You want this process to take about thirty seconds, maybe forty-five, no more. Close your eyes and create a picture, making sure it's vivid and crystal clear. Then think of an action, a dynamic, crazy action. Do this now.◆

The second thing we want to remember is bacon. Where does it go? On the second peg on your Body List, which is the knees. Create a vivid picture of your knees and a vivid picture of bacon. To help yourself create the picture, think back to that exercise about the lemon and do the same thing with bacon. What does the bacon look like? Is it frozen? Is it in a package? Is the package open? What's the color of the bacon? How greasy is it? Now put that bacon on your knee using action.

Here are several examples of how someone might do this. "Maybe I'll just nail the bacon to my knee." There's a lot of action there, and it's ridiculous (if somewhat painful!), something that would never happen in real life. Here's another example. "Well, maybe I'm frying bacon all over my knee, and it's getting real hot and my knee feels hot." Someone else might think, "Maybe I'm taking bacon and shining my knee." One last example: "I'm putting my knees together and wrapping bacon around them in a knot, and I'm trying to walk, but I can't."

The examples in the above paragraph weren't boring because they all had strong action. (In the first example the action was nailing. In the second it was frying. The third was shining. The action in the fourth example, tying, wasn't as good as the other three, but it's still okay, especially if you keep the action going.)

Ask yourself, "What is my action?" to tell whether your peg is a good one. If you can answer that question clearly, and you're vividly picturing it, you have a good peg. In real-life situations, it is the vivid action that will serve up on a silver platter whatever you want to recall.

All right, close the book, and in your mind's eye, peg bacon to your knee.◆

The third thing we want to remember is hamburger. It goes on the third peg on the Body List, which is the muscle. Vividly picture that thigh muscle and vividly picture hamburger, and using action, put hamburger on your thigh. Maybe your hamburger is raw, and you're rubbing it all over your muscle in your mind's eye, and your muscle is getting very greasy and gooey. Even better: You're bouncing hamburger balls on your muscle, and they're getting bigger and bigger and bouncing higher and higher. Don't be afraid of exaggeration—the crazier and more ludicrous the picture, the better. Close the book and do it now.◆

The fourth thing we want to remember is milk, and you won't be surprised to learn that it goes on the fourth peg on the Body List, which is your rear. You're probably laughing right now, thinking of a whole bunch of crazy things to do with milk and your rear. That's something else I'm always trying to remind you of: Have fun. Laughing makes Mega Memory much more effective! Maybe very cold milk is being poured on your rear. Maybe you're playing with a friend in an ocean of milk, and you're splashing each other in the rear. Close the book, and peg milk all over your rear in your own mind's eye.◆

The fifth thing we want to remember is bananas, and it goes on the fifth peg, which is love handles. Peg bananas to your love handles. Maybe you're seeing banana trees sprouting out of your love handles all over the place. Because you want to exaggerate the picture, perhaps you're peeling a huge banana and wrapping it around your love handles. Maybe the banana is blue or red. Close the book and peg bananas to your love handles now.◆

Let's go back and review what we've pegged so far. If you can't answer each of these questions instantly, you need to go back and intensify the images. What's on your toes? What's on your knees? What's on your muscle? What's on your rear? What's on your love handles? Notice when we go back to each one of the pegs, what pops into your mind? The pictures, the action. If you had lots of action, and vivid pictures, the peg comes back because it has been locked into your knowledge bank. You used the right software for the mind, which is pictures. And you used strong "glue," which is action.

Let's go to the sixth peg. The sixth peg on your Body List is shoulders. I want you to peg bread to your shoulders. Make sure you get a vivid picture of the type of bread you're using. Is it Italian bread? Is it whole wheat? Fresh and crisp, or old and hard? Make sure you exaggerate the picture. And don't do something obvious, which is easy to do with number 6. "I'll just put bread as shoulder pads," is not good because it has no action. In one of my seminars someone once said, "I see a giant loaf of bread on my shoulders and I'm slicing off a piece. I go too far and . . . Oh! I cut myself." Now that's action!

Here's another tip regarding pegging: We've had a number of images that involve pain because pain is very memorable. It's a good thing to have in your pegs. Of course, if you don't want to be thinking of painful images all the time, other emotions make for very good pegs, too: love, fear, or anger, anything comical, or with a sexual overtone—they're all memorable as well. So in your mind's eye, create a vivid picture of your shoulders and bread, using lots of memorable action. Close the book and do it now.◆

The seventh peg is collar and the seventh thing you need to remember is lettuce. In your mind's eye, peg lettuce to your collar. Maybe you have a big lettuce leaf flapping in the breeze around your collar. Maybe it's purple or silver. Maybe you're adding more and more lettuce leaves. Close the book and do this now.◆

Let's review. If you can't answer each of these instantly, you need to go back and intensify the images. What's on your shoulders? What's on your love handles? What's on your rear? What's on your toes? How about your muscle? What's on your knee? What's on your collar? What's on your shoulder?

Let's go to the eighth peg, which is face. I want you to peg a pie to your face. Now, I know what your thinking. "Kevin, that's easy. We're just going to smash a pie in our face." But what have I been saying? When the action is obvious or possible in real life, it usually isn't very memorable. Smashing a pie in someone's face is very obvious, we've all seen it on TV or in the movies.

But here's a twist. The action in this picture, smashing, is good. From experience, I know that when you're pegging, you can't always come up with a "perfect" action, action that's both active and origi-

nal. So in this case of smashing a pie into your face, you can compen-
sate by making sure that your picture is vivid, vivid, vivid. Create
a peg by answering the following questions: What type of pie is it?
Does it smell delicious? Is it crusty? How big is it? Smell the smells,
get your taste buds involved, feel what you'd feel if you had the pie
right in front of you. The more you can picture yourself in the
scene, the better.

Now close the book and peg a pie to your face.◆

The ninth peg is your point, the top of your head. Remember,
it's your point because you can point to it. I want you to peg carrots
to your point. Some good pictures: "I see a giant carrot and someone
is holding it like a baseball bat and just beating me over the head
with it." "I'm taking golden carrots one by one and tacking them
to my head." "There are two giant carrots up there on my head
and they're dancing with each other."

In your own mind's eye, get a vivid, crystal clear picture of
carrots to peg them to your point. Close the book and do it now.◆

The tenth peg is the ceiling. I want you to peg hot dog buns
to the ceiling. Maybe you're putting butter or mustard on hot dog
buns, throwing them up one by one, and sticking them to the ceiling.
Or maybe you're standing on a ladder, trying to paint the ceiling
with a hot dog bun instead of a paint brush, and paint is getting
all over your hands.

In your own mind's eye, put hot dog buns on the ceiling. Keep
in mind, you can exaggerate it, which means there can be thousands
of hot dog buns or a giant one. We've also been talking about
making the picture dynamic, full of action. Maybe it's a live hot dog
bun trying to get away from you and running around on the ceiling.
The more nonsensical the picture, the better it is. And don't forget
to include feelings, and other sensations. Maybe you're hungry, can
smell that delicious hot dog, and that's why it's trying to run away.
Lots of action and movement; more is always better than less. Do
it now.◆

Time to review. What's on your toes? What's on your knees?
What's on your shoulders? Where are the bananas? Where are the

carrots? What's on the ceiling? What's on your collar? Where are the eggs? Where's the hamburger? Where's the milk? Where are the bananas? Where's the pie? Where are the carrots? Where are the hot dog buns? Where's the lettuce? Where are the eggs?

What's on your knees? What's on your love handles? What's on your shoulders? What's on your collar? What's on your face? What's on your point? What's on the ceiling? What's number 5 on the Tree List? What's number 7 on the Tree List? What number is bowling ball on the Tree List? What number is paycheck?

Who is in the backseat of the limousine? What is he wearing? What's in his mouth? What do the purple pennies fall on? Where is the thing the purple pennies fall on? It is being pulled by what? Who is sitting next to John Travolta? What is that person wearing? What's on her lap? What is on top of the Statue of Liberty? What's in someone's right hand? What's in the left hand?

What number is dice on the Tree List? What number is eggs on the Tree List? What is the number for witch? What number is light switch? What word is 18 on the Tree List? What word is 20 on the Tree List? What word is nineteen on the Tree List?

What's happened? The answers to all of these questions have popped right out of your memory in the form of the pictures you had earlier put there. Even questions from previous exercises and chapters. And we're just getting started.

Let's review pegging. You create a vivid picture of an established peg and a vivid picture of something you want to recall. Using VIA (vivid visualization, imagination, and action), you then put both pictures together in your mind. You make your pictures funny, ludicrous, nonsensical, something that could never happen in real life. You exaggerate, animate. Include feelings and other sensations. Remember that more is always better than less. Get that imagination going. And smile. You are creating a foundation that will let your memory do everything it is capable of doing.

Chapter 5—Review

Pegging
Linking in a ludicrous, nonsensical fashion a vivid picture of a preestablished peg and a vivid picture of the information you want to remember.

Key to Pegging
VIA: vivid visualization, imagination, and active action.

Characteristics of Vivid Pictures
    Crystal clear and in color.
    Specific, filled with detail.
    Include sounds, smells, other sensations.
    Include yourself and your feelings.
    Include active action.

Active Action
Any type of fast movement—running, jumping, smashing. Passive action—talking sitting, walking—is weak mental glue and thus is not useful when pegging.

Things to Keep in Mind While Pegging
1. Exaggeration: Always exaggerate your pictures, making them bigger than life.
2. The senses: Pictures should be extremely vivid, in color, and so real you can smell, hear, and feel them.
3. Animation: Use your imagination to make pictures of inanimate objects come to life.
4. Action: The best type is nonsensical, ludicrous, crazy.
5. More is better than less.
6. If it's boring, it's bad.

A Key Question When Pegging
What was my action?

The Three Basic Steps of Remembering
1. a place to put the information, which is a peg
2. a vivid picture of what you want to remember
3. mental glue holding the picture on the peg, which is action

Chapter 5—Required Mental Exercises

Exercise 1
Review your Body List (toes, knees, muscle, etc.), by asking yourself
the following two questions for each peg:

1. What item did I peg to my toes, knees, muscle, etc.
2. What was my action?

Exercise 2
Do the same exercise as above, but think of another action for
each item!

6   Playing Concentration

This is going to be a fun lesson because we're going to be playing a game. It's a game that was on television several years ago and which still gets shown in syndication from time to time. The game is called Concentration. If you remember, Concentration consisted of a hidden puzzle on a board. The board was divided into numbers, and different pieces of the puzzle were revealed as contestants matched numbers and prizes. Once they saw enough pieces of the puzzle, the contestants tried to guess what it was.

The puzzle could be a familiar phrase, a well-known saying, a particular object. It was make up of pictures, pictures that represented syllables of words. When you put all the pictures together, you came up with whole words and sentences. For exmaple, the picture of an eyeball and a tin can, "eye" and "can," would give you "I can."

We're going to play Concentration in this lesson, but we're going to do it in reverse. Instead of my giving you pictures and having you tell me what words they represent, I'm going to give you words that we're going to break down into syllables, turning the syllables into pictures. We'll do one word at a time. I'll lead you through a few examples step by step, and then I'll ask you to do some on your own. It's fun to work with someone else on this particular exercise.

When you are trying to come up with a picture for each syllable, think of what this syllable sounds like to you—the way you would pronounce it—not necessarily the way the syllable is actually spelled. Then choose the picture, what I call a sound-alike picture. (Like "eye," which sounds like "I" in "I can.") We're going to repeat this process for each syllable of the word, so that you will have two or three pictures for every word. Remember, the pictures won't have anything to do with the meaning of the word, they will only sound like each syllable.

Let's take the word "building." What's the first syllable? "Buil." I think of bills to be paid or a dollar bill. Let's use a picture of a dollar bill, that's easier. What's the second syllable? "Ding." How about two bells ringing—ding! "Bill-ding." "Building."

Let's take another word, "management." "Man-age-ment." How about a picture of a man for the first syllable; that's easy. Now how about "age"? That's harder because it's a concept. In Concentration, the pictures in the puzzle could represent not only sounds, but concepts, too. How do you represent the concept of age? How about a picture of an old person? Or three people side by side—a child, someone middle-aged, someone old? Now "ment." What sounds like "ment"? How about "mints" or "mince," a picture of cookies with a green filling or meat being chopped up? Let's choose the cookies. "Man-age-mints." "Management."

How about the word "category"? What's the first syllable in "category"? "Cat." Most people immediately think of a cat. What's the next syllable? "E," which sounds like "eh." That doesn't really help us, and in cases like this, you could combine syllables in Concentration, too. So what's the next syllable? "Gor." "Eh-gor." That still doesn't sound like anything. Let's add the last syllable, "y," which sounds like "ee." We now have "eh-gor-ee." "Eh-gor-ee." Something gory. What's a picture of something gory? A face with blood running down it? Frankenstein? Another monster? "Category," if we broke it down by syllables, would give you a picture of a cat and something gory. "Cat-gory." "Category." Sorry, cat lovers.

As you can see from the three words above, you have a lot of choices in the sound-alike pictures you come up with for each syllable. Some are easier than others. You can combine syllables if you find that helpful. If you prefer, you can ignore the sound and choose a picture that represents the entire word. There is no one right way to do this.

When teaching Mega Memory, I always stress "good, better, best." What I mean by this is that if something works for you, it's okay, because there's rarely only one choice for anything. Try to do what you think is best for *your* Mega Memory; it might be second best for someone else, but if you feel it works for you, it's definitely allowed. The most important point here is to *stimulate the imagination,* getting you to think in new ways that you might not have done before. Remember, at this point we are still trying to build a solid foundation for our memories. The more ways you allow your imagination to work, the firmer that foundation will be.

Breaking Down Words into Sound-Alike Pictures

Now for some exercises. I'll be giving you some words. After you read the word, I want you to close the book. Say each syllable out loud several times, and then create a picture for each syllable. If you want to combine syllables, that's okay. But—this is important—don't write anything down. You might be tempted to write down the syllable or the picture. Don't. Remember, no note taking in this book. Trust your memory; it will work. Say the syllable out loud several times, think of a picture, and go on to the next syllable. Spend only a few minutes on each word. Then come back to the book and read what pictures I chose for the word.

The first word is "trading." Close the book and do it now.◆

Let's break "trading" down. The first syllable is "tray." What sound-alike picture can represent "tray"? How about a silver serving tray. What's the last syllable in "trading"? "Ding." How about those ringing bells, or a picture of a scratch or dent in something, which is referred to as a "ding." So you might have a picture of a tray and a picture of two bells, while someone else may have a tray and a picture of something with a scratch in it.

The next word is "conduit." Close the book and do it now.◆

The first syllable is "con." What did you imagine as a picture for "con"? You may have thought of a convict. Or maybe you thought of a convent or con artist. This brings up an interesting point about choosing a good picture. As we've been considering the different words, you may have noticed that the sound-alike pictures that represent abstract ideas or general concepts are much harder to come up with than those that represent a concrete thing. Why? Because something abstract can be represented by many pictures, while a concrete object usually requires a simpler, clearer image. If you have a choice, you want to think of a picture that's more specific and exact.

For "con," if you use the image of a convict, you would have a pretty clear picture of a person in a striped uniform, with a ball and chain around his feet, maybe standing behind bars. If you want to use con artist, a good picture is harder to imagine. It's not as specific because you have many choices. It's as if I asked you to give me a picture of a teacher or a picture of a lawyer. "Teacher" or "lawyer" could be represented by so many pictures—a man, woman, someone young or old, with glasses or without—it's not as clear.

Let's finish "conduit." The last two syllables are "do" and "et." You probably want to combine them. How about a picture of two people singing, a duet. So your pictures for "conduit" would be a con and two people singing.

Let's do a few more words. "Patience." Close the book and turn "patience" into sound-alike pictures.◆

Many of you probably broke down "patience" into two syllables. The first syllable, "pay," might be a picture of someone at a counter or booth handing over money. The next syllable is "tience." What does that sound like? How about "cents." "Pay-cents." "Patience." You may also have thought a person in a hospital bed, a patient, and used only one picture for the entire word. That's fine. "Change" is another word you can represent with one picture. Most people think of coins on a counter or in a cash register.

Let's try "proud." Close the book and come up with something that represents proud.◆

"Proud" is an abstract term. What makes you think of the word "proud"? Maybe a bald eagle, or a peacock? Other choices are a father holding a newborn baby, a Marine ("the few and the proud"), or someone getting a gold medal. I would choose peacock or a Marine.

How about "peace"? Close the book and think of a sound-alike picture for peace.◆

Was the first thing you thought of a "piece" of something? You focused on the sound of the word, maybe coming up with a slice of pie or pizza. Or you could have focused on the concept, coming up with a peace symbol, an olive branch or a dove. Those are all good pictures that can be used for "peace."

Here's another tricky one. Close the book and turn "find" into a picture.◆

"Find" is one syllable, so you had to choose something that either sounds like "find," or something that represents the idea of finding something. A word that sounds like "find" is "fined." How can you represent "fined" with a picture? How about being fined for speeding? Your picture would have been a traffic ticket, or a police officer writing one out, or even a judge in a courtroom. Instead of something that sounds like "find," you may have thought of a picture that represents finding something. How about a treasure chest—that's a pretty good find.

One more: "freedom"? Close the book and give me a sound-alike picture for freedom.◆

Breaking it down by syllable, you would have "free" and "dom." I find both of those rather tough, so I would try to think of a picture that represents freedom. When I asked for this in one of my workshops once, a young man in the back of the room yelled out, "Lottery ticket." Well, the whole group laughed, and I laughed. But then I thought to myself that this was quite legitimate. A lottery ticket was this man's picture of freedom. Other people might think of the American flag, revolutionary soldiers, the Liberty Bell, the Statue of Liberty.

The key with "freedom," as with all the other words, is to use what works for you. There are no right or wrong answers—the important thing has been getting you into the habit of breaking words down by syllable and turning them into pictures. Sound to picture. Abstract term to picture. It's a great way to bend and stretch and stimulate the imagination, and motivate you to think in new and exciting ways.

The Jumping Flea

Many of my workshop participants tell me that the Concentration exercises are not easy to do—at least when I first expose them to it. If someone complains, I like to repeat the following story about how they train fleas in the South.

I'm not an expert, but I'm told that fleas ride dogs, they jump, and that's about all they do. I'm told if you have a flea and you put it in a jar, it will jump right out of the jar. In order to train it, you put a lid on the jar. Watch what happens when the flea tries to jump out. It whacks its head on the inside of the lid. You come back an hour later, and this flea is still jumping and whacking its head on the inside of the lid. You come back two hours later and it's still jumping and whacking its head. In three hours, it's still jumping, but by now it's not hitting the lid anymore but is jumping to about an inch below it. Then, you can take the lid off, and the flea still won't jump out of the jar. You have trained the flea to alter its jumping pattern.

I have to ask you—can the flea jump out of that jar? The answer is no. It can't jump out of the jar anymore because it doesn't know the difference between the real limitation of the lid and a self-imposed limitation that it put on itself.

You and I are the same way. We go into business. We go into life. We put limitations on ourselves, and many times we don't know the difference between real limitations and those that we have artificially imposed upon ourselves.

The exercises in this chapter teach you how to release your imagination by thinking of new ways. If the exercises seem difficult, do them again, more slowly. First focus on creating pictures that remind you of the sounds; then create pictures that represent concepts. Then combine the two.

I want you to keep jumping out of that jar. I want you to know that there is no lid there. You can jump as high as you want. You can go as far as you want. You can do what you want to do and be what you want to be. Just allow yourself to be open to new ways of thinking and believe that the answer is yes, instead of no.

Chapter 6—Review of Lesson

Rules for Turning Abstract Words into Pictures

1. Break down the word by syllables.
2. Ignore how the word is spelled.
3. Focus on the syllable's sound.
4. Repeat each syllable out loud.
5. Create a sound-alike or symbolic picture based on the syllable's sound.
6. Relax and have fun!

Chapter 6—Required Mental Exercises

Exercise 1

For following words, create vivid mental pictures of each of their syllables. If a syllable does not conjure up a picture for you, combine it with the next syllable and work with the sound created by both syllables. And be sure to always say the syllables out loud.

1. handsome
2. denial
3. conform
4. carriage
5. article

Exercise 2

Say the following words out loud, then imagine a sound-alike picture for each.

1. trust
2. peace
3. change
4. love
5. happiness

Once you've done that, also create a picture of something that symbolizes or represents each word.

7   Pegging the Tree List

We are going to do another pegging exercise in this chapter. In Chapter 5, we pegged ten items to our Body List. This time we are going to peg twenty items to our Tree List from Chapter 2.

Let's first go back and review the Tree List pegs. Say each one out loud. "Number 1, tree. Number 2, light switch. Number 3, stool. Number 4, car. Number 6, gun, Number 7, dice. Number 8, skate. Number 9, cat. Number 20, cigarettes. Number 5, glove. Number 10, bowling ball. Number 11, goalpost. Number 19, golf club. Number 18, voting booth. Number 15, paycheck. Number 16, candy. Number 17, magazine. Number 14, ring. Number 13, witch. Number 12, eggs."

What number is glove? Five. What number is bowling ball? Ten. What number is paycheck? Fifteen. What number is witch? Thirteen. What number is stool? Three. What number is cigarettes? Twenty. What number is gun? Six. What number is goalpost? Eleven.

I'd like you to review the Tree List on your own for about three to five minutes. Go backward and forward, to make sure you instantly know what numbers and pictures go together. Being able to recall everything instantly is important, so if you keep getting stuck on a particular number, go back to Chapter 2 and review the association. The Tree List should be fresh in your memory before you can continue with this chapter.◆

Okay, we're now going to start pegging to our Tree List. When I give you the number, you will create a vivid picture of the Tree List peg that corresponds to that number. For example, when I say, "Number 1," you will get a vivid picture of a tree. Then I will give you an item that I want you to remember. You will link this item to your Tree List peg, putting them together using action.

Keep in mind what's important in pegging. The pictures have to be vivid, full of detail, and as colorful and exaggerated as you can make them. You're going to use a lot of movement and action—active action. Include yourself in the pictures, which helps get your emotions and different senses involved. Create pictures that are funny and nonsensical, making sure that such a scene could never take place in real life. Remember, if it's boring, it will be bad. If it's funny and ridiculous, it will be good.

Let me give you a few more pegging tips. You can close your eyes if you want; that helps you focus. Some people prefer to leave their eyes open, as if they were daydreaming. That's okay, too. Work on one item at a time. When we're on number 5 or 6, don't worry about what we pegged to the tree or to the light switch or to the stool. Just be concerned with what we are doing at that moment. Trust your memory—that's what this chapter is all about. After you've done these exercises, you'll really appreciate what a powerful tool it is.

One more important thing. When we get to about number 14, you may have a little voice that says, "Hey! Do you think we're going to remember all these things?" That's stress, which produces a negative attitude. Don't let stress hold you back. Just relax. Breathe easy, smile, and keep on reading and doing the exercises. The important thing is to let your imagination go wild and have fun. That's the best way to learn how to trust your memory.

Pegging to the Tree List

Now please follow along with me carefully. I will start each item by giving you the number, and you will spend no more than a minute or two pegging the item to the Tree List. To help you along, I will give you my pictures for the first example.

Number 1. You should have a vivid picture right now of a tree in your mind's eye. The word that I want you to peg to it is "elephant." So get a vivid picture of an elephant and peg it to the tree using action. Include yourself if you can, and have lots of movement. If you have the elephant sitting next to the tree, that's bad because it's boring. Maybe you're riding the elephant and the elephant is stampeding into the tree. Maybe he sits on the tree, and you're in the tree, so he threatens to sit on you, too. Maybe he's wrapping his trunk around the tree, pulling it out of the ground and beating you over the head with it. Or maybe you're Superman; you rip up the tree and start beating the elephant. Use your imagination. More is better than less. Number 1 is "elephant." Close your eyes if you want to, and spend no more than a minute or two pegging "elephant" to "tree." Do it now.◆

Number 2. There should be a vivid picture of a light switch just waiting to pop into your mind. The second item is "ketchup." Peg ketchup to a light switch. You may be thinking ketchup doesn't belong on a light switch. But you'll make it belong. Use your imagination and peg ketchup to a light switch in a funny, nonsensical way. Don't forget the action, and remind yourself you're having fun with this, that anything is possible. Number 2 is "ketchup." Do it now.◆

Number 3. You know the third peg is a stool. The third item is "Scotch tape." Peg Scotch tape to a stool. Put yourself in this picture. Exaggerate the action as much as you can. And feel the feelings, smell the smells, and experience the sensations. Number 3 is "Scotch tape." Do it now.◆

Now forget the Scotch tape. Go back to number 2 very quickly. Do it now. You should have immediately come up with your picture of the light switch and ketchup. Notice how fast that happened.

Go back to number 1 very quickly. Do it now. Notice how the picture of the elephant and the tree pops right into your mind. You are recalling things easily and at will. Go back to number 3 now.

The stool and the Scotch tape were right there in your mind's eye. They have been locked into your memory.

Number 4. You know the fourth peg is car. I want you to remember "water." Don't create a picture of it raining on a car. There's not enough action in that picture, and it's boring. Include yourself if you can, maybe experiencing fear or other emotions. Exaggerate the water; make the car a funny size or painted brilliant colors. Number 4 is "water." Do it now.◆

Now forget about the car and the water. Go back to number 2 very quickly. You received a picture of ketchup and a light switch and whatever action you had used to peg them together. Go back to number 3. The scene with the stool and the Scotch tape popped right into your mind. Now go back to number 4, water. There's the picture of the car and the water again.

Number 5. You know the fifth peg is glove. Peg "bubble gum" to it. Relax and focus on a crazy action for bubble gum and a glove. Don't just wrap it around the glove, which is obvious. Exaggerate it and make it ludicrous. More is better than less. And make the picture vivid, of course—there's a lot you can do with bubble gum! Let your imagination go wild. The object is to have fun, remember? Five is "bubble gum." Do it now.◆

Go back to number 4 now. You saw the car and the water in your mind's eye, and reviewed the action that links them together. Go back to number 2 now. In an instant you reviewed the picture and the action. You can now appreciate that you have instant recall—at will. Now go back to number 5, the glove and the bubble gum. Your mind's eye reviewed the scene in pictures that were crystal clear.

Number 6. You know the sixth peg is gun. The sixth item I want you to remember is "pillow." Peg a pillow to a gun. Make it funny. Make it ludicrous. Exaggerate it. And don't forget movement—vivid, crystal clear pictures with movement. Six is "pillow." Do it now.◆

Forget the pillow and the gun. Go back to number 5. The picture of the bubble gum and the glove flashed through your mind. Go back to number 4. You instantly saw the car and the water and whatever action you used. Your great memory has locked them into the knowledge bank. Now go back to number 6 and review the gun and the pillow.

Number 7. You know the seventh peg is dice. I want you to remember "rug." Get a vivid picture of a rug. Now exaggerate the action, keeping in mind that more is always better than less. Stay away from the obvious, like someone throwing dice on a rug. Make it fantastic, including yourself and your emotions in the picture ... pain, excitement, fear, pleasure. Make it memorable. Seven is "rug." Do it now.◆

Forget about the rug and dice. Go back to number 6 and review your scene with the pillow and the gun. Your pictures are vivid; your actions are clear because they're locked into your knowledge bank. Go back to number 5, bubble gum and glove. Now go back to number 7, the dice and the rug. Your imagination is getting stronger and stronger. You picture things easily, your actions are animated and funny, and you're relaxed and having fun. Take a deep breath and relax, allowing your mind to wander for a while....

Number 8. You know the eighth peg is skate. I want you to remember "window." What can you do with a window and a skate? You're avoiding the obvious, like watching someone skating through a window. Your picture is much more alive and ridiculous. It has lots of action. Perhaps it's funny, or perhaps there's another emotion involved. Number 8 is "window." Do it now.◆

Forget number 8. Go back to number 7. You reviewed the dice and the rug. It's like running a movie in your mind's eye. The pictures get more and more vivid, and the scene comes back more and more easily. Go back to number 6. Now go back to number 8, the skate and the window. That picture is right there in your mind's eye.

Number 9. You know the ninth peg is cat. The ninth thing I want you to remember is "jeep." Create a picture of a cat and a jeep. Exaggerate. Animate. Maybe the cat is a giant one; maybe there are a lot of them. And of course, there's movement and outrageous action. Number 9 is "jeep." Do it now.◆

Forget about the cats and the jeep; go back to number 8 now. The skate and the window and whatever actions were going on instantly popped right back into your mind. Go to number 7. Now number 9, the cat and the jeep. The pictures and the action for both of them come right back.

Number 10. You know the tenth peg is bowling ball. I want you to peg your "foot" to it. Not your shoe, not your feet, your *foot.* Remember, you're being as specific as you can. And you're avoiding the obvious. Come up with something impossible, funny, a bowling ball made of some crazy material. Do something with your foot that you can't in real life, like picking up the bowling ball and playing catch. And keep the action coming. More is better than less. Number 10 is your "foot." Peg it to a bowling ball now.◆

Forget Number 10. Go back to number 9, the jeep and the cat. Now review number 8. Now relax. Remember, we're just doing one at a time, and I don't want you to trip over yourself. But I do hope you are trusting your memory more and more. You are seeing how great it is, how quickly it can remember things. Now review number 10 again, the bowling ball and your foot.

Number 11. You know the eleventh peg is goalpost. I want you to remember a man's "necktie." What are the most vivid pictures you can create involving a necktie and a goalpost? Perhaps you can make them really big and very colorful. Include yourself in it and make it as exaggerated as possible. One of my favorites is a huge, pink-flowered necktie tied to the ends of the goalpost, and I'm swinging in it wildly, about to fall out. That's exaggerated, it's got a lot of action, and is full of emotion, too. Number 11 is "necktie." Peg it to goalpost now.◆

Go back to number 10. In your mind's eye you saw the bowling ball and foot, pictured each thing clearly, and reviewed the action. Go back to number 9. Now go back to 11, the goalpost and the man's necktie. I hope you see vivid pictures with lots of action.

Number 12. You know the twelfth peg is eggs. I want you to remember "mustard." The first thing I think of about mustard is its texture.

If you want, focus on that as you create your picture. And think of all the different shades of yellow mustard comes in. Now come up with an exaggerated action for eggs and mustard. You can have a lot of fun with this one. Just don't use logic. Focus on the fun you can have with this. And don't forget to taste it, smell it, and feel the texture. Number 12 is "mustard." Peg mustard to eggs now.◆

Go back to Number 11. You saw the necktie and the goalpost. Go to number 10. Remind yourself to stay relaxed. By now you know you have a powerful memory and a vivid imagination. The pictures come easily. Take a deep breath and review number 12 again.

Number 13. You know the thirteenth peg is witch. The thirteenth thing I want you to remember is "book." Get a vivid, crystal clear picture of a book. Using action and exaggeration, put a witch and book together.◆

Go back to number 12 quickly. You saw the eggs and the mustard. The pictures instantly pop back into your mind. Look at number 11 now. Now go back to Number 13. The witch and the book are back in your mind with whatever action was involved.

Number 14. You know the fourteenth peg is ring. You want to remember "chair." Maybe it's your favorite chair. Maybe it's a chair you've seen in a store window and would like to buy. How can you put a ring and a chair together? Perhaps the ring can be bigger than life. Perhaps the chair is precariously balancing on it. Perhaps you're sitting in that chair, afraid of falling over. Or maybe the chair is turning around and around on that ring, and you're holding on for dear life. Or maybe the chair is suspended from a huge ring that is hanging from the ceiling and you're doing gymnastics. These are things that could never happen in real life—at least not in my life. Keep it outrageous; have fun with it. Number 14 is "chair." Peg it to a ring now.◆

Go back to number 13 quickly and picture the witch and a book. What was the action? Now go to number 12. What was that action? Now go back to number 14. What is the action involving the ring and the chair?

Number 15. You know the fifteenth peg is paycheck. I want you to remember a "cup of coffee." Peg coffee to a paycheck. No, don't spill coffee on a paycheck. That's boring, predictable—at least in my life. We want bigger than life. And don't forget to include different emotions and feel different sensations. Put yourself right in the heart of the action. Number 15 is "cup of coffee." Peg it to a paycheck now.◆

Forget the coffee and paycheck. Picture number 14. You immediately saw the chair and the ring. Picture number 13. You saw the witch and the book. Now go back to number 15, the paycheck and the cup of coffee.

Number 16. You know the sixteenth peg is candy. Making sure you have a detailed, crystal clear picture of the type of candy you want, peg an "alligator" to it. Include yourself in this picture—that always makes this picture a lot of fun. Maybe you're losing a limb as you give your pet alligator a lick of your candy, or better yet, maybe the alligator is losing a limb because you're the one taking a big bite. Maybe the alligator lets you lie on top of him, and both of you swim up the river, eating candy and having the time of your lives. And don't forget to create as vivid a picture as you can of the alligator. Let your imagination really go wild with this one. Number 16 is "alligator." Peg an alligator to candy now.◆

Go back to number 15. The paycheck and cup of coffee have instantly popped back into your mind without any effort on your part. Now go to number 14. You're seeing the ring and the chair. Go back to number 16. There are the alligator and the candy.

Number 17. The seventeenth peg is a magazine. I want you to remember "baseball bat." What's the magazine look like? How does the baseball bat feel? What color are they? Now what's the action? What can you do with a baseball bat and a magazine in your mind's eye that you can't do in real life? Can you include yourself in the picture? What are your emotions? Is your scene funny? Frightening? Sad? Number 17 is "baseball bat." Peg it to a magazine now.◆

Now picture number 16. Did you see candy and an alligator—and yourself—involved in some crazy action? Look at number 15.

You saw the paycheck and the cup of coffee. Go back to number 17, the magazine and the baseball bat. Make sure your pictures are vivid and that action is continuing.

Number 18. The eighteenth peg is a voting booth, and we want to remember "beer." Beer and a voting booth. That shouldn't be too hard. But remember, it has to be exaggerated and nonsensical. Make it funny. Make it ludicrous. Make it bigger than life. Include a lot of movement. Number 18 is "beer." Picture a voting booth and beer and peg them together now.◆

Go back to number 17 and your picture of the magazine and the baseball bat. Now go to number 16, the alligator and the candy. Now go back to number 18, the voting booth and beer.

Number 19. The nineteenth peg is a golf club, and we want to remember a "basketball" with it. How can you put a basketball and a golf club together? They don't have very much to do with each other in real life, and that's exactly the point of this exercise. Using vivid images and lots of crazy action, think of a way you could link them to each other. Number 19 is "basketball." Peg it to the golf club now.◆

Go back to number 18 and your picture of the voting booth and the beer. Now picture number 17, the magazine and the baseball bat. Now go back to number 19, the basketball and golf club.

Number 20. One more—number 20. We know the twentieth peg is cigarettes. The twentieth item is "piano." How do you peg a piano to a pack of cigarettes? Since a piano is so big and cigarettes are so small, how about doing the opposite—make the piano tiny and the pack of cigarettes the size of a piano. Now choose animated action, and include yourself in this picture. Make it funny, ludicrous, and full of emotion. Number 20 is "piano." Peg it to cigarettes now.◆

Go back to number 19, the golf club and the basketball. Now go to number 18, the voting booth and the beer. Now go back to number 20, the cigarettes and the piano.

Now I want you to take out a sheet of paper and number 1 through 20 down the left side. When I tell you to, you will write down from memory the twenty words that I asked you to remember. When you get to number 1, you will ask yourself, what was my first peg? And your mind will respond with the picture of a tree, which will pop right into your mind. And almost at the same time, whatever you put on the tree will be right there in your mind's eye. Don't write down any of the action. Just write the word that I asked you to remember. When you get to number 2, look for the second peg in your mind, which is the light switch. Whatever picture you created with the light switch will pop into your mind, vividly and automatically.

To help yourself along, you can ask two questions. The first, "What is my peg?" will bring up the appropriate picture. The second question is about action: "What was my action?" or "What was happening?" or "What was I doing?" This second question will help you focus on the action and give you a picture of the item you are trying to remember. You should be able to recall most if not all of them.

Stay relaxed and don't rush through this exercise. The more relaxed you are the more easily the pictures will come back to you. If you get stuck on one, go to the next. Close the book and do it now.◆

Now, let's review the twenty items for you and you can see how well you did. Number 1, elephant. Number 2, ketchup. Number 3, Scotch tape. Number 4, water. Number 5, bubble gum. Number 6, pillow. Number 7, rug. Number 8, window. Number 9, jeep. Number 10, foot. Number 11, necktie. Number 12, mustard. Number 13, book. Number 14, chair. Number 15, cup of coffee. Number 16, alligator. Number 17, baseball bat. Number 18, beer. Number 19, basketball. Number 20, piano.

If you missed any, it's only because of one of four reasons:

1. *You didn't know your pegs.* If you didn't know the Tree List well enough, then this exercise would have failed. That's the first thing to ask yourself.
2. *Your pictures weren't vivid and specific enough.* If you wrote down "glass" for number 8 (instead of "window") or "shoe" for number 10 (instead of "foot"), you were close, but you didn't get it right. The close-but-incorrect answer is an indication that you need more practice creating vivid pictures.

3. *Your action was boring.* That is why people usually forget an item. If I ask you what your action is and you can't remember, nine times out of ten, it's because your action was boring. Boring action means you didn't stimulate your imagination enough. You need to work on developing more action that is zany and animated.

4. *Stress was affecting you.* Stress does play havoc with your memory, and it can block any information from getting out. We'll be talking about stress in a later lesson. For now, it's important to remember to stay as relaxed as possible when pegging and let your memory do the work. You'll be amazed at how it cooperates.

Congratulations! You not only committed twenty things to memory without writing them down, you have given your memory and your imagination a great workout. And most of all, I hope you've become more confident and are really learning to respect your memory's power. The more you can trust it, the further along you are on your way to developing a Mega Memory.

Chapter 7—Review

Pegging to the Tree List
You need a vivid, crystal clear, picture of the peg (tree, light switch, stool, etc.) and a vivid, crystal clear, picture of what you want to remember. You peg them together using action.

The first thing you want to remember always goes on the first peg and the second thing you want to remember always goes on the second peg, etc.

Helpful Hints
1. Include yourself in the picture.
2. Close your eyes to help you focus.
3. Concentrate on one peg at a time.
4. Ask two questions:

a. What is my peg?

b. What am I doing to my peg?

Reasons Why People Forget Their Pegs

1. They weren't sure of their pegs.
2. Pictures weren't vivid enough.
3. There was not enough of the right kind of action.
4. Stress.

Chapter 7—Required Mental Exercises

Exercise 1

Review what you did in Chapter 7 by pegging the twenty items to the Tree List again. But this time, try to come up with action that is different from what we have already used.

Exercise 2

Go to the video store and rent videocassettes containing the following characters:

1. Bullwinkle
2. The Road Runner
3. Bugs Bunny
4. Daffy Duck
5. Sylvester and Tweety Bird

Watching these cartoons will help you regain your powers of imagination and loosen up your sense of fun and fantasy. Cartoons are also good examples for what to strive for when turning words into mental pictures: exaggerated, colorful, nonsensical action.

8 How Your Body Affects Your Memory

It's time to take a break from exercises. In the last few chapters, you've learned how to create pegs, on which you will be able to store new information. You've played a form of Concentration and have pegged twenty words to the Tree List, which not only has helped you think in new ways but has also shown you how quick and powerful your memory can be. And above all, you're learning to trust your memory, starting to let go more and more so that your memory can do the work it's capable of.

But just as in any exercise program, it's time to rest. In this chapter, I will review how your mind works in processing information so that you will have a better appreciation of the exercises you've been doing. I will also provide information on how your body and mind are connected, discussing how stress and the foods you eat affect your memory. I will also share what I have learned about certain diseases that affect your mind, and what you can do to create not only a stronger, more powerful memory, but also a healthier, more balanced life for yourself.

A book obviously can't replace a doctor. Based on my own experiences, the points raised here are provided as guidelines for you to explore further, perhaps to help you talk to your doctor or to another health practitioner about a particular problem. Maybe something you read here will lead to a solution. Maybe this chapter will simply inspire you to take better care of yourself. As with the rest of the book, the responsibility rests with you. Take the information provided here and use it to your best advantage.

How Your Mind Works:
The Five Stages of Processing Information

I want to talk about your mind and how it works. In order to do this, we need to be clear on one thing: Your mind is not your brain. When we talk about the brain, we talk about that mass of gray matter inside your skull. We talk about chemicals and neurotransmitters.

When we talk about your mind, we talk about what happens when your brain does its work. It's really the essence of your brain, and that's what we're concerned with in this book. We're looking at both the conscious and unconscious processes that are under way when all those neurotransmitters are firing away. How does memory fit into this scenario? Why is it that you remember things when you're not trying to?

Imagine this particular scene: You walk into a bank or a grocery store and you see someone you've previously met. You say, "Oh, hi—" As soon as you say "hi," your mind goes completely blank and you forget the person's name. Has that ever happened to you? Of course it has. It has happened to all of us. And we agonize the whole day, trying to remember the person's name, but we can't remember it. Three days later, at two A.M., we wake up and from nowhere the person's name pops into our mind. "Oh, it was Jack Smith."

The same phenomenon also occurs in problem solving. How many times has the following happened to you at work, at school, or at home. You are trying to figure out a particular problem, and you begin wrestling with it, one day, the next, and the next. Perhaps your business is riding on the solution to a personnel problem or you're trying to figure out your finances. You keep thinking about this particular problem, trying to analyze all the angles, but you can't come up with a satisfying answer. Three or four days later you're at the movies. You're not thinking about the problem anymore, either having given up or (more healthfully) having decided to take a break from your ruminations. And what happens? A light bulb goes off. You come up with a perfect solution. It seems so simple you ask yourself, "Why didn't I see this earlier?"

What is happening in each of these cases? How does the mind work when you are trying to recall something? In the examples above, the answers you were looking for did come to you, though not at the time you wanted them to. So they were obviously there in your long-term memory, your knowledge bank. The knowledge just wasn't accessible at the time. Why not? The best way to understand what is going on in each of the above cases is to think of memory as a five-step process. When you are processing information or trying to recall something, your mind goes through five stages, or levels, of thought. These five stages are:

1. think stage
2. emote stage
3. look/search stage
4. create stage
5. know stage (the knowledge bank)

The first stage, the think stage, is what you do consciously. You know you want to remember a particular piece of information or solve a problem, so you analyze, you compare, you ask yourself questions that you hope will lead you to the right answer. As in the examples above, at some level you know that you know the person's name or can find a solution to your problem. But no matter how hard you think, you don't receive the answer you are looking for. Why? Because the information isn't accessible until stage five. You're stuck in the think stage.

One of the ways to get to level five is through level two, your emotions. Think of your emotions as the bridge between your conscious mind, represented by stage one, and your unconscious mind, represented by stages three through five. Emotions are your "gut" feelings. They are a slightly deeper stage of your mind than stage one. Remember that when you were pegging information in Chapter 5, I kept saying that adding some type of feeling helps reinforce the peg? When you add pain, fear, anger, love, or any other emotion, your mind is working at a deeper level. You can let go of your analytical thoughts because your emotions are now involved in the recall process. And once your emotions are involved, you automatically go to the next stage, the look/search stage.

Your mind works on many different levels. We say the deeper levels of thought are unconscious because you're not aware of them. But there's a lot going on, and as a matter of fact, your unconscious is much more powerful than the conscious part of your mind. When you are trying to remember something, step three, the look/search stage is very important. Signaled by your emotions that it's time to get to work, your unconscious mind begins freely accessing all of the information that is stored in your memory. I've been using the metaphor of your mind as a big file cabinet where everything you've seen, heard, or thought about is stored in files. When you're in the look/search stage, your unconscious mind can go through all those files in seconds, searching for whatever it needs to find. Pictures are the primary way it goes about this task, and you've already seen how quickly all this can happen.

Now something interesting happens. Sometimes your unconscious goes right to step five, going into the knowledge bank and giving you whatever information you are looking for. Other times, the solution isn't very accessible, and it takes our unconscious a while to give us the information as shown by the example of the person in the grocery store. Researchers still aren't sure why certain things take longer to come "to the surface" than others. The point is, however, once the unconscious gets involved, there is very little it *can't* do.

In the case of the second example, when you are trying to come up with a solution to a problem, your mind has to go to another level, the create stage, before it can give you an answer. Why? Because there is no one file with the solution to your problem. Your mind has to keep going through different files, everything you already know, and then devise something new as the solution. It has to create a new file for you. That takes time as well, during which time you may have consciously stopped thinking about a problem but in which your unconscious has been busy working on it.

Sometimes the create stage can be entered very quickly. A good example is the Statue of Liberty story. What was going on in your mind when I mentioned purple pennies? Without being consciously aware of it, you entered the look/search stage. Your unconscious found a file named "purple," and a file named "pennies." But with all the trillions of bits of information that it looked through, it probably didn't have a file named "purple pennies." So what did it do? It created a new file. It's as if your unconscious was saying, "I've got a purple file. I've got a pennies file. Now I'm going to combine the two and create a file called 'purple pennies.'"

In the create stage, your mind is taking different files, bits of information, and creating new files in different combinations. When you create new files, you are creating new pathways of information in the brain, which serves to further reinforce your memory. The more you create, the better your memory gets. Your mind thinks faster and more clearly. And the whole process becomes progressively easier.

And here's something even more important: When you create something, you know it. You've arrived at level five, the know stage. You are just like the person at the office with the cluttered desk who knows where everything is. Why? Because they've created the mess. That's also why I keep insisting that you don't take notes. When you create something, you know it. The only problem is in learning how to access it.

I also hope that as you continue going through the exercises in this book and work through the examples I give you, you'll be creating your own examples. My examples should provide a framework and give you different ideas of how to proceed. The most important thing is for you to build creatively on these ideas so that you keep training your memory and expand your unconscious capabilities.

Stress and Your Memory

When you are trying to recall something, there is a menace that keeps you in the think stage. And that menace is called stress. Stress plays havoc with your memory because it causes you to spin your mental wheels, preventing you from releasing the unconscious thought processes that get you to level five.

There are two types of stress—emotional and physiological. Emotional stress is a heightened level of a particular emotion. You struggle to "keep control" so that the emotions don't get the better of you. The emotions can be positive, like joy, or negative like fear or anger. Physical stress is caused by overloading the functioning of your body in some way: lifting material that is very heavy, overeating, working too hard, even reading too much.

Have you heard of the fight-or-flight syndrome? When you are feeling stress, your brain tells your body to mount all of its defenses in order to protect itself. Your heart beats faster, your blood pressure rises, your muscles are tense—in other words, you are not relaxed. Far from it. Your brain knows that now is not the time to allow the unconscious thought processes free rein. It's time to hunker down, and prepare to defend yourself, not release your deeper levels of thought.

Sometimes, just the very act of trying to remember something causes you stress. Usually, the harder you try, the worse it gets, just like when you're trying to remember someone's name or find a solution to a problem. Telling yourself to relax doesn't work, either. The more you tell yourself not to bother, to let go, the more stressful you are apt to feel.

I use two techniques to cut down on my stress level. One is fasting. Depending on your particular fast, this process cleanses your entire system in a matter of days. By ridding yourself of various toxins, you give the body a fresh start. You function more efficiently and energetically, and this includes your thinking and memory as well. Always keep in mind that fasting has to be carefully planned, and done under the supervision of a physician. Never undertake fasting alone.

In relation to fasting, I want to mention one other thing. There is another insidious way poisons can build up in your body—through your drinking water. There are so many chemicals in our water supply—the lead, chlorine, synthetic organic chemicals, and the many other chemicals introduced by municipal water treatment itself—which are really, literally poisonous. I recommend that you get your water tested right away and consider some kind of purification system. But please, don't be taken in by the advertisements of unscrupulous dealers and distributors who push water filters that would actually put more poisons into your system than they're taking out. Seek out some professionals who can test your water properly and give you the right information.

The second way to reduce stress involves a simple action that you can perform whenever you wish. If you are trying to remember something, it's a great way to get out of the think stage and release your unconscious thought processes. This action involves your eyes. Take a moment to stop what you're doing and look up, either to the right or the left. Hold your eyes in that upward position for a few seconds. That simple action allows the left and right brain hemispheres to work more in sync, which allows you to access information more readily.

You can see this process at work by comparing talk shows and movies. When someone is relating a personal anecdote or telling a story about their life, their stress level is heightened because there are a lot of emotions associated with recalling past events. Watch what happens during interviews on talk shows. When guests are talking about themselves, especially when it's about something that seems important to them, they periodically look up. It's because they're trying to reduce the stress produced by the emotions that are arising. Now watch what happens in many movies during emotional scenes when a character is revealing some important information or telling a story. The actors keep facing forward and the drama feels a little forced. I feel this at the movies all the time. At some level, the actors' responses always seemed false to me, yet I had no idea why. Now I love to point it out to anyone I'm at the movies with.

Keep this eye action in mind throughout the book when I ask

you to recall something. Don't look down and stare. And don't try so hard, thinking, thinking, thinking. When I say relax and take a breath, I also want you to take a moment and look up to the right, up to the left. It's the quickest, easiest way I know of to get out of the think stage.

Nutrition and Memory

The body and mind work synergistically. One affects the other. If you are feeling bad physically, your emotions are affected negatively as well, which in turn hampers memory. On the other hand, if you are physically healthy and everything in your body is in balance, you feel better emotionally as well: The same problems seem a little bit less pressing, you're a little more optimistic about life in general, and everything about you is a little more dynamic and vibrant. Your memory capacity soars, too.

You function best when everything in your body is in balance. The word for this state is *homeostasis,* defined by Webster's as "a relatively stable state of equilibrium or a tendency toward such a state between different but interdependent elements of an organism." Your body operates at peak efficiency when all its interdependent elements—the physical, emotional, mental—are in sync. The single biggest way you can make sure that you stay physically healthy is by the foods you eat.

Unfortunately, the study of nutrition is a very young discipline. And there is much disagreement as to what is good or bad for you. As soon as one study indicates that you should eat food X, another study comes along indicating just the opposite. While the effects of the foods you eat are very real, they're also very subtle and interconnected in a myriad of ways. We're all different, and that goes for body chemistry as well. The guidelines below are based on my own experiences, things that helped me on my road to a fantastic memory. I hope they help you, too. But as I have been saying throughout the book, if you disagree with something, or the opposite seems to work for you, trust your own experience. Use these guidelines as a springboard to do further research. And using the address at the end of Chapter 28, write me a letter telling me what you have learned. We will both be able to share it with others.

One more reminder: As you are doing the exercises in this book—or any other heavy "brain work"—be aware of the digestive times of different foods. As one of the ground rules in Chapter 1, I cautioned you not to eat a heavy meal before doing these exercises. You have only so much blood in your body, and it goes to the areas where it is most needed. After a heavy meal, of course, blood goes to the digestive organs. You should also be aware that it's not only how much you eat that matters. Certain foods take longer to digest than others. Pork, for example, takes longer to digest than other meat. Beef takes a little less time. Then come poultry and fish. When it comes to carbohydrates, complex carbohydrates such as whole-wheat pasta are healthy choices, but they tend to take longer to digest than simple carbohydrates such as regular pasta. Vegetables, fruit, and fruit juices are digested the most quickly. If you must have a big meal before doing a lot of mind work, have a meal with more vegetables and fruit. You won't be as lethargic and will stay mentally alert because the digestion will be relatively easy.

Foods to Be Avoided

Turkey. There is one particular food that should be avoided for the few hours prior to which you want to have optimal mental capacity: turkey. Turkey is rich in tryptophan, an amino acid that promotes sleep. Have you noticed that people fall asleep all over the place after Thanksgiving dinner? Think back to any dinner where a lot of turkey was served. You were tired, lethargic, not moving very fast. It wasn't just because you ate a lot. It's because tryptophan makes you mentally slow. So stay away from turkey when you want to be thinking quickly and clearly. You can have as much turkey as you want after that business deal, test at school, or marathon working spree.

Sugar. Sugar is terrible for your memory. Why? The ingestion of sugar into your body causes the pancreas to secrete insulin, which is the hormone essential in breaking down sugar so that it can be metabolized properly. A sudden onrush of sugar makes the pancreas go crazy as it produces higher amounts of insulin to cope with the demand. You may get a sugar rush or sugar high for an hour or two, but what happens after that big high? You "crash," which is another way of saying everything slows down, including your thought processes.

When I speak of the negative effects of sugar, I'm referring primarily to processed or refined sugar. It's the sugar found in baked goods, candy, soda, and the white sugar found on your table. Foods with brown sugar should be included in this list as well.

Fructose, on the other hand, which is the simple sugar found in fuits, does not produce the dramatic highs and lows of processed sugar. It is absorbed more slowly by the bloodstream, and its effect on the pancreas is much more mild, causing less insulin release.

White flour. The next food on the proscribed list is white flour. White flour? Yes, white flour in the pasta and bread products you buy at the supermarket. White flour is a simple carbohydrate. There is a popular misconception that all carbohydrates are good for you. The more you eat, the better off you are. There is a difference, however, between simple and complex carbohydrates. Simple carbohydrates such as white-flour pasta and breads have a high glucidic rate. What that means is that they are high in sugar and that the pancreas has to secrete relatively high levels of insulin in order to have them broken down.

White-flour products are hard on the digestive tract as well. If you need to be convinced of this further, just mix white flour and water together as you used to do in school. What do you get? Pastelike glue. That's what's lining your intestines. You become con-stipated to a degree and your whole digestive system is out of whack while the paste is slowly broken down. More blood is needed for that work, which means less blood is available for your brain.

If you take some whole wheat floor, however, and mix it with water, nothing happens. It will not harden. Whole wheat is a com-plex carbohydrate, which has a relatively low glucidic rate. The pancreas doesn't have to work very hard to break it down and the blood levels of insulin stay relatively stable. You have fewer of those sugar highs and lows.

Coffee and Alcohol. We need to mention *coffee* and *alcohol* as well, two "foods" that we are told to stay away from and which most of us consume anyway. As far as coffee is concerned, we all know that caffeine makes us more mentally alert. It does kickstart those neurotransmitters in the brain, making them fire more rapidly. But there is a point of diminishing returns. Caffeine also makes many people jittery as well as causing other physical problems. Alcohol, on the other hand, has the opposite effect of coffee. It numbs the neurotransmitters so that you think more slowly. But there is a side benefit to this, which I hate to admit. It reduces stress—which, as we've already discussed, helps you recall things more easily.

Though both coffee and alcohol have what may seem some short-term benefits for your memory, you should never drink one or the other with the assumption that they will aid memory in the long run. The point of diminishing returns for both coffee and alcohol comes very quickly as well as causing a host of other physical problems.

Aspartame and MSG. *Stay away* from these "excitotoxins"! The research is mixed and controversial; however, here's a simple test to see if these substances may be affecting you: Stay off aspartame (NutraSweet) and MSG (monosodium glutamate, also sometimes listed as "hydrolyzed vegetable protein") for two weeks. Then eat something containing one or both of these substances (a diet soda is likely to contain aspartame, for example) and watch how you feel! I'm especially concerned about children eating foods containing aspartame or MSG. My opinion: *"Stay away! Danger!"*

Lecithin and Other Memory Boosters

If you want to increase your memory power, eat foods rich in lecithin. Lecithin is a phospholipid, which is a class of fats. Lecithin contains choline, a building block of one of the many neurotransmitters in the brain that form the basis of thought and memory. If you have high levels of lecithin in your brain, you think quicker, faster, more efficiently. If you don't, you think more slowly. Geniuses, people with IQs in the 150–200 range, have incredible amounts of lecithin in their brains. Foods rich in lecithin are soybeans, organ meats, eggs, and wheat germ.

Lecithin is also sold separately as a supplement. There is much controversy about food supplements, of course, as researchers try to determine the effectiveness of supplements as opposed to getting what you need from the foods you eat. The side effects of overly high dosages are also a problem with certain supplements. I believe that supplements can be an effective aid to good nutrition—but an aid, not a substitute.

If you do buy lecithin supplements at a health food store, make sure you inquire about the product's PC concentration. That refers to the purity of the lecithin you are buying, which varies from product to product. Although there are no official FDA guidelines on this, most people who take it agree the PC concentration should be in the 30–35 percent range.

There are also some exotic (to us Americans) herbs that have a positive effect on brain function and memory. A wonderful herb used in China and Europe for centuries is called ginkgo biloba. Extracted from the leaves of the ginkgo tree, ginkgo biloba improves oxygenation to the brain, makes you more alert, mentally and substantially increases your brain power and memory function.

For people who need a quick mental boost, guarana is an option. An herb, guarana is a naturally occurring source of caffeine. It usually has the same positive effects as caffeine but doesn't produce the jittery feeling that many people associate with coffee. Used all over the world, guarana is sold in health food stores.

Candidiasis and Epstein-Barr Syndrome

A number of diseases have received much attention in the papers in the last few years. Their myriad symptoms have made them hard to diagnose. Sometimes the symptoms are subtle, involving a whole list of vague complaints. Doctors often told people who came for help that everything was "in their minds." Sometimes, aware that something was not quite right but not really feeling terribly sick, people avoided going to doctors for the same reason. Even though awareness of these diseases is growing, there are still many misconceptions about them. Since they both affect memory, I want to discuss two of them here. They are candidiasis and Epstein-Barr syndrome.

Discussing candidiasis is very important to me because a few years ago I was diagnosed with candidiasis. Over a period of months, I slowly noticed that I was sleeping more and more, sometimes up to twelve hours a day. There were also other subtle problems. I felt bloated and gassy. I also had a harder time concentrating and remembering things. At first, I thought it was due to my stressful lifestyle: I was traveling around the country constantly, conducting my seminars and taking care of other business related to the American Memory Institute. But no matter how much I slept, how much I tried to take care of myself, the symptoms continued. I began a merry-go-round of doctor visits, most of whom said the problem was in my mind.

Luckily, I finally went to a doctor who diagnosed me as having candidiasis. Over the next few months, with dietary changes, holistic remedies, and vitamin supplementation, I began to feel better. My energy returned, my mental clarity improved, the bloated feeling disappeared. I was finally back to my old self.

Candidiasis is an intestinal overabundance of a fungus, *Candida albicans,* that resembles yeast. The problem with diagnosing candidiasis is that, as in my case, the symptoms are so varied and begin subtly, progressing over a long period of time. People who later are diagnosed with this illness say they feel "spacy." They may crave sugar and white flour and have a hard time getting up in the morning. One of the most common symptoms is lack of energy. "I'm always tired by the afternoon. I just can't think that well. I'm anxious and nervous. Is there anything wrong with me?" is a typical series of complaints. Candidiasis can affect your thinking and memory as well.

I also feel that if you suspect you may have candidiasis or any other combination of vague and debilitating problems, it's very important to go to a doctor who is aware of holistic medicine. Practitioners of traditional Western medicine are trained to focus on specific problems and treat those problems with drugs and surgery. In contrast, doctors practicing holistic medicine look at the body as a whole entity, studying how all the parts function together. In the holistic approach, treatment focuses on natural substances as well as dietary and lifestyle changes.

The other disease I want to discuss is the one caused by the Epstein-Barr virus. Although there is still some debate, it is now generally referred to as chronic fatigue syndrome. It is another disease with subtle but very real symptoms.

Consider a young friend of mine who suffered from this syndrome for years without knowing what was going on. Hearing about my experience with candidiasis, she came to me one day and started telling me her symptoms. She said that all through her years at school she could never think very clearly. Concepts that other children grasped quickly took her a long time to grasp. She felt it was because she was "not very smart." Looking back, she realized she had always been somewhat mentally lethargic, having a hard time concentrating, unable to focus very well. That, too, she felt was "just the way she was." Deciding she was not cut out for college, she had stopped studying and taken a low-paying, stress-free job just to get by.

We took her to a clinic where clients are evaluated from a holistic standpoint. The doctor diagnosed her with Epstein-Barr virus. As is normal with Epstein-Barr, the virus had lodged itself in my friend's central nervous system, affecting not only her memory but her other thinking processes as well. With a few homeopathic injections, in a couple of weeks the Epstein-Barr virus was under control, and this young woman is now back in school, and doing very well.

As with candidiasis, we're finding that Epstein-Barr can be controlled through the holistic approach. I highly recommend that you seek out the people who are specialists in homeopathic medicine and experienced in treating candidiasis, Epstein-Barr syndrome, and other related diseases. Too many of these ailments remain untested, undiagnosed, and untreated. I've seen people all over the country who can't seem to function at peak mental capacity. Whether they suffer from an inability to think clearly or have a poor recall of information, they are not very productive in their work or in school. There are practitioners who can simply and inexpensively diagnose and treat these particular problems.

In reading the material presented in this section, I hope you've reached one basic, but very important conclusion: All too often, there are physiological reasons why we can't think clearly and our memory is adversely affected. Keep aware of what's happening to your own body, seek out articles and books on these issues, and find out which doctors are knowledgeable about these diseases.

For a listing of recommended homeopathic clinics, call the American Memory Institute at 219-736-6172.

Chapter 8—Review

The Five Stages of Processing Information
1. think
2. emote
3. look/search
4. create
5. know

The Two Types of Stress
emotional
physical

Reducing Stress
Looking up, either to the right or to the left.

Digestion Rates of Basic Foods (from slowest to fastest)
pork
beef
poultry, fish
vegetables
fruits
fruit juices

Foods to Be Avoided
turkey
sugar
white-flour products
coffee and alcohol

9   Pegging the House List

It's time to do another pegging exercise. I think you will be even more impressed with your memory by the end of this chapter because we are going to be working on increasing speed.

I'd like to go back to the House List. First we will review it. All this will be done in your mind's eye—no pencil or paper allowed. Just sit back and relax. What I will want you to do is take that mental journey through the four rooms that you chose for your House List. I will ask you to see vividly, in order, every peg on that list. You will begin with the first room and spend no more than a few seconds visualizing the first peg. Then you will go in sequence to peg numbers 2, 3, 4, and 5. After you've finished the first room, continue on to the next room, and proceed in order through all the pegs until you've gone through all four rooms. Review these pegs in sequence three times, going forward from 1 through 20, seeing each peg vividly. The pegs will come to mind instantly.

Close the book and start the exercise now.◆

As you were doing this exercise, you probably thought to yourself, "That was fairly easy. I reviewed the House List just a few chapters ago, Kevin, and it's still locked into my memory." Yes, I know it is. It should be right there, and it should be firm.

Now that you've reviewed your House List, we are going to

do another exercise with it. I am going to give you a list of ten words to peg to your House List. As with all pegging, you will create vivid, colorful pictures for these words. You'll smell the smells, feel the feelings, include any sounds you can, and add yourself if you like. Then you will take a picture of one of your House List pegs and join the two together, using some kind of ludicrous action.

An important point to keep in mind: When you peg to your House List, you will be creating slightly stronger pegs than if you were pegging to the Body List or the Tree List. Why? You created this list. These are items from your house, not mine or anyone else's. And when something is yours, there's more emotion associated with it. (Damaging a rental car isn't the same as damaging your own car, is it?) This will help you later when you want to recall what you put on your House List pegs. As we learned in the last chapter, the fact that you used more emotion will more easily lead you out of the think stage and into the look/search stage of your unconscious. And as an added bonus, you'll see that pegging to the House List will be easier as well.

One more important reminder: When pegging, do not use association. Remember, association is based on logic. Way back in Chapter 2, we linked "tree" and the number 1 because the trunk of a tree looks like the number 1. Pegging is the exact opposite: You're putting your two pictures together in a nonsensical way, creating something that could never happen in real life. Like a lion wearing a fur coat.

As I mentioned at the beginning of the chapter, you're going to be working on speed this time. This exercise works a little more easily with a partner, but you can do it by yourself, too. When I tell you to, I want you to look at the first item on the list of ten words below and create a vivid picture of it. Then take the first peg from your House List and put the two pictures together using action. Go through the entire list. Do this as fast as you can, spending no more than five seconds on each word. We'll peg only ten words so that you'll use only half your House List, but that will give you a good idea of how powerful and fast your recall abilities are. If you're working with a partner, have him or her read the words to you at five-second intervals. If you're alone, probably the easiest way to work is by sliding a straightedge down the page.

Before we continue, I want you to close the book and review your House List one final time. Make sure that your pegs are committed to memory so that you can scan them very, very quickly. Make sure that you have the sequence down. Close the book and do it now.◆

Okay, now sit back, relax, and take a deep breath. As a beginning student, if you wish you may shut your eyes between words to help you focus. Visualize the item, then the House List peg, and put them together, spending no more than five seconds on each item. Take another deep breath. Exhale.... Now take your straightedge and begin pegging in five-second intervals:

  1. a man's suit
  2. a bottle of beer
  3. Donald Duck
  4. dollar bills
  5. turkey
  6. a pencil
  7. a pig
  8. a wig
  9. hot dogs
  10. a wedding cake

Now close the book, number 1 through 10 down the left side of a clean sheet of paper, and from memory, write down the ten words. Do it now.◆

Now check yourself. How did you do? I'm sure you're feeling pretty pleased with yourself because you remembered most, if not all, of the words. And I'm sure you noticed that when you went back to each House List peg, its image came to you instantly.

If you missed one or two items, ask yourself the four pertinent questions:

1. Did you know your House List pegs well enough?
2. Were your pictures vivid enough?
3. Was your pegging action strong and clear?
4. Were you stressed while doing this?

Perhaps you were nervous, putting pressure on yourself to succeed. That would have caused you to stay stuck in the think stage. If your problem was in using strong, clear action, don't worry. In the following chapters, you will get plenty more practice at it.

If you did well, you now have established fifty pegs for yourself, fifty places to store information. Think of them as fifty file folders in your Mega Memory inventory. You will be using these file folders to remember all sorts of useful things, things you never thought were practical or possible. Can you see why they say your mind thinks faster than the speed of light, which is 186,000 miles per second? You spent only five seconds on each item in the above exercise.

Think back to the story of the flea and our discussion of self-imposed limitations in Chapter 6. You don't have them anymore. They're gone. Do you now really believe your mind is incredibly powerful, your memory photographic? And can you say you have learned that it's available for you to use any time you want?

If the answers to the above questions are yes, you have reached an important milestone in your Mega Memory program. You're now ready to walk into that room of fifty people and remember everyone's name. . . .

Chapter 9—Review

How We Program Our Memories to Fail
"I have a terrible memory."
"I never remember people's names."
"I better write this down or I'll forget."
"I just know I'll forget that appointment."
Begin reprogramming yourself today by making positive statements.

Chapter 9—Required Mental Exercises

Exercise 1
Review your House List mentally while your mind's eye sees the pegs vividly, in detail and in the exact order you chose them.

Exercise 2
Peg a different list to the House List from the one we did in Chapter 9.

Exercise 3
Say out loud three times daily until you finish this course:

> "I have a great memory."
> "I remember easily."
> "I recall easily."

This is the beginning of reprogramming your unconscious mind.

10 Remembering Names: Part 1

You're ready to put your Mega Memory to use in real life! As a result of the exercises in the first nine chapters of this book, you have established a Mega Memory inventory for yourself—fifty pegs that you will be using as reference points in the future on which to store information. And just as important, if you have done the exercises faithfully and have followed the chapters in sequence as I have been advising, you now trust your memory enough to release its vast power. In the last chapter, by pegging ten words at five-second intervals, you learned to appreciate the speed of your memory, too. Now you will apply both its speed and its power to remembering people's names.

I am going to break one of my major ground rules now: You may read this and all the following chapers more than once. As you begin to use your Mega Memory in real life, I want you to feel free to use these chapters for reference. You may want to reread certain sections or review an entire chapter. Feel free to do whatever you feel necessary to build your memory skills. I keep emphasizing that everybody learns different concepts at different rates, and I have found that the best way to utilize the Mega Memory program is by allowing everyone to go at his or her natural pace. So feel free to practice, play with, or put a different spin on whatever techniques you find on the following pages. They are there for your use.

What's Your Name Again?

How many times has this happened to you? You walked into a room, met someone, shook hands, heard the person's name, and then, as soon as the handshake broke, forgot the name you had heard? And a few minutes later, when trying to recall that name, you were forced to say, "I'm sorry. What's your name again?" It's happened to all of us. And it's very embarrassing.

Now just think how great it would be not to have to ask that question ever again. People will be amazed with the ability you have to walk into a room, meet forty or fifty people, and in a few hours leave and say good-bye using everyone's name. I've had so many students come up to me at my seminars and say, "Kevin, I can meet fifty, sixty, or seventy-five people and remember their names. When I do, they all remember *me*!" People will be very impressed, because the most important thing you can remember about a person is his or her name. It's the sweetest sound in any language to that person. It commands attention—and that person's respect—every time it is used. And you can bet that the person will remember you because something like that doesn't happen very often.

Once you know someone, that person's name stays with you. For example, think back to the last time you started a new job. On the first day, you were introduced to all the people in your department, and even if your department was rather small, let's say four people, you promptly forgot their names. By the end of the first week, however, you knew everybody's name. You did that by repetition. After hearing each person's name a couple of times, you were able to reinforce it in your memory. With only four people, you didn't have too much information to process, so that you were able to commit everyone's name to memory very easily.

When you walk into a room of forty or fifty people, however, you don't have the luxury of repetition. At most you have a few hours, and usually much less, to remember whatever names you can. This is where the power of your newly trained Mega Memory comes into play. In the next three chapters of this book, we're going to learn how to take someone's name, put it into short-term memory, and keep it there long enough that it goes into long-term memory and becomes knowledge.

As we've discussed previously, there are three basic steps to remembering anything:

    1. a place to put the information, called a peg
    2. the information turned into a picture
    3. mental glue to hold the picture on the peg, which is action

We've spent the first nine chapters doing each of these basic steps in a variety of ways. Now we are going to use these steps in remembering names. Each of these next three chapters will focus on one of the steps. Once you have finished Chapter 12 and done the review lessons, you will be walking into meetings and parties and recalling more names than you ever thought possible. You probably won't remember fifty or sixty right off the bat—like everything else in life, it will take some time to become that proficient—but I guarantee that you won't be putting yourself into the embarrassing position of having to say, "I'm sorry. What's your name again?"

Creating a See Peg

As we've been learning over and over, the first thing you need in order to remember anything is a place to store the information. In Mega Memory, that place is a peg. In learning names, we will be using what I call a see peg. I call it a see peg because it's something you see, the first thing you notice about a person. It could be something the person is wearing: a big red tie, a bright flowered print dress, a bow in the hair. It could be something about the person's face or body (big hands, dark eyes) or a striking piece of jewelry. It could even be the person's gestures or body language—someone speaking with a loud voice, waving their hands excitedly, or striking a particular pose. It can be anything, but it's the first thing that strikes you about the person.

Sometimes we can pick out a see peg very quickly. We can often glance around a room, spot someone, and immediately notice something that pops out at us about that person. At other times, no one trait strikes us immediately and we have to make a choice—pick one thing that we want to associate with that person. "That's a great red blouse she's wearing," we might think. We call that person Miss Red Blouse. "Look at that guy with the ugly yellow polka-dot tie," we say of someone else. That person becomes Mr. Yellow Tie. Then there might be Mr. Ponytail, Ms. Almond Eyes, Mr. Thin Lips. Learn to pay attention to these things. They become your see pegs.

Here's a tip on choosing your see pegs. Pick concrete things rather than abstract concepts. In your exercises, you have already learned that concrete images are easier to visualize, and the same goes for see pegs. For example, if you notice someone who seems pompous and full of himself, talking about all the money he's made or how everyone should believe what he believes, don't name him Mr. Obnoxious or Mr. Attitude. It would be better to choose Mr. Loudmouth or Mr. Moneybags. Having a simple, concrete see peg will help you in step two, which we will discuss in the following chapter.

In certain situations, you don't have the luxury of standing around and observing someone from far away. There will be times you will be introduced to someone you've never laid eyes on before. Picking out see pegs at a time like that is harder for most people because you're face-to-face with someone, concentrating on interacting with that other person. My advice for such situations is to take a genuine concern in the person you have just met. Just focus on giving the other person your attention and really *listening* to them. You will find that that will give you a chance to relax, which will allow you to start noticing their hair, their clothes, their mannerisms. The see pegs will stand out. And over time, you will notice the see pegs more and more quickly and easily.

Taking a genuine interest in someone, by the way, is not only helpful for your memory, but will pay big dividends in your communications and "people" skills. Sensing your concern, people will respond to you much more warmly, openly, and genuinely themselves. You will be rewarded with their attention in what you have to say or do.

As you can see, creating see pegs is a very simple task. You are engaging the memory because you are *focusing* on something. If you remember, just by focusing you are getting those neurotransmitters in the brain to fire away and reinforce the memory, even if it's for a hundredth or a thousandth of a second. That's all it takes. And by creating pictures, you are using the software your brain needs for recall.

At this point I want you to do an exercise in choosing see pegs. Look at the photographs on page 110 and choose see pegs for the four people pictured. And one more reminder. "Good, better, best" applies here. There's no one right answer for each picture. Do what works best for *you*. It's what *you* notice about the person, what *you* choose as a see peg. The important thing is that you focus on one aspect of the person pictured.

Take a look at the pictures and choose a see peg for each person now.◆

Now go to the end of the chapter and look at the see pegs I chose for each of the pictures.◆

I hope the exercise was fun. As you can see, it's very simple to do. Most important, it forces you to observe the people you meet. And when you observe, you focus. Instead of merely looking at someone and then quickly forgetting what you just saw, you are training yourself to commit it all to memory.

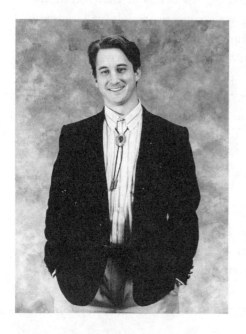

Chapter 10—Review

See Peg
The first thing you notice about a person.

Two Types of See Pegs
1. Permanent: something about the features of the individual, either facial or bodily. This may also include their gestures.
2. Temporary: something noticeable but transient about a person's appearance, such as an article of clothing or jewelry.

By picking see pegs, we fulfilled the first of three steps toward remembering anything: We found a place to put the information.

Chapter 10—Required Mental Exercise

Exercise
Try to pick a see peg for five people you meet today. At the end of the day, sit down and visualize the five see pegs as clearly as you can.

Kevin's Answers to See Pegs
1. Mr. Bolo Tie
2. Ms. Striped Shirt
3. Mr. Star Sweatshirt
4. Ms. Brass Buttons

11 Remembering Names: Part 2

In the previous chapter, you learned how to create see pegs, which is the first step in remembering someone's name. Now what is the second of the three basic steps in remembering any piece of information? It's taking that information and turning it into a picture. And that's what we're going to practice doing in this chapter: turning people's first and last names into pictures.

Let's say you meet a person named Bill. We need to turn "Bill" into a picture using the same method we used earlier in Chapter 6 when we played Concentration. In Concentration we took words, broke them down into syllables, and then created sound-alike pictures for each syllable. When we put the syllables together, we came up with the entire word. If the word was one syllable, we came up with of a sound-alike picture for the entire word.

Our rule for turning each syllable into a picture was to focus on the way the syllable sounded, not the way it was written. Sometimes the syllables reminded us of abstract things or concepts, and sometimes they reminded us of a particular object. We decided that simple, concrete objects were easier to work with, though syllables that reminded us of abstract terms were allowed as well.

We'll be doing the same thing in picturing names. The object of creating pictures is building a vocabulary—a vocabulary of names. It's just like learning a new language. Once you've learned the meanings of certain words, their meaning is instantly clear when you hear the words again in the future. Remembering names will work the same way. In this chapter, we are creating our vocabulary. In the next, you will see how we use that vocabulary to recall the names of people we meet in any and every situation.

Picturing First Names

Let us go over a few examples of picturing first names. Remember, what you are doing now is building a vocabulary, setting the groundwork for the future.

When you hear someone's name, break down the name into syllables, and think of what the syllables sound like to you. If you meet a man named Bill, for example, you'd probably think of a dollar bill or a duck's bill. Either one is a good picture. If someone's name is Mike, you might picture a microphone. John?—my choice is a toilet! If someone is named Donald, you might picture Donald Duck, instead of breaking his name down into two syllables. Remember, combining syllables is allowed, too.

Here's a tougher one: Sue. If you focus on the way it sounds, you might think of a Sioux Indian or suing someone in court, both of which are pretty abstract concepts. Keep in mind that the key to picturing abstracts is choosing as simple and clear a picture as possible. If you use suing someone in court for the name "Sue," you may choose a picture of a judge, with his gavel and black robe, or perhaps imagine a summons or the scales of justice. Your picture has to be vivid and clear, as I've been emphasizing throughout the book. Some of my seminar participants choose to picture a man's suit because "suit" and "Sue" sound so much alike. That's allowed too—the two words don't have to sound exactly alike, just enough so that one reminds you of the other.

Here are a couple of longer names. Roseanne sounds like "rose" and "ant," "rose-ant," so you could create a picture of those two things. For Robert, I would choose "rob," and "hurt," picturing a robber in a ski mask and a finger with a Band-Aid around it. When I hear "Beverly," I think of a lever of some kind and leaves, "lever-leaves." I hope you understand how it works.

Some people in my seminars wonder whether creating pictures every time they hear someone's name is too much effort. "We don't want to be doing this for everyone we meet," they tell me. But here is the beauty of this system. Once you create a picture, you can use that picture over and over again. Let's use Mike as an example. Once you've decided to use a picture of a microphone for the name "Mike," you can use it again for every Mike that you meet. As I've said, you are building a vocabulary. Just as in learning any new language, it might take a little while at first to get the meanings of certain words, but once those meanings become clear to you, you use the words effortlessly.

To understand how this will work, think back to Chapter 7 when we pegged twenty words to our Tree List. When I call out number 7, for example, what image comes to your mind? It's dice, isn't it? How about ten? It's bowling ball. Twelve is no longer 12, but eggs. The picture vocabulary of names will work the same way. In your memory, the *picture* of the name will replace the name itself.

Now I would like you to do an exercise. Below is a list of ten common first names. Look at each name and spend no more than a few seconds creating a picture for it. Make sure it feels right to you—chances are if it comes easily it will be memorable to you and thus useful over and over. Write down your choices for each name in the space provided. Yes, I want you to write down your choices—you'll see why in a moment. After you've gone through the entire list, go to the end of the chapter and compare my choices with yours. Go to the list and do the exercise now.◆

List of Names	Your Choice of Pictures
1. Waldo	1.
2. Wallace	2.
3. Dolly	3.
4. Debbie	4.
5. Nicole	5.
6. Jan	6.
7. Ann	7.
8. Jim	8.
9. Joe	9.
10. Mark	10.

Now go to the end of the chapter and look at my choices, then come back here.◆

How did your choices compare with mine? I hope you could see how I chose pictures that were simple and clear. They are objects that you can visualize easily. Here's an important point. For number 3, I have heard many people choose Dolly Parton. Never use celebrities. People don't make good pictures. Here's another reminder: Keep your picture small. For number 8, Jim, for example, a picture of a basketball or a Slim Jim is better than imagining an entire gymnasium. Keeping the picture simple and clear makes it easier to keep in your memory.

Okay. In a moment you'll return to the list above. To reinforce the link between the pictures and the names you have just created, I want you to cover your choice of pictures, so all you see are the first names to the left. Review the names and see if you remember the pictures you chose. Spend some time doing this, covering up the picture word and seeing if you can recall the picture just by looking at the first names. Repeat this several times, because some of them are difficult. Four or five times on a tough one, and you'll remember it. It's important to have this picture vocabulary established. Do that now.◆

Now I want you to do the exact opposite. Cover up the first names, look at each picture you've chosen, and see if you can remember what first name that picture represents. If you've been doing all the exercises in this chapter correctly, you will have instantaneous recall. The names will pop into your head right away. Go back up to the list and do the exercise now.◆

Okay. At this point you should have established a beginning picture vocabulary for ten first names. Let me remind you once more that you can make this vocabulary grow by practicing this technique with everyone you meet. Over time, you will develop pictures for many first names. And the larger your vocabulary is, the easier it will be for your memory to function at peak capacity.

Picturing Last Names

Now we are going to practice picturing last names. Working with last names is usually harder than with first names. In the first place, last names tend to be longer and less familiar. You need to do a little more work in breaking down the names into syllables and creating pictures for them. And building a picture vocabulary that you can use over and over again is harder, too. For example, how many Kowalskis and Martinellis are you going to meet over the course of your life?

You may not want to make a practice of remembering the full name of everyone you meet, but there will be times when you will be happy to remember someone's full name. And I do have students in my seminars who immediately start working on both first and last names. They're good at it and they enjoy it.

I do want to remind you, though: Walk before you run. When you start doing this for real, make sure you are confident with first names before you attempt last names. As I've just said, some people can do both immediately. Most people, however, need a few days to a week or so practicing on first names before they feel comfortable enough with last names. Success builds confidence, and failure does the opposite. So if it takes you a while to begin working with last names, don't be too hard on yourself. You are like the majority of my students.

Turning last names into pictures is the same as doing it for first names. We break the name we have just heard into syllables. We then take each syllable and turn it into a picture based on the way it sounds or what it represents to us. You can combine syllables, and you can choose sounds that are similar to, but not exactly like, the syllable you're trying to picture. Let's go over a few examples.

We meet someone with the last name Johnson. Breaking Johnson into syllables, we get "john" and "son." My picture for "john" is a toilet. For the second syllable, "son," you can picture either the sun in the sky or a son, someone's male offspring. Picturing the sun in the sky is better because it's simpler and clearer than son, which is more vague. So take a few seconds to vividly picture a toilet and a big, bright yellow sun in the clear blue sky. "Johnson." You've created a picture for Johnson.

Let's take the name Maskowitz. "Mask-kow-itz." The first syllable is "mask," for which I picture a Halloween mask. The next syllable is "kow," which makes me think of a big brown cow. The last syllable, "witz," is a little tougher. My choices are a witch, or perhaps a whip. So you're picturing a mask, a cow, and a witch. "Mask-cow-witch." "Maskowitz." They're close enough to work very well.

What if someone pronounces Maskowitz differently, as people with the same last name sometimes do? For example, someone might say "Mas-kow-itz." What do you do then? Well, how about picturing a mass, the Catholic ceremony, plus a cow, plus an itch? "Mas-cow-itch." "Maskowitz." It still works, doesn't it? Remember, it's the sound that matters. How you pronounce the name is how you turn it into pictures.

How about the last name Saffron? Some people may think of saffron rice. Others might break it into syllables, "saf" and "ron." They may picture a safe for the first syllable. It doesn't sound exactly the same but it's close. For the second syllable, they may choose a picture of someone's feet running. "Safe-run." "Saffron."

How about Kowalski? You have two choices. "Kow-wal-ski" gives you a cow, a wall, and a ski. "Cow-wall-ski." "Kowalski." Or you can put the first two syllables together. "Kowal" sounds like "koala" bear "Koala-ski." "Kowalski." That works just as well.

Let's do one more name, Jeffries. The first syllable is "jeff." What sounds like "Jeff"? How about "chef." A picture of a chef's hat would be good for this. Now how about "fries"—pronounced "freez"? "Freez." Think of something frozen like an ice cube or an image of someone with chattering teeth. Some people would use "fries" as in french fries. It's close enough. Either one of these picture combinations sounds like the name we want to remember.

Now I'd like you to go to the list of ten last names below and choose sound-alike pictures for each one, just as you did for first names. Take a few seconds to break each name down by syllable, create pictures, and next to each name write what you visualized. Do this exercise now.

List of Names	**Your Choice of Pictures**
1. Atwater	1.
2. Carmichael	2.
3. Crawford	3.
4. Gardner	4.
5. Hawkins	5.
6. Jarrett	6.
7. Rabinowitz	7.
8. Schuster	8.
9. Shelton	9.
10. Wayne	10.

Now turn to the end of this chapter and look at my choices, then come back here.◆

How did your choices compare with mine? Let's review a few of them. Are you wondering about number 2, Carmichael? "Car-bicycle" sounds close to Carmichael, doesn't it? How about the white glove? If you remember, when we discussed picturing first names, I told you not to use celebrities as subjects of pictures. So for Michael, you can't picture Michael Jackson. However, what object is closely linked with Michael Jackson? A white glove. Objects that represent celebrities are fine to use.

How about number 9, Shelton? The first syllable can be pictured by a seashell and the second by a representation of something that weighs a ton or a tin. Tin is better because it's less vague (and probably smaller!). "Shell-tin." Shelton.

Now I want you to do the same exercise you did with first names. I want you to cover your picture choices, so all you see are the names to the left. Go through the names and see if you remember the pictures you chose. Review each name several times. Do that now.◆

Now do it in reverse. Cover up the first names, look at each picture you've chosen, and see if you can remember what name that picture represents. Do the exercise now.◆

Let's review what you have done in this chapter. You've worked on mastering step two in the process of remembering, which is creating pictures. We've gone over pictures for both first names and last names. First names are a little easier. If you find last names a bit overwhelming, stick with first names for a while. As you practice this technique more and more, it will become easier and easier and you will want to graduate to last names. But do it at your own pace.

Now it's time to combine these pictures with our see pegs from the previous chapter. But make sure you do the review exercises before you go on to Chapter 12. Once you feel comfortable with turning names into pictures, learning how to put these pictures onto your see pegs will be a snap.

Kevin's Pictures for First Names

1. Waldo—a wall with dough on it
2. Wallace—a wall with lace on it or a walrus
3. Dolly—a doll or a mechanical dolly
4. Debbie—a dead bee
5. Nicole—a nick on a piece of coal or a nickel
6. Jan—jam
7. Ann—an ant
8. Jim—basketball or a Slim Jim (better than gymnasium)
9. Joe—a hoe or G.I. Joe or coffee
10. Mark—a marking pen or marker

Kevin's Pictures for Last Names

1. Atwater—ants in water
2. Carmichael—car and a bicycle or car and a white sequined glove
3. Crawford—a crow driving a Ford (car)
4. Gardner—a gardener
5. Hawkins—hawk with fins or a hawk entering an inn
6. Jarrett—a jar and a rat or a chair and a rat
7. Rabinowitz—a robin and a witch
8. Schuster—a shoe stirring or a shoe store
9. Shelton—a shell weighing a ton or a shell made of tin
10. Wayne—a cane

Chapter 11—Review of Lesson

Turning Names into Pictures

This is essentially the same as turning any abstracts into pictures.

1. Break the name into syllables; if the name is one syllable, use the whole name.
2. Close your eyes and say the syllable (or whole name) several times out loud.
3. Create a sound-alike picture or something representative or symbolic of the sound.

Helpful Hints for Turning Names into Pictures

1. Never use celebrities, though you may use something representative of a celebrity.

    Example: for Michael, many people picture Michael Jackson, which will not work. However, a white sequined glove, representative of Michael Jackson, will work.

    Exception: You can use cartoon characters.

2. Anytime you have a large picture, simplify it.

Example: If for Jim you have a large picture of a gymnasium, reduce that to a smaller picture, such as a basketball.

Turning Last Names into Mental Pictures

This is done exactly the same way we turned first names and abstracts into pictures. If possible, divide the words into syllables; close
your eyes, say the syllables out loud (combining two or more if
necessary); and create sound-alike or representative images. Avoid
creating a picture of a real person who has that last name.

Chapter 11—Required Mental Exercise

Exercise 1

Create a picture word for each of the following names, and write
it in the space provided. If you get stuck, you can refer to the Name
Guide at the end of the book, but I highly recommend you do it
on your own first.

Al

Andy

Art

Barry

Ben

Bob

Carl

Dan

Donald

Ed

Frank

Harry

Jack

Jeff

Martin

Anita

Betty

Carol
Cindy
Diane
Dorothy
Elizabeth
Fran
Jean
Kris
Mary
Nancy
Pat
Ruth
Toni

Exercise 2

Each day for the next twenty-one days, pick out last names of five people whom you know. Create a mental picture for each one. Make the pictures either sound-alike or symbolic of that person in some way.

12 Remembering Names: Part 3

Let me tell you a quick story. I was visiting a sales organization in New York City to conduct business having to do with my American Memory Institute. The woman I was talking to interrupted me for a second and conducted some other business with a young man who had just walked by. After they exchanged a few sentences, the woman turned back to me, apologized again for the interruption, and introduced the young man to me, saying, "Kevin, this is Tom So-and-so, our general manager from Atlanta."

"Hi, Tom. Kevin Trudeau. Nice to meet you," I said.

"It was a pleasure meeting you, too," said the young man and walked away.

About six months later, I was in the lobby of the same building in New York, waiting for an elevator. The elevator doors opened, and out came about twenty or thirty people. I recognized the young man, and he seemed to recognize me, too.

"You're the memory guy," he said coming up to me and smiling. "Hi."

"Hi. You're Tom So-and-so," I said, remembering both his first and last names.

This guy was shocked. "I can't believe you remembered my name!" he stammered.

I laughed. "I can't believe I remembered your name, either!" The young man was literally beaming, the smile on his face broader and broader. We both had a good laugh; then he asked me if I had a few minutes, and would I pop by his office when I was finished with my other business.

I love seeing people react when I remember their names. A big broad smile spreads across their face. I can tell that they instantly have become a little more open to me, impressed that I took the time to remember their name. On a personal level, it's a great way to get to know people better. And it opens up opportunities in business situations as well.

Once you finish this chapter, you will be well on your way to making this one of your talents, too. This is the third and final lesson in remembering names. Using action—active action—we are going to take our see pegs from Chapter 10 and peg them to the sound-alike pictures we learned to create in the previous chapter. We've already done a lot of pegging exercises in the book, so this should come very easily to you. Putting it all together is actually the icing on the cake.

By pegging various names to see pegs, you will be training your memory to file away information for the future, preparing it to remember the names of people you encounter every day. Combining all three steps of our name-remembering process might feel a little cumbersome at first—like driving a stick shift or learning a foreign language—but it will become easier and easier, and in time you will be doing it without even thinking.

If this sounds like a hard promise for me to keep, let me remind you that in Chapter 9 you were able to peg ten items to the House List in five-second intervals. Until then, you probably didn't believe you could do that, either. So keep your faith now. You've seen the speed and power of your memory—continue to trust it. It will do the work if you just let it. And of course, I'll lead you through the exercises step by step.

Just make sure you apply the techniques exactly as I describe them. You will look at photographs of various people. Then you will pick a see peg for each person, turn the name into a picture, and put both pictures together using exaggerated, nonsensical action. Remember, both pictures have to be linked together illogically. They can't make sense. And don't forget some of our other tips for good pegging: If the action is logical or boring, it's bad. Include emotions and yourself in the scene, hear the sounds, smell the smells, feel the feelings. Keep the scene going—more is always better than less.

Now look at the first photograph below. There are six photographs in all. We will pretend as though we are meeting these people for the first time. After looking at each photograph, I will lead you through all three steps of remembering, slowly and methodically. You will get a sense of how you will be doing this for real.

Step 3: Putting It All Together

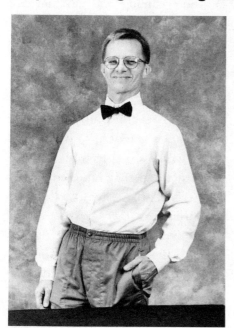

Photo 1. Look at the first photo. Let's call this gentlemen Mr. Bow Tie. The bow tie is his see peg because it's the first thing I notice about this man when I look at his picture. Take a few seconds to observe his bow tie, noticing its size, the material it's made of, the patterns.

Let's say this man tells you his first name is Harry. Say it out loud, as if you were repeating it while shaking hands: "Harry." Meanwhile, how do we create a sound-alike picture for "Harry"? You may think of a few things. I'm going to visualize hair. I always use hair for the name Harry. In your mind's eye, create a vivid picture of hair: its color, thickness, how it may feel to you.

Now for step three. Peg the hair to the bow tie, which is the see peg. Remember to use active action. Perhaps you're sewing hair on the bow tie. Or perhaps you're wrapping the hair around and around the bow tie in a faster and faster motion. Pick a clear, simple action and peg the two pictures together now. See it all as vividly as you can.

What was our see peg in the above exercise? Bow tie. What did we peg to it? Hair, because "hair" sounds like "Harry."◆

Photo 2. Look at this woman and decide what you would use as a see peg. You could use several items she is wearing, but I'm going to use earrings. Take a few seconds to really observe those earrings so that they are embedded in your memory.

This woman tells you her name is Judy. "Judy." Say it out loud. Now what would be a good picture for Judy? "Judy." Breaking Judy into two syllables is tough, so I don't use a sound-alike picture. I'll use something that represents Judy to me: red shoes. Why red shoes? They remind me of Judy Garland in *The Wizard of Oz*. Remember, in the last chapter I told you that you could use an object that reminded you of someone? Like a white glove for Michael Jackson? Red shoes always remind me of Judy Garland.

Now in your mind's eye you need to peg the red shoes to the earrings using strong, clear action. Maybe you see these red shoes attached to the woman's earrings, and they are whirling around and around. Maybe you're walking up to the woman, saying, "I love those earrings," and trying to pull the red shoes off them as she jerks back, saying "Ouch!" In your mind's eye, create a scene with the earrings and the red shoes. See everything vividly: the colors, the action. Use your imagination and make everything bigger than life.

Let's review photo 2. What's your see peg? Earrings. What picture have you pegged to the see peg? Red shoes. Why? They represent Judy.◆

Photo 3. Let's look at the third photo. We're going to call this man Mr. Striped Shirt. Observe him, really look at this man's shirt for a few seconds, so that the picture is reinforced in your memory.

This gentleman goes by the name of Bill. What's a sound-alike picture for "Bill"? We've come across this one before. Let's use a dollar bill. In your mind's eye, link dollar bills to this striped shirt. "Ow! Ow! Ow!" Maybe you're tacking dollar bills to this man's shirt and he's trying to pull away. Maybe huge dollar bills are wrapping themselves around this man's shirt. Maybe there are two bills that look like wings attached to the shirt, and the man flies away.

As you're pegging the bills to the shirt, keep the action vivid and exaggerated. Make sure you picture the dollar bills clearly: Are they big, small? Are there many of them or just a few? Don't forget to include emotion in your scene, as well as other sensations. Maybe the dollar bills are new, and you can feel their crispness and smell that newly minted smell.

Let's review. What was your see peg for photo 3? A striped shirt. What did you peg to the shirt? Dollar bills because the man's name is Bill.◆

Now go back and look at the first photo. What's the see peg? Bow tie. What do we put on the bow tie? Hair. And what's the man's name? Harry.

Photo number 2. What is the see peg? Earrings. What do we put on the earrings? Red shoes. And what's the woman's name? Judy.

Photo number 3. What's your see peg? The striped shirt. What do we put on the striped shirt? Dollar bills. What's the man's name? Bill.

Photo 4. Now look at photo 4. We're going to call this person Miss Glasses. That's her see peg. And her name is going to be Mary.

How do we turn Mary into a picture? Getting sound-alike pictures for the two syllables "Ma-ry" seems kind of difficult to me. How about the whole word. What sounds like Mary? How about "marry." What's a good picture for "marry"—remember, we want something simple. How about a wedding dress or a wedding cake? What are other choices for Mary? Some people think of "merry"-go-round, which is fine. Some people link the name to Christmas, because they are thinking of the Virgin Mary. What's a good picture for Christmas? How about a Christmas tree or a wreath. My picture for the name Mary is a horse. Can you guess why? Mare. "Mare" sounds like "Mary," and it's even a common nickname for Mary.

Do you see how far you can make your imagination go when you're creating pictures? Even if it's a little awkward at first, the more you do it the more fun you can have imagining outrageous combinations. I use "mare" for Mary, but you may think of something no one has ever thought of before. And that's great because that's what Mega Memory is all about.

Now let's peg a mare to our see peg, glasses. I see the glasses as being very big and silver-colored, and the mare is eating them. The woman is yelling, "Oh, no! Oh, no!" but the horse just keeps gobbling up more and more. Visualize this in your mind's eye. Or perhaps the woman is taking off these big glasses and beating the mare over the head with them. "Stay away from me! Stay away from me!" Or even better, put both pictures together. The mare is trying to bite the glasses off. The woman rips the glasses off and starts pummeling the mare with them. See all this in your mind's eye.

Let's review. What is our see peg? Glasses. What is our picture? A mare, for the woman's name, Mary.◆

Photo 5. Here is the fifth photo. We're going to call this person Mr. Pocket Silk because of that striking silk handkerchief in his breast pocket. Your see peg may have been different from mine. You could choose anything—hair, eyes, shirt, ears, etc., but I'm going to call him Mr. Pocket Silk.

The man tells you his name is Mark. How would you turn Mark into a picture? "Mark." How about a Magic Marker, a big, red Magic Marker? Other people think of marks on a report card, and others of a marker on a piece of property to distinguish boundaries, like a stone or a post. For now, let's use my choice, the Magic Marker. In your mind's eye, put a big, red Magic Marker to the silk handkerchief. Remember to use action that's ludicrous and exaggerated. What can we think of? You're marking up that beautiful silk handkerchief with big, red streaks. And what does the man do? He's nodding and saying, "Wow! That looks great! It really looks great!" And the handkerchief keeps getting bigger and redder and both of you are nodding excitedly, very pleased with the results!

Let's review. What's your see peg for this man? Pocket silk. What's his name? Mark. What picture did you choose for Mark? A Magic Marker, which you pegged to the handkerchief in a vivid, ludicrous way.◆

Photo 6. We're going to call the woman in Photo 6 Miss Scarf. Again, we could choose other things for see pegs, but we're going to use a scarf.

This woman's name is Janet. "Janet." "Jan-et." "Jan-net." How can you create a sound-alike picture for these syllables? How about "jam," for "jan"? And the second syllable? That's easy, a picture of a net, either a volleyball net that's high up in the air, or a tennis net that's nearer to the ground. Other people might think of a butterfly net. They're all great pictures. Let's use a tennis net. Create a picture of jam on a tennis net, and see that vividly in your mind: the color of the jam, the gooey texture, whether the net is taut or sagging against the ground.

Now in your mind's eye, peg that picture to the scarf, which is your see peg for this woman. Perhaps you're playing tennis over this net with jam all over it, but instead of tennis balls you're using the woman's scarf. She's terrified that the scarf will get stuck on that gooey net. But you keep playing, hitting volleys and ground strokes, and the scarf keeps sailing over the net at all angles, missing the jam by inches. The woman keeps yelling more loudly, and you keep playing more and more recklessly, trying to win each point. This scene has action, emotion, and is certainly exaggerated and ludicrous. I want you to create a similar scene in your mind's eye now.

Let's review. What is your see peg for this woman? A scarf. What picture is pegged to the scarf? "Jam" and a "net," for the woman's name, Janet.◆

Now go back to the first photo. What was your see peg? Bow tie. And what's the picture we pegged to the bow tie? Hair. And what does that give us for a name? Harry.

Photo 2. What was your see peg? Earrings. What's the picture on the earrings? Red shoes. What's the woman's name? Judy.

Photo 3. What was your see peg? A striped shirt. What picture did you peg to it in your mind's eye? Dollar bills. What's the man's name? Bill.

Photo 4. What was your see peg? Glasses. What picture was pegged to the glasses? A female horse, a mare. And what's the name you're trying to put into your memory? Mary.

Photo 5. What was your see peg? Pocket silk. What picture did we put on the pocket silk? A Magic Marker. And what's the man's name? Mark.

Photo 6. What is the see peg? Scarf. What picture did we put on the scarf? A net with jam all over it. What name are we trying to remember? Janet.

How Your Mega Memory Recalls Names

Now, how does putting these three steps together help you in remembering names? Let's examine what happens when you later meet one of these people. Let's use Janet, the woman from the last photo, as an example.

One day, you run into Janet again, let's say at the supermarket, a scenario we referred to a few chapters ago. We've all been in that situation. We know we've met the person, but we just can't remember the name. Instead of saying, "Excuse me, I forget your name," with a trained memory you do the following:

First ask yourself, "What was my peg?" If you have done the exercises correctly, I promise you that the picture of the see peg, the scarf, will pop into your mind, even though the woman may no longer be wearing it. Then ask yourself, "What was I doing to the scarf? What was the action?" I guarantee you, your picture of playing tennis with the scarf over the net with jam on it will come to you. "Net-jam." "Jam-net." "Jan-et." Janet! The name will come to you.

Let's return to another photo, number 3. You've met the man with the striped shirt at a party, you talked to him for a few minutes, and then went on to talk to someone else. It is three hours later and you're approaching him to say good-bye. What was your see peg for this man? A striped shirt. What was your action involving the striped shirt? You were tacking dollar bills to his shirt. Bills. Bill! The man's name is Bill.

Now keep in mind that this process is happening in your unconscious mind, which is very powerful and very quick. In the beginning, the process might take a while, and you might not always remember all the steps correctly, especially when you're in a rush. However, as with all the individual steps you've been practicing, the more you do this, the more automatically everything will happen.

As you keep going, you won't even have to ask yourself these questions consciously. Sometimes you'll see the person, and in a few seconds the name will pop into your mind. That will happen more and more as you practice. Your memory will have learned to go through these questions on its own and will give you the name you are searching for. And instead of waking up in the middle of the night three days later with the name of the person on the tip of your tongue, you'll have it when you need it.

At this point in my seminars, I am always asked a lot of questions, and I sense that people are experiencing a lot of resistance. "Kevin, how will I ever learn to meet fifty people and remember all their names in the space of a few hours?" "Kevin, everything we're doing seems pretty strange and complicated. Is it really worth all that effort?"

In answer to the first question, I tell everybody, "You learn how to remember the names of fifty people the same way you learned to eat a big piece of steak as a child. One bite at a time. Take it slowly. Have fun with the different pieces. Over time you'll learn how to put all the pieces together and you'll be remembering all those names without even thinking about it, just like you now eat that big piece of steak. That's the best thing about Mega Memory. You let everything happen at its own pace."

As for the second question, I want to quote you a line from Zig Ziglar, America's premier motivational speaker and author of several books on motivation and attitude. He says, "We don't pay the price of success, we enjoy the benefits of success." Yes, there is some time and effort involved in learning how to use this technique easily. But think of the benefits. You will generate goodwill. People will be appreciative that you made the effort to remember their names, and they will in turn remember you. And think how important that is in business. Making a good impression and generating goodwill might be just that "small" edge that gets you the job or the contract. We often don't consider these small interpersonal factors when thinking about business, but they are the engine that usually generates business deals, gets contracts signed, and opens up opportunities. When you remember people's names, you will be giving yourself that small but vital edge.

Remembering Last Names

I have some students in every seminar who pick up these techniques in a few days. If you're one of these fast learners who wants even more of an edge, here are some exercises that involve adding last names to the Mega Memory equation.

Again, I'm going to recommend that you feel confident with first names before you start adding last names to your repertoire. As you become more and more successful with first names, you will be able to build on that confidence as you start playing with remembering last names. The procedure is the same. We just add another step to our technique. We still pick a see peg in the beginning. We still turn the first name into a picture. Then we create another picture for the last name before pegging everything together.

For our examples, let's go back to the photos we used for first names, staring on page 125. The man in the first photo is named Harry. Our see peg is the bow tie, and we've pegged hair to it. Let's assume this fellow's full name is Harry Johnson. How do we turn the last name, Johnson, into a picture? Say it out loud upon hearing it, that always helps. "John-son." We pictured "Johnson" in the last chapter. We used a picture of a john, representing a toilet, and the picture of the sun in the sky. So picture a toilet in a great big field with the sun shining brightly on it. Add that picture to the bow tie and the picture you created for the first name in your mind's eye.◆

Let's go to the second photo. Let's assume the woman's last name is Wilbond, Judy Wilbond. "Wil-bond." How do we turn it into a picture? What's a good picture for the first syllable, "wil"? Maybe a will that someone has written. And what does "bond" remind you of? It reminds me of cement, bonding cement. What else for bond? A ring? Or bonds, as in stocks and bonds? Or tying something, binding something up. I can picture a will being tied and bound to a chair in my mind's eye. Add that picture to the red shoes.◆

Let's go to our third photo, Mr. Striped Shirt. What is pegged to the stripes? Dollar bills. His first name is Bill. Let's assume his last name is Conant. Breaking it into syllables would give us "Co-nant" or "Con-ant." What picture can you use for the first syllable? It depends on how you pronounced it, "con" or "cone." Let's say "cone." Let's picture an ant, a big black ant for the second syllable. Now put both pictures together. How about big black ants eating a scrumptious pistachio cone? Add that picture to the dollar bills on the man's striped shirt.◆

Now we'll do some exercises involving the other three photos. I'm going to give you last names and I want you to turn them into vivid pictures and vividly peg the pictures to the see pegs.

Go to the fourth person. Our see peg for her is glasses, and our picture is the horse eating the big silver-colored glasses. The woman's last name is Nightingale. Say it out loud. "Nightingale." Repeat it out loud, breaking it down into syllables. "Night-in-gale." Repeat the first syllable. "Night." "Night." What does that give you a picture of? Now take the other syllables, say them out loud several times, and turn them into pictures. Now close the book and turn Nightingale into a picture using as much action as you can.◆

Go to the fifth person, Mr. Pocket Silk. His last name is Yamagishi. Repeat it out loud. "Yamagishi." "Yam-a-gi-shi." "Yam-a-gi-shi." How can you turn the first syllable, "yam," into a picture? Now repeat the other syllables out loud. "A-gi-shi." Repeat them either singly or in combination. How can you turn them into pictures? Close the book and do that now.◆

Let's go to our last photo, Miss Scarf. Let's assume her last name is Shafeet. "Shafeet." Say it out loud, breaking it down by syllable. "Sha-feet." "Shaf-fet." Take each syllable and see if you can break them down into pictures. Close the book and do that now.◆

How did you do? As you can see, turning last names into pictures is the same as doing it with first names. And pegging those pictures to our see pegs works the same way as well; it's just another step in the entire process. Once you become comfortable with breaking down the names into syllables and turning the syllables into pictures, the rest comes easily. And you can have a lot of fun with the pegging, which I hope you have been doing already, letting your imagination get as crazy as it wants.

By doing these exercises—by letting your imagination go wild, by picking see pegs and creating vivid pictures, by pegging things together in interesting ways, and above all by having fun with this technique—you will develop great skill at remembering people's names. You won't remember just one name, or two or three names, but you'll be able to walk into a room, meet forty or fifty people and a few hours later go back and recall everyone's name. I can do it, and I've seen many of my seminar participants do it in the practice "cocktail parties" we stage. So go to it—start pegging! I promise you, when you leave your next cocktail party or business meeting, you'll have a lot of people remembering you.

Chapter 12—Review

The Three Steps for Remembering Names
1. Pick the see peg.
2. Turn the name into a picture.
3. Put the picture on the see peg with *action* in a ludicrous way.

Chapter 12—Required Mental Exercise

Practice pegging the name of anyone you meet today by doing the three basic steps reviewed in this chapter. If you have a partner, you can also have your partner introduce himself/herself to you using a made-up name.

13　Basic Day-to-day Applications

One of the most gratifying comments I hear from my seminar participants is "Kevin, I just can't believe how powerful my memory is. I'm remembering all sorts of things when I'm not even trying to apply your techniques!" That's perhaps the most satisfying aspect of Mega Memory. As you really get into the various exercises and techniques on a day-to-day basis, your unconscious literally takes over and performs what you've been training it to do—except even more so. A great memory becomes habit, part of your makeup, just as deep lung capacity or great stamina is developed by any well-trained athlete.

I hope you had fun learning how to remember names—and I hope you're already dazzling your friends and business colleagues with these techniques! In this chapter I'm going to begin teaching some additional real-life applications of Mega Memory. Again, we'll be taking it very slowly—one step at a time. I'll discuss the techniques with you, explain why I'm doing what I am, and then let you try the same thing. While you're learning them, these techniques will begin to work on your unconscious. Slowly but very surely, when you see, hear, and experience various things, you will be automatically filing them away for instantaneous recall in the future.

Before beginning to discuss the various applications, I want to reemphasize one important thing. All of these techniques are grounded in certain fundamentals. I will be very specific in describing each technique, but it doesn't mean that you can't apply what you've just learned to another situation. If something's not touched upon in this book, it doesn't matter. If a technique seems useful, go ahead and use it. By the end of this book, you will have learned to use techniques that are applicable to many situations in daily life. So keep your mind open to the possibilities—they're virtually endless.

The Daily Schedule

To remind themselves of their daily schedule, most people keep a written to-do list or a pocket calendar. Used almost universally, it's a widely accepted practice for everybody, including businesspeople. Keeping a written list or a calendar is well and good at the office or on your kitchen table, but the problem is, it's not enough. What happens if you think of something when you're not in a position to write it down? When you're driving a car, in the shower, or in a meeting? That's often when you think of things like, "Oh, I've got to stop by the dry cleaners." Or, "I've got to pick up milk at the grocery store." Or, "I'd better not forget to mail that letter again today!"

Let me say this, even with a Mega Memory, your memory will not replace the written word; it will supplement it. That's very, very important. *It will not replace; it will supplement.* I've been saying throughout this book that I don't want you to write things down. I don't want you to do it when it will interfere with your memory and get you in the bad habit of not trying to remember a piece of information. By writing something down when you think of it, you are really telling yourself that you don't need to remember it, your pen and paper will do the work for you. It's just like the employee whose boss goes over his work in great detail. The employee knows he doesn't have to try very hard because his boss hasn't really given him much responsibility.

What I'm telling you here is to give your memory real responsibility. Train it to remember things; you then go back and write something down to reinforce what it is you're trying to remember. But as I've been repeating, the more you train your memory, the less you will need to rely on pen and paper. Just like a good boss with a good employee, you may have to be there occasionally to give some guidance and provide support, but basically your employee will want to keep growing and taking on more and more tasks. The paper and pencil will be needed less and less.

I always find it funny when I'm out on one of my speaking or teaching engagements and someone asks me to send some information or a set of tapes. I'll say, "Sure, give me your address." The person responds with, "Oh, jeez, I don't have a pen." I laugh and say, "That's okay, I don't have a pen, either, but I have a memory." And we both laugh, though I can see the person just dying to say, "You're really going to remember?" Yes, I'm going to remember!

I'm going to ask you to establish a Things to Do Today list for yourself. When you're keeping a mental to-do list, what do you need first? You need a place to put the information—a peg. Since you'll want room for more than one thing, you'll need a few pegs. You'll want to use one of your peg lists. The pegs I use for my Things to Do Today list are from my Body List. Whenever I think of something I need to do—pick something up, make a phone call, complete a task—I turn it into a picture and peg it to my Body List. I put the first thing I think of on my first peg, which is my toes. I put the second thing I think of on my second peg, which is my knees, and so on. Then throughout the day all I need to do is periodically scan this list and see what's on my pegs, just as I would look to see what's on a written to-do list.

When I'm teaching this in my seminars, inevitably someone will say, "But Kevin, what if I forget to look at my Body List? What do I do then?" The only answer I have for that person is "What if you forgot to look at a written to-do list? What if you forget to look in your mailbox?" That's not the point. You'll always know you have things to do. You just might forget the specifics. All you need to do is get in the habit of scanning your mental to-do list. Look at each of the pegs and ask yourself, "What's on my toes?

What's on my knees? What's on my muscle?" You can go through the whole list in a few seconds.

In a moment I'll ask you to close the book and think of five things that you want to do today. They should be very ordinary, perhaps going to buy some groceries, picking up your dry cleaning, purchasing a particular book. Do not write down these tasks. Close the book and think of five tasks now.◆

Now let's take the first thing you want to do and turn it into a vivid picture. Then, in your mind's eye, using action, peg that picture to your toes. Make sure the action is exaggerated. Include emotion, like joy, sorrow, or pain. Include yourself in the picture, too, and make sure the action could never happen in real life. Close the book and do it now.◆

Let's review what you've just done. If you needed to buy some milk, for example, perhaps you pictured ten milk cartons on your toes. You were walking on them, feeling lighter than air. Or perhaps you were picturing a giant cow nibbling on your toes. Perhaps you pictured yourself as very thirsty while all of this was happening, just dying for that tall, cold glass of milk.

Now, close the book and repeat the same procedure with the other four tasks you've set for yourself. Turn each one into a picture and peg it to your Body List. Your second picture will go on your knees, the third on your muscle, the fourth on your rear, and the fifth on your love handles. See the pictures clearly. Use strong, simple action. Turn each task into a picture and peg it to your Body List now.◆

Now that you have done this, just scan this list to remind yourself of your five tasks. The pictures that you pegged to your Body List should flash through your mind. That's exactly how you would do this in real life.

Keep in mind that you can peg anything in seconds, anywhere you are: right before you go to sleep; in the shower; in an elevator; while doing the laundry; even while you're doing something like cooking or gardening or cleaning and just don't want to take the time to write things down. I even do it when I'm on a phone call and something pops into my mind. You will be able to peg that quickly. It's that easy and convenient. You always have your memory, and can always process and organize the information in mental file folders so that it's right there at your mental fingertips.

Where Are My Keys?

How often have you asked yourself, "Where are my keys?" You've come home from work, thrown down the keys, grabbed a quick sandwich because you wanted to go out again soon, and twenty minutes later you're frantically searching for your keys, not knowing where you threw them down. Or perhaps you've overslept and are going to be late for work, so you shower and dress quickly, and start out the door, when you realize you don't have your keys. You search frantically through the clothes you wore yesterday, your purse, your coat. They're not there. How would you like never to have this problem again?

You forget where your keys are because you are not focusing on the keys when you put them down in the first place. Your memory is not connected to what your hand is doing. You're throwing down the keys, but consciously you're thinking about your upcoming date or what you'll have for supper or how horrible your boss is. The movement of placing the keys somewhere is being accomplished without any link to the memory. And this doesn't just happen with keys. It happens with many small items you use on a regular basis: glasses, umbrellas, a favorite pen, a comb, a brush. I always used to forget where I put my sunglasses.

To prevent this from happening, all we need to do is get into the habit of focusing and adding action when putting down the keys. Let's say you come home from work and throw your keys down on the coffee table. To practice this technique, picture the coffee table blowing up with the keys on it. That's all you have to do. You're still applying the three basic steps of remembering. You've got a picture of the coffee table, which is your peg and you've got a picture of the keys, which is the information you want to remember. Put both pictures together using action. Blowing up the coffee table is strong and simple. But you could choose other action as well: nailing the keys to the table, or imagining the keys being huge as you throw them down.

The result of doing this? Thirty minutes or a day later, when you ask yourself, "Where are my keys?" your memory will produce a picture of the coffee table blowing up, in a sense telling you, "You blew up the coffee table with them, dummy." And there they'll be, on the coffee table. The very act of imagining that action of blowing up the coffee table—even if that imagining lasts one hundredth of a second or even less—engages the memory. What you're doing is focusing, making sure you connect the movement of your hand to your memory, and by doing that you're locking in a piece of information for recall later.

You might very well ask, "Well, Kevin, what if I put my keys down on the coffee table today and on the microwave oven tomorrow, and on the TV the day after that? Won't I get confused? What's going to happen if I blow them all up!" First of all, let's take the worst-case scenario. Your keys will be in one of three places: the coffee table, the microwave, or the TV. Having three places to search in is still better than running around the entire house, isn't it?

But if you get in the habit of practicing this technique, the more likely scenario is the following: When you ask yourself where the keys are the first day, a picture of the coffee table blowing up will flash through your mind. When you ask the same question the next day, a picture of the microwave blowing up will flash through your mind. The third day a picture of the TV blowing up will come to you. If you've been practicing this technique, your memory will tell you where you put the keys most recently.

Let me repeat a very important point I mentioned when we first started this chapter. In the beginning, you will be applying this technique consciously. That is, you will have to make yourself think about blowing up the table, or imagine nailing to a desk a pair of glasses you always misplace. In a very short time, just a few weeks, you'll be applying these techniques on an unconscious level. You really won't be thinking about blowing up the coffee table or applying any other action when you put down the keys or glasses.

Your unconscious will do it automatically for you because you will have trained your memory to be engaged when you take that action.

Don't be surprised one day when you find yourself saying something like this: "Where did I put that contract? Oh yeah, it's on this chair." And you'll think, "You know, I didn't peg it to the chair, but I guess I have a great memory." The technique was applied unconsciously, and you have recalled the information seemingly without trying to.

Remembering Addresses

Memorizing addresses involves using the pegging and chaining techniques we've already learned. Remembering an address, such as 15 Wilshire Boulevard, Los Angeles, involves breaking it down into three parts: the number, the street name, and the city.

The number. Let's use the above address as our example. To remember the number, you first select a peg list on which you will peg the information. You have three lists to choose from: the Body List, Tree List, and House List. Let's say you choose the Body List, and your first peg on it, toes. Visualize toes.

Now create a picture for your number by going to the Tree List and picking the appropriate word. In this example it's number 15, which is "paycheck." In your mind's eye, link the two pictures together using action. How about a big paycheck falling down and cutting your toe? So from now on you may decide that anything pegged to your toes will be address. The next time you ask yourself what number this particular house is on, a picture of the check cutting your toe will flash through your mind, and you'll be able to decode it: "Toes" represents an address; "paycheck" is number 15.

A few tips: Don't worry if there's a zero in the address; you can use a doughnut, for example, as a picture for zero. If the number is 21 or above, divide the number into smaller pieces. Create a picture for each piece and then peg or chain them together. (In Part II, "Advanced Mega Memory," I will give you some techniques so you can easily remember much longer numbers.)

Street name. Break the street name into syllables. Here's how the address above would sound: "wil-shire-boul-e-vard." Create a sound-alike or representative picture for each syllable. Peg the pictures to a peg list or chain them together. For "wil-shire" how about a picture of a will being cut in two by scissors or shears? "Will-shears." For "boul-e-vard" how about a bull carrying a work of art—"Bull-art"? "Will-shears-bull-art"? "Wilshire Boulevard."

City. Follow the same initial steps you did for the street name. Break the city into syllables and create pictures for each syllable. Los Angeles might be "lost-angles" or "lost-angels." Now you can peg the city name to an entirely new peg; in which case each picture for the number and the street would have its own peg. Or you can chain the pictures for the city name to the street.

For example, you might picture a will being cut by huge shears, being followed by a bull with art on its back, being chased by a group of lost angels. To include the number, start your chaining sequence with the paycheck cutting your toe, and then follow through with the rest of the chain.

Once you practice using the different lists and techniques, you will find the ones that suit you best in various situations. I think being able to remember addresses is not only practical, it's fun. So the next time someone asks you whether you have a pen and paper with which to record an address, take a breath and say, "No, I don't have a pen, but I have a memory," and use one of your Mega Memory techniques!

Remembering Driving Directions

How many times has this happened to you? You're driving some-place with a friend, and you get lost. Your friend, who's driving, asks you to roll down the window and ask someone for directions. This person, being very helpful, decides to give you very explicit directions. "Well," she says, "you go down this road for about a mile. Then there's a hill, take a left at that street. Then you take a right and continue for about a mile. When you come to a fork in the road, bear right." While the woman is talking, you're nodding. "Uh-huh, okay. Right, up the hill, then left. Uh-huh. Okay. Then right or left? Right. Uh-huh, after the fork another right." When you're finished, you roll the window back up and turn to the driver. "Okay, did you get that?" Your friend shakes his head. "You're the navigator." "But you're the driver!"

Between the two of you—if you're lucky—you might remember that you go down the same road for a while, then up a hill to the left. If you're really resourceful, you might have had a pencil and notebook handy, and you would have started scribbling down as best you could what the woman was saying. Then you would start driving, and suddenly what you had written in the notebook wouldn't make sense. Time to pull over again.

You can save yourself a lot of trouble when you use your Mega Memory techniques. And, again, when receiving driving instructions, the techniques are very basic: pictures and action.

Rule number one for directions: Always ask for a landmark. Why? You can use the landmark as a peg. If the person says, "You go down a road ... I think to the third light, and at the second street after the third light take a right," ask for a landmark. "Is there anything at that right?" The landmark can be either man-made, like a gas station or a building, or natural, like a pond or stream. Usually, man-made landmarks stand out more. Then, even if you get a bit confused, you can still search for that landmark. For example, if the person giving you directions tells you there's an Exxon station at the third light, you can use that information to orient yourself.

There is something else you can do. Very often you forget whether someone told you to take a right or a left at a particular place. To reinforce the information, you need to establish a picture for right and left. From now on after reading this book, your picture for right is going to be one of rats. Your picture for left is going to be leaves. (Yes, these are mnemonics; as I've said before, in certain situations they are very helpful!) When you hear someone tell you to take a right, create a picture of rats in your mind. When you hear someone tell you to take a left, visualize leaves.

In the above example, let's say the person tells you to take a right at an Exxon station. Create a picture in your mind of an Exxon station with—you guessed it!—rats pumping gas. Big, old, gray, very helpful, rats. See that in your mind's eye.

Now this is how your trained Mega Memory will work. You'll be driving along, and even if you've forgotten the details, you don't have to worry. When you see an Exxon gas station, the picture of those rats pumping gas will flash through your mind and you'll remember you have to take a right.

Let's say you're asking for another set of directions from someone. That person tells you, "Go down the road, past two intersections, I think. At the second intersection, take a left." Ask for a landmark. "What's at the intersection?" "There's a bank." Get a clearer picture. "What does the bank look like?" "It's a big white building."

Then, visualize the big, white bank, and since you've been told you should take a left, guess what you peg to that bank? Leaves. Add action. Maybe the leaves are on fire. Maybe they're huge and brightly colored.

You will have given your unconscious enough information to get you where you're going. As you're driving along and you pass by a white bank, you'll remember that you have to take a left because the picture of the white building with the leaves on it will spring to your mind.

The same thing happens in an unplanned way when you're driving through a place you've been to before and can't quite remember where you go next. If you're with a friend and your friend asks you for directions, you might say you don't know but, "as soon as we get there, I'll know." At some level you know that you know—you know that your unconscious remembers and you only hope that at the right time the correct information will spring to your mind. With a Mega Memory, you don't have to leave things to chance. You train your mind to provide this information when you need it.

Again, let me emphasize that, as you're first reading this book, it may seem like you have to do a lot of work—picking a peg, creating a picture, thinking of an action—in order to remember a simple piece of information, like whether to turn right or left. But, always keep in mind that as the days and weeks go by, you'll get better and better, faster and faster with these techniques. The more you train your memory, the more quickly you'll be able to do all these steps and combine them in all sorts of interesting combinations. Whenever you feel the need, these mental tools will be there for you, allowing you to operate much more efficiently in many different situations.

Creating Your Own Applications

Now I'd like to review a couple of other situations in which you would use these same techniques, and I want you to figure out how to apply them. Whatever the scenario will be, however, remember that the basic steps are always the same:

1. a place to put the information, which is your peg
2. the information turned into a vivid picture
3. mental glue holding the pictures together, which is action

Scenario 1. Let's say you're a real estate agent, and that you're going on tour to look at new homes. You want to make sure you remember specific things about each home. Sure, you can write things down. But you don't want to be a slave to pen and paper. With so many homes and so many clients, you want to make sure that when you're talking to someone about each home, these things will come right to your mind.

Let's say you visit three homes. The first one has very big bathrooms, a swimming pool, and a master bedroom with a balcony. The second home has beautiful wood paneling and a spacious two-car garage. The third home is small, but is situated on top of a hill and has lovely views.

Think of the three-step procedure you would use to remember these things about each particular home. Close the book and do it now.◆

Let me show you how I would remember the outstanding features of the first home. The first step is to pick a peg on which to place our information. I could choose any of my three peg lists, the Tree List, the Body List, or the House List, and then I could create pictures of the bathrooms, the swimming pool, and the master bedroom, and peg them to one of the lists.

There's another way to create a peg. Let's say I've noticed that this first house has a huge oak tree in the front lawn. I can use the oak tree as a peg. This is a form of association we learned in the very beginning of the book when we discussed the mnemonic HOMES for remembering the Great Lakes. You use association when you need to remember something that you can logically link to a piece of information already in your memory. Something you know, with something you don't know.

Because I already associate the oak tree with the first house, let's use option two. Make that oak tree your peg. Now create pictures for your three features and peg them to the tree. The first picture would be a toilet bowl for "john"; the second picture could involve water, which would represent the swimming pool; and the third picture might be one of pillows, which would represent the master bedroom. Then, using exaggerated, nonsensical action, you would peg these pictures to the three.

To emphasize again, once you've become adept at these techniques, you would be doing this *as you go through the house,* simultaneously seeing its various features. That's what makes Mega Memory so practical. You need to waste precious little time later, writing down everything or reviewing everything in your head. The information gets locked in as you are seeing, hearing, or experiencing it. Now try the same techniques with the other two houses.◆

Scenario 2. Let's practice another scenario. Assume you're in the automotive business and you want to have a better recall of the cars you have and their different features. You start with your first car, a used model that you think is a good deal. You want to remember that the car has 13,000 miles on it and has air conditioning. What would you do to remember those two pieces of information about this car? Close the book and do the exercise now.◆

What's our first memory rule? We need a peg, a place to put the information. Have you observed anything outstanding about the car? Let's assume it has mag wheels. That would be my peg. (Other pegs: a dent on the body, a shiny color, a missing light.) Now we need to take the two pieces of information and create pictures for them. This car has 13,000 miles on it, so I'd get a picture of a witch, because that's 13 on the Tree List. And I'd also make the witch seem cold or frozen, her teeth chattering away to remember the air conditioning. How would I do step three? I'd put the witch on the mag wheels using a lot of action. Perhaps she's spinning with the wheels; perhaps she's rotating the wheels trying to keep warm.

The next time I talk to a customer about her needs for a car, what happens? If she tells me she's looking for a used car, I'll flip through my mental file folders of used cars. One of them will be of this particular car. The pictures I've created will flash through my mind. The witch reminds me of 13, her chattering teeth remind me of cold, and I'll remember that car has 13,000 miles on it and air conditioning. Without needing to look things up, I'll be able to tell my customers this information right away and find out whether she's interested. Remembering that one used car has 13,000 miles on it and air conditioning may not seem like a great achievement to you. But multiply this by twenty, fifty, a hundred cars, all with their different features, and you'll get an idea of how useful your Mega Memory can be.

Scenario 3. Let's try one more application. Assume you're going to make a speech and you have an outline. There are ten points in your outline. How would you make the speech without the use of notes? Close the book and think about the procedure right now.◆

Here's my solution. The first thing you need is a peg on which to put the information. I would probably pick one of the lists, Tree List, House List, or Body List, because all the information in my notes is new. If I were going to use association, I'd already have to be pretty familiar with my speech so I could use certain parts as preexisting pegs.

Next, we need to turn each of the ten points in our outline into pictures. Let's say our topic for this speech is making money in real estate, and the first point in your outline is how to become an astute investor. Focus on the most important part of point one, which is on being astute, and turn it into a picture. "As-tute." "Ass-toot." Maybe you'd see a jackass tooting a horn. And you'd put that on the first peg on a list.

Your second point might be choosing your sales categories. What's the main idea of point two? Sales categories, choosing categories. We've already turned categories into a picture when we played Concentration. We came up with a bloody, gory cat ("cat-gory"). Peg the picture to the second peg on whichever list you are using. Then complete the process with the rest of the items in your outline.

When making your speech, in your mind's eye you'll be able to look at the first peg, and you see what? A jackass tooting a horn. "Folks, I want to talk about how to become an astute investor." After you've finished discussing point one, you'll take a look at your second peg, and you'll see a bloody cat. "The next thing I want to talk about is categories. Sales categories . . ." And you'll continue down your list until you have finished your speech. It may take you a while to become that confident in using your Mega Memory, but believe me, it happens. Whatever you're doing and wherever you are, just keep practicing those three rules of memory:

1. a place to store the data, which is a peg
2. the information turned into a picture
3. mental glue to hold it there, which is action

Chapter 13—Review

Daily To-Do List
1. Choose a peg list (Tree List, Body List, House List).
2. Create a picture of each thing you would like to do or remember.
2. Peg each picture to the pegs on the list you have chosen.

Where Are My Keys?

1. Get into the habit of focusing on the piece of furniture or place where you put down your keys.
2. In your mind's eye, add action.

Remembering an Address

The Number Part of an Address

1. Select a peg list you already know (Tree List, Body List, House List).
2. Choose a picture for your number.
3. Peg the picture to one of the pegs on the list you chose.
4. Create a mental picture linking the two.
5. If there's a zero in the address, use a doughnut for your picture.
6. Divide longer numbers into sections and follow the same rules as above.

The Street Name

1. Break the street name into syllables.
2. Create sound-alike or representative pictures for each syllable in the street (remember, you can combine syllables).
3. Peg them sequentially to a peg list. Or:
4. Chain them together and peg just the first one to a peg list.

The City Name

1. Follow same first two steps you did for the street name.
2. Peg the pictures on an entirely new peg. Or:
3. Chain them to the street name.

Remembering Directions

1. Ask for a landmark.
2. Convert the street names into pictures—as when memorizing addresses.
3. Use pictures for directions, as below:
   Indicating right and left:
   Right—picture rats.
   Left—picture leaves.

Indicating additional directions:
North—north pole.
South—sow (female pig).
East—chopsticks.
West—cowboy hat.

Chapter 13—Required Mental Exercises

Exercise 1
Peg the following activities to one of your lists, pretending this is today's to-do list.

1. Go to the post office to mail a package.
2. Buy a trash can.
3. Return a defective flea collar.
4. Buy a light bulb.
5. Go to the grocery store for condensed milk.
6. Pick up some flowers for your significant other.
7. Spend fifteen minutes reading a positive-think book.
8. Get your car washed.
9. Do thirty minutes of aerobics.
10. Get your shoes polished.

Exercise 2
Using the steps described above, peg the following addresses:

1. 100 Nightingale Court
   Peoria
2. 1512 Main Street
   Boston
3. 9 Phillips Circle
   Fort Hood
4. 723 Jackson Drive
   Wheeling

5. 1902 Tremont
   Seattle

Exercise 2

Practice pegging at least fifteen sets of directions per week. You can begin with the ones below.

1. Turn left on Ashbury.
2. Go south on East Maple.
3. Drive west on Eagleton Way.
4. Turn right on Ramsdale Road.
5. Go north on Belleview Avenue.

14   Reading and Mega Memory

We're now going to apply our Mega Memory techniques to reading comprehension. Do you always remember what you have read? Has the following ever happened to you: You're reading along, and suddenly you notice with a start that you have no idea what you're reading or even how far you've gone in the book? You have, quite literally, lost the train of thought.

That happens because even though your eyes are going over each word, your mind is focused on something else. It's similar to your throwing keys down someplace but not paying attention to what you are doing with your hand. In this case you're not paying attention to the words. Your mind is wandering, focusing on something else, and the meaning of the words doesn't register.

You lose interest in the words for many reasons: The material is difficult or complicated. Sometimes, it's simply a case of the book not being written well, and you're bored. Textbooks with a lot of data can often feel overwhelming and incomprehensible. You can also have trouble focusing for physiological reasons: You're tired; you're upset about something; or you are feeling stressed because you are studying for a test. Whatever the situation, the bottom line is that you need to absorb the information better.

Reading and Remembering

To help people become more focused readers, I've developed a technique using the Mega Memory system that is very simple. But when done properly, the results are quite astonishing. The technique is this: When you are reading, you must always read as though you are imparting the information presented in the book to someone else.

Let me rephrase that. When you are reading, in your mind's eye you should picture yourself speaking the words to someone else. Why? As we've said a number of times, we are our own favorite subject. We always pay more attention to what we say than whatever anyone else might ever say. When we imagine ourselves speaking the words that we are reading, we make the process and material personal, because we are in the picture. The emotions come into play. And being the bridge to our unconscious, our emotions start the wheels of those deeper thought processes going, and our memory becomes engaged. We start paying attention.

There's another reason why this technique works well. Your conscious mind can focus upon—and picture—only one thing at a time. It can't be in two places at once, so to speak. By picturing yourself saying these words as you're reading, you are forcing yourself to mentally stay put. i.e., not wander or daydream. You are engaging your memory instead, and locking in the information. That one simple step will also help you to recall infinitely more data than reading normally, because the process of engaging the memory will increase recall substantially.

I want you to practice this technique right now. Imagine saying, "I want you to practice this technique right now." Pick whomever you want as your audience. In your mind's eye, take whatever position you want, sitting or standing up. Your audience is facing you. Tell that person or persons, "I want you to practice this technique right now." Do it now.◆

How did it feel? Most people tell me it's a bit difficult at first, because in their mind's eye *they have to concentrate on what they are saying.* And that's exactly the point. Concentrating means focusing, which means engaging the memory. Like other techniques in Mega Memory, this will make you read a little more slowly at first. But when you get used to it, you will be reading with more comprehension.

Here's another twist we can add to this technique. What if you don't understand what you're reading? You come across words and concepts that are unknown or seem too difficult to grasp. What do you ordinarily do in situations like that? Try to reread the material once or twice? Look up words in the dictionary? How long do you do that before you give up?

If you encounter something that you don't understand, in your mind's eye see yourself not only as the teacher, but as the student as well. And, as the student, ask yourself a question: What did you mean by that sentence? What does that word mean? Can you explain that again?

Got that? If you read past something you don't fully understand, you disengage from it, your memory is turned off. If you continue to read, you stop paying attention because at a certain level you're still thinking about what you didn't understand. It's as if you're actually saying to yourself, "Now, wait a minute. What was that? I didn't get it, I don't understand. Stop!" If you don't stop, your mind disengages. There's too much stress involved in trying to figure out the meaning of an earlier word or sentence and keep up with what you're reading presently. Remember, your mind can't be in two places at once.

Use this to your advantage. When you come to a word you don't understand, for example, stop. In your mind's eye, ask yourself a question. "What does that word mean?" If you can't figure it out, in your mind's eye say, "Let's go to a dictionary and find out." Go and look the word up in a dictionary, and explain it to your imaginary student. That causes you to engage and to focus. It's that one little extra thing to do which makes you cognizant of what you're reading or studying.

When you imagine yourself as the student, you can also ask

yourself to *rephrase* something. For example, you're reading along and you come to a sentence that you don't understand. Ask yourself, "Could you please rephrase that?" "What are you really saying?" And you will be amazed that if you take this step, the meaning of the sentence that seemed incomprehensible a minute before will suddenly make sense. Again, this happens because you make use of the power of your unconscious. By imagining yourself asking these questions, you engage those deeper levels of thought.

Rephrasing in your mind's eye is one of the most powerful tools you can use to lock in memory. When you rephrase, it causes your unconscious to go into the look/search stage, pop out all the data, and come up with an explanation you understand. Rephrasing makes you re-create the material (know it), and infinitely increases recall ability, whether it be for a test, a meeting, or in any situation.

Studying for a Test

Let us take our discussion of reading yet another step further. Let's assume you're reading a chapter for a test and doing it as described above, that is, in your mind's eye seeing yourself telling an imaginary student what you are reading. You are also asking yourself questions like, "Could you rephrase that?" "I don't understand this word." You look things up. All well and good. Now here's something you can do when you come to a passage or selection of data that you think you'll be tested on.

In your mind's eye, tell your imaginary student, "By the way, make sure you remember this because it will probably be on the test." After playing that little scene in your mind's eye, jot down a note. The note should be a buzzword or a phrase about what you just read, something that, if brought into the classroom, would jog your memory and let the information come back when you needed it. What you jot down can be a summary of a passage, a particular word, an outstanding fact, an important phrase, any reminder of what you just read. After you have jotted this note down, continue reading.

You may be doing a double take right now. After all I told

you in this book about not writing things down, now I seem to be switching gears. But as I said in Chapter 13, I don't want you to use note taking as an excuse not to remember something. This technique is very different. By jotting things down, you are making a list, a reference, telling yourself *what* to commit to memory later. You will come back to this list later and use Mega Memory techniques to reinforce these bits of information in your memory.

Once you're finished with your list, review it and make sure that everything is condensed as much as possible. Ideas, words, and concepts; that's what I want you to jot down. Now just think how well you would do on the exam if you could bring that list to class with you. One word or one small phrase would bring back a lot of information to you. It would be great if you could refer to it.

Well you can—in your mind! All you have to do is apply our memory techniques to this list. Take the words and phrases and turn them into pictures using the techniques taught in the previous lessons. Break the words down by syllable, and turn the syllables into sound-alike pictures. One at a time. Take your time. It may take you fifteen minutes or half an hour for a one-page list, but just think how relaxed you will be once you're in the classroom, knowing you have this "sheet" to work from. Once you've completed the process, connect, or chain, these vivid pictures into a story as we did with the Statue of Liberty. You may have thirty, forty, or even one hundred pictures. Make a wonderful, ludicrous, nonsensical story out of them. Review it two or three times, and I guarantee that you have all the information committed to memory.

This technique is one of the most powerful tools available to help us remember information for tests. Even a story with five hundred pictures can be run through entirely in your mind's eye in a minute or two. Each picture would give you a phrase or a key word, and each phrase or key word would being back large amounts of information. This is the technique law students use for recalling tremendous amounts of case law.

Keep in mind, we can either work hard or work smart. You can spend hours per night studying using the rote method—repeating, repeating, repeating—and hope that information will penetrate your mind. Or you can use the smart method. Not only does using Mega Memory techniques accomplish the goal, but it actually reduces stress on the body. You're using your imagination. You're having fun thinking ludicrous, nonsensical thoughts and being imaginative. It's enjoyable. And most important, you remember every single thing. You walk into the exam room with confidence, and you'll be the first person done. It will feel wonderful.

As a final test, let me ask you right now: in the Statue of Liberty story, who's driving the limousine? John Travolta. What is the limousine pulling? A long house trailer. Doesn't it feel good to know your recall is instantaneous?

Listening to Lectures

Now I'd like to give you some tips on how to listen to lectures to absorb the maximum amount of information. Whether you're listening to a lecture in class, are participating in a seminar of some kind, or are in any other situation where a speaker is sharing information, the basics are similar to what you do when reading.

I first have to remind you again, of course, not to take notes. When you are at a lecture, you need to pay attention to what is being said. And you can't do that fully if you're trying to write down things at the same time. As I've already mentioned, your conscious mind can't be in "two places" at once. Also, there is stress involved in note taking. You're not only putting pressure on yourself ("I've got to get this down!"), you're also struggling to write something as quickly as possible while the speaker has already moved onto something else. You are playing catch-up constantly, and because of that you retain less information.

Your basic rule in listening to a speaker at a lecture is this: In your mind's eye, pretend that the speaker is talking only to you. Make believe there's no one else in the room. Have you ever had a tutor or been the lone student in a class? If you have, you will understand how different that experience is from being one of twenty or thirty students. You really have to concentrate and respond to what the teacher is saying. The energy between you and the teacher is heightened. And because the teacher has only you to focus on, all the information is tailored to you and you alone.

You can create a similar situation in your mind's eye. And, just as you would in real life, ask questions in your mind's eye. During pauses, breaks, or any other interruption in the lecture, imagine yourself raising your hand and saying, "Excuse me. Could you re-phrase that?" Obviously you won't get an answer, but just taking those few seconds to focus on that will help lock in a particular piece of information into memory.

You can take this strategy one step further by imagining your-self saying, "Excuse me, just to clarify my own thinking, do you mean . . . ?" That's even better because you have rephrased the infor-mation. And when you rephrase you re-create, right? Which means you've caused those neurons in your brain to fire away, for that incremental sliver of time, and engaged your memory.

I do recommend that you tape lectures. When you go home, listen to the tape of the lecture. Buy yourself a variable-speed tape recorder, and you can double the playback speed. There's also a pitch adjustment on some recorders so the playback doesn't sound like Mickey Mouse talking, which I find annoying. As you listen to the lecture a second time, do the same thing: Rephrase things in your mind's eye. This time, however, when you come to something that you feel is important or that you think you'll be tested on, press the pause button and jot down a note.

Follow the same procedures I described in the section on read-ing. Condense the notes, turn each of the condensed notes into pic-tures and make a ludicrous, nonsensical, and funny story out of them, a story similar to our Statue of Liberty example in Chapter 2. Now everything will be committed to memory.

Even if you don't want to go through this last step of creating pictures from your notes, you're still ahead of the game. If you have just listened to the tape, you have already intently listened to the lecture twice. People who were taking notes didn't listen intently even once. I would bet that you are already capable of doing very well if you were tested on the material in that lecture.

I cannot emphasize enough the value of using the simple

methods I have described in these sections on reading and listening to lectures. The techniques work. They worked for me as I began applying them after my experience at St. Mary's High School, when I was told I had a learning disability, and I've seen them work for many of my seminar participants. They work because they cause you to focus on the information being presented to you. They work because you can have fun with them. And they work much better than repetition, which is boring and doesn't engage your unconscious to help you. When people ask you why you have this great memory, you'll think, "Because I know how to study. I know how to learn the information properly. I know how the mind works and I know how to process and organize information in my mind so it can be there when I need it, at my mental fingertips."

By the way, you can also employ this technique in conversations. Ask people to rephrase things. Or say something like, "Just to clarify, do you mean ... ?" and rephrase it for them. Don't be afraid to ask someone to repeat something. Everyone likes to be listened to, and when you ask someone to repeat something, you are telling that person that you are really interested in what he or she is saying. That kind of gesture always elicits a great response.

Chapter 14—Review

Reading for Better Comprehension

1. Read the information as if you are saying it to someone else.
2. Question yourself about things in the text you don't understand. ("Could you rephrase that?" "I don't understand.")
3. Tell yourself to remember particular items of information; at the same time, jot down a brief note to yourself.
4. Condense your notes into single-word phases if possible, each phrase representing lots of information.
5. Convert the phrases, one syllable at a time, into pictures.
6. Combine the pictures into a nonsensical story similar to the Statue of Liberty story we learned earlier in the book.

Studying for a Test

Follow the same steps as above, but when you come to a section that you suspect you will be tested on, tell your imaginary student, "Make sure you remember this because it will probably be on the test."

Listening to a Lecture or Speech

1. Pretend that the speaker is talking only to you.
2. In your mind's eye, ask questions.
3. Tape the lecture and listen to the tape (on fast speed if you like).
4. Follow steps 4, 5, and 6 from the "Reading for Better Comprehension" section, above.

Chapter 14—Required Mental Exercises

Exercise 1

Take a book that you have previously had trouble with. Try reading it again using Mega Memory techniques. (You can also do this with just one chapter in a book that you otherwise liked.) Is it easier to read? Do you remember more?

Exercise 2

The next time you go to a lecture or a speech, don't take notes. Try Mega Memory techniques instead. How well do you remember what was said?

15 Vocabulary, Spelling, and Mega Memory

Remembering Vocabulary Words

How do you memorize a word and its definition? You could do it by repetition, which we've all been taught, and which we all know is boring and takes a long time. Or, you can turn it into vivid pictures with action.

Let's take the word "consternation." Consternation means paralyzing amazement, dismay, or a confounding terror. How do we turn consternation into a picture? What are its syllables? Repeat out loud. "Con-ster-na-tion." Or "con-stern-nation." The first syllable, "con," might be your picture of a convict. For the second syllable you could have a picture of a spoon going around in a bowl (stir), or a stern of a boat. "Na-tion" is trickier. I prefer creating a picture of both syllables together, something that represents a nation, like the United Nations, an atlas, or a globe. So perhaps you see a convict sitting on the stern of a boat going to something that represents a nation.

Once you've created your picture from your syllables, take the meaning of the word and make it part of your picture. "Consternation" means to be in paralyzing amazement or dismay.

In your mind's eye, picture the convict being confused, dumb-founded and in despair. He's experiencing what? Consternation, of course.

What you are doing is reinforcing the meaning of the word by turning it into a picture. The next time you come across consternation, you will have a much better idea of what it is. If you relied on repetition, you would have to look it up any number of times before its meaning got locked into your memory.

You can also use this technique in learning foreign language words. Learning foreign language words is the same as learning vocabulary in our own language. Divide the word into syllables, turn the syllables into sound-alike pictures, turn the meaning itself into a picture, and put all the pictures together, just as we did with "consternation." As an example, let's take the word *pelo* (pronounced "paylow"), which in Spanish means "hair." *Pelo* needs to be converted into a picture, which means first turning it into syllables. Repeat out loud, *"Pe-lo." "Pe-lo."* What does *pelo* sound like? How about a picture of a halo? Your sound-alike picture is "halo." Create a vivid picture in your mind of a halo. Now what's all over the halo? You guessed it—hair. Make sure your picture is vivid and clear. You've created a picture from the syllables of the word, and you've created a picture of its meaning, and you have put them together. You're finished memorizing the word.

If you were taking a test, you'd be asked one of two questions. The first one would be, What is "hair" in Spanish? When you ask yourself that question what pops into your mind? A picture of hair. And guess what it's covering. A halo. "Halo" reminds you of *pelo*. The second question would be the opposite of the first: "What is the definition of *pelo*?" When you ask yourself that question, what pops into your mind's eye? A picture of a halo. And guess what's all over it? Hair. It works both ways.

Let's take one more foreign word, something more difficult. It's a Portuguese word, *amesuis*. *Amesuis* means "clam" in Portuguese and is pronounced "ah-mess-yu-is." "Ah-mess-yu-is." Repeat the syllables out loud. "A." "Mes." "A-mess." "Yu." "Is." "A-mess-yu-is," meaning clam.

To reinforce the word in your memory, perform the following visualization: You are standing on a beach. The waves are coming in, and the water is rolling up to your feet. Looking out to sea, you see a giant clam walking out of the water. He's got legs. He's got arms. He's got eyes. And this clam is covered with dirt: muck, goo, barnacles, seaweed. I want you to point to him in your mind's eye and repeat out loud, "What a mess you is." Say it out loud: "What a mess you is, *amesuis*." Repeat it several times, "A mess you is, *amesuis*." "A mess you is, *amesuis*." If you see that scene vividly in your mind, guess what? You'll always remember that *amesuis* means "clam" in Portuguese.

It took us less than thirty seconds to commit the meaning of that word to memory. You used our basic equation, vivid pictures plus action equal memory. By using your imagination, you can increase your vocabulary and learn foreign language words, medical terms, and any other information more easily than you can by repetition.

Keep in mind that you are not associating, using mnemonics. Association is taking something you know and something you don't know and putting them together in a logical way. We are linking these things *illogically*. We're taking a vivid, crystal clear picture of one thing and a vivid, crystal clear picture of something else, and putting them together in a ludicrous, nonsensical way using as much action as possible.

I love teaching this technique, because I remember how I used to sit in front of flash cards, repeating words over and over again. Instead of spending half an hour on each vocabulary word, using the rote method of learning, just think what it would be like to take one or two minutes on each word. Turn the word into a picture, turn the definition into a picture, and put them both together. You are using your imagination, you are having fun, you are reducing stress, and it doesn't take any more time, and guess what ...? You remember 100 percent of the words. It's the difference between working hard or working smart.

Spelling

So many kids and adults come to me and say, "I'm terrible at spelling." I tell them that if they memorize the spelling of a word using Mega Memory techniques, they'll remember how to spell that word forever. And I mean it.

Usually, in any given word, there is only a two- or three-letter combination that's confusing to you. To remember the correct spelling, isolate the letter combination that's giving you trouble, and create a vivid picture of it. That's it.

Let's take the word "weight." It's the *e* and *i* that usually bother people. How do we remember that the "e" comes before the "i" in "weight"? In your mind's eye, think of an elephant. This elephant walks up to a scale and gets on it to weigh himself. Looking down he cries in shock, "Oh no, I'm so fat!" He's so depressed because he weighs so much that he begins to cry ice cubes. He's crying, and the cubes hit the scale—clink, clink, clink. Your picture is done.

Review the sequence of events. The elephant walks up to the scale, and, after seeing how much he weighs, he cries ice cubes. In the sequence, elephant, which represents *e,* comes first. The ice cubes, which represent *i,* come second. Now, forever more, the picture of the elephant crying ice cubes will tell you that *e* comes before *i* in "weight."

Let's do another one. "Necessary" gives people fits Is it one *c* and two *s*'s, or the opposite, two *c*'s and one *s*?

Picture a cat—your cat?—prowling around in your living room. All of sudden, he sees a skunk run from behind your couch and jump onto your coffee table. Then another skunk joins the first and the two of them begin dancing on the coffee table. The cat runs to the coffee table, trying to attack the skunks. It is doing what is necessary, trying to jump up and bat its paw at them, but they don't care. There are two of them, and your cat is powerless against them, so they keep dancing, waltzing back and forth over your coffee table.

I guarantee that from now on, if you have committed this story to memory, the image of your cat confronting two dancing skunks will remind you that "necessary" has one *c* and two *s*'s.

Chapter 15—Review

Committing the Meaning of Words to Memory
1. Look up the meaning of the word.
2. Break down the word into syllables.
3. Create sound-alike or representational pictures for each syllable.
4. Chain the pictures together.
5. Take the meaning of the word and make it part of your picture.

Committing the Spelling of Words to Memory
1. Look up the correct spelling of a word.
2. Pick out the combination of letters in the word that you find difficult.
3. Choose pictures that represent the letter combination.
4. Chain the pictures together into a ludicrous story.

Chapter 15—Required Mental Exercises

Exercise 1
Using the process we discussed in this chapter, commit the meaning of the following words to memory.

1. bookkeeping
2. precede
3. liaison
4. receivable

5. census
6. questionnaire
7. pneumonia
8. subtle
9. macabre
10. wreckage

Exercise 2
Use the same list of words and commit their spelling to memory.

16   Numbers and Mega Memory

Not too long ago, I was visiting a grammar school in Connecticut. In one of the classrooms, I asked a student what 7 times 7 was. He opened up his desk, grabbed a calculator, and punched in the numbers. "Do you sneak that calculator into class?" I asked him. "Oh, no," he replied. "We're required to have it for math." My eyes were wide open in disbelief. "Required in math class?" I asked him. He looked at me as if I was from the moon. "Yeah. How else are you supposed to add stuff?"

We really have let our minds get flabby, and nowhere else does this show up more than in doing math. I sometimes find it hard to believe how lazy we've become with numbers and how afraid of them we are. And I'm not just talking about children in school. A lot of adults can't do simple addition in their heads. Without the use of a calculator, many of us can't balance a checkbook. Simple multiplication and division require a calculator, too, and anything slightly more complicated seems way beyond us. Believe me, there's a price to pay for all this. Just as your body pays a price when you don't exercise, your brain suffers when you don't use it.

Calculating the math in our minds instead of using calculators should be a priority for everyone. It's a great way to keep those neurons firing away, those pathways of thought fresh and active. And the more you do it, the more clearly and quickly your mind works. That's the message I've been emphasizing throughout this entire book.

I have to admit, though, there's a reason why we've embraced calculators so thoroughly. For many of us, learning numbers was not easy—and definitely not fun. Let's take multiplication tables. I am told by educators that learning multiplication is one of the most difficult and even traumatic experiences for many, many students. Why? Like vocabulary words and many other things, multiplication tables are taught by rote memorization. And as I've been saying, not only is repetition boring, it's not a very efficient way to stimulate those brain cells. "Memorizing" becomes a very frightening and demoralizing thing for many schoolchildren.

I think there's a better way.

Learning Multiplication Tables

What is 4 times 3? Here's my answer:

Picture the following scene in your mind's eye. You are standing outside your house right next to your father's brand-new car. You're angry, so you pick up a stool and smash it over the hood of the car. You do it again. And again. All of a sudden, your father appears in the doorway. Seeing what's going on, he thinks you've gone bonkers. He is angry, too—about what you've just done to his car. He's got a big basket of eggs in his hand, and he starts to throw the eggs at you. You yell, "No, Dad! Don't hit me!" But then, smack! An egg hits you in the back. You catch another egg your father has thrown, and throw it back at him. Another egg hits you in the back of your head. You and your dad both have egg all over your faces.

Now I'm sure that if you give this answer for 4 times 3 to your fourth-grade math teacher, she would think you'd gone bonkers, too. But can you guess what we just did? We created a picture for the equation.

Think of our Tree List. What number on the list is car? 4. What number is stool? 3. What number is egg? 12. And 4 times 3 equals 12. I created that little scene in about thirty seconds, and you can too.

In order to teach yourself or anyone else the multiplication tables, you follow our three basic steps for remembering any piece of information. You need a peg for each number. You create pictures for each number. And then you put the pictures together using action. In the example above, I used elements of the Tree List as pegs. You can also use your House List or the Body List.

Let's try another example: 2 times 4 equals 8. Using your Body List, close the book and create a scene for this equation now.◆

Here's my equation: I am walking along the street and all of a sudden my knees being to tickle. I look down and I notice a big pink mosquito buzzing around my knees ready to strike. I swat it away, and what does he do? He lands on my rear. I swat it away and he goes to my face. I slap my face, but I miss and he goes back to my knees. And we keep chasing each other, and my knees and rear tickle, and my face hurts from slapping.

Simple. Knees, rear, face: 2 times 4 equals 8. It's not only fun to create these stories, it's easy. And thinking along these lines gets your mind working at those deeper creative levels, so that you really remember the answers. When you create, you know.

We all love to do what we do well. If children can do well, they'll love to go to school. If they do well playing basketball, they'll like to play basketball. If they do well remembering things for tests, then they'll love doing it. It's the same thing with anything else you might be trying to memorize. Turn anything into a picture and put both pictures together using action. After a few seconds, the information will be committed to memory. I'm sure you can think of a lot more examples.

Creating Additional Peg Lists

You might have wanted to ask one question when we were creating pictures for our multiplication examples. How do we picture 5 times 6 equals 30? Or 7 times 8 equals 56? We have pegs for 5 and 6, and 7 and 8, but what about higher numbers? We've only gone as far as 20 on our House and Tree lists, and 10 on our Body List.

There are two primary ways to expand the lists that you have. You can expand each list by simply adding more items. Since the House List is the most powerful (you created it; they are your items), you can use that as your primary peg list. Add more rooms and more objects in each room, and you will have a very long and reliable peg list.

The second way to get additional "peg space" is to create entire new lists. For example, an office list is a very useful peg list. There are a lot of things in your office that you see and touch every day, so you are very familiar with them. In creating the list, think of different ways you use these objects.

For example, I've created what I call a Reach List from the items in my office. The list consists of things I can reach while sitting at my desk. From where I sit, I can pick up a staple gun, which is my first Reach peg. My paper clip holder is my second peg, my pen and pad my third. Then comes my blotter, my telephone, my desk lamp, my in-box, and so on down the line. Once you put your mind to it, you will be amazed at how many pegs you can create. And let me remind you again, you know these items already. All you need to do is remember the sequence.

Remembering a Series of Numbers

Remembering a string of numbers is another talent you can develop with a Mega Memory. For my example, I'll use a license plate number, though this would work well for telephone numbers, lock combinations, account numbers, even those ridiculously long credit card numbers. We'll be discussing the longer numbers in Part II: "Advanced Mega Memory," where you'll learn other, even simpler and more useful techniques for committing numbers to memory.

Let's consider license plate number A71416D. How do you remember that? You simply turn each item into a picture and put the pictures together in a ludicrous, nonsensical story.

Picture the following in your mind's eye: You're holding an apple in your hand. Take that apple and throw it at some very big dice on the floor. Make sure you hit the dice. When you hit them, the dice break open, and inside is a whole bunch of diamond rings. You walk over, pick up the diamond rings and say, "Wow, this is great! Look at all these diamond rings! But I'm really hungry. What I would really love are some candy bars." You go to a store, give the clerk diamond rings, he gives you a whole bunch of candy bars, and you're happy. You're walking out of the store eating the candy bars, when a dog jumps on you and begins eating the candy bars, too.

You just committed to memory that license plate number by using the pegs on your Tree List. We start with mnemonic, picturing an apple for A. You throw the apple at what? The dice; that's what number in your Tree List? 7. When the dice crack open, what's in them? Diamond rings. Ring is number 14 on the Tree List. When you take the rings into the store, what do you buy? Candy? What number is candy on the Tree List? Number 16. And when you walk out of the store, who jumps on you? A dog; that's another mnemonic, dog for D.

apple–dice–rings–candy–dog equals A–7–14–16–D

The above equation is your story, and your story is your number. With a trained memory it takes about thirty seconds to create these pictures and commit them to memory. Obviously, you won't be at that level immediately. To begin training yourself to use this technique, take a telephone number you would like to remember. Or a checking or savings account number. Sit down and spend a few minutes creating a story from it. Break the numbers into smaller chunks, just as you break words into syllables. Then, put it out of your mind, your conscious mind, and do something else. The next day see if you can remember the number without looking it up. It will have been committed to memory.◆

Chapter 16—Review

Learning the Multiplication Table
   1. Turn each number into a picture using one of your peg lists.
   2. Chain the pictures together by creating a story.

3. If you need larger numbers, create additional pegs or entirely new peg lists.

Remembering License Plate Numbers
1. Convert each item of the license plate into mental pictures.
2. Chain the pictures together into a ludicrous Statue of Liberty-type story.

Chapter 16—Required Mental Exercises

Exercise 1
Memorize the following license plate numbers using the methods we learned in this chapter.

1. A11H13D
2. 18194C
3. B4U28RT

Exercise 2
Go to your office or school and create a new peg list of ten items for yourself.

Part II

Advanced

Mega Memory

17   Advanced Mega Memory: Review and Introduction

Welcome to Advanced Mega Memory! At this point in their Mega Memory training, many people come to me and say something like, "You know, Kevin, I'm glad I stuck this out. I can't believe how much I've already improved my memory. And I can't believe that I thought having a bad memory was something I could never change. Thanks a lot!" As we start on our Advanced Mega Memory techniques, I hope you feel the same way.

Advanced Mega Memory builds upon the foundation laid in the first part of the book to provide you with a graduate-level course in recall systems. We'll quickly review the basic skills you learned in Part I, then begin learning techniques that will enable you to remember things you never thought possible. By pushing the boundaries of what your memory can do, Advanced Mega Memory enters the realm of enhanced mental capability. You will be dramatically increasing your powers of calculation and your ability to recall complex bits of information. Besides strengthening your memory, you will also be developing important new tools that improve many aspects of your life.

You will be able to think more quickly, more creatively. De-stress. Sleep better. You will be able to break bad habits you couldn't conquer previously. I lost forty-eight pounds by using these techniques. In a later chapter, I'll share with you exactly how you can "re-link" the memories in your mind, allowing unconscious programs to help you break habits and change other unwanted patterns of behavior.

The Ground Rules

Just as in Part I, I want to quickly review the ground rules so that you get the most out of Part II.

1. *Proceed through the chapters in order.* The material in this section, just as in the first, is carefully arranged to help you learn the Mega Memory techniques. You will compromise yourself if you jump ahead.

2. *Go through each chapter without interruptions.* Lock the doors if you have to, turn on the answering machine, and don't take a break while you are in the middle of a chapter unless I specifically tell you to. If you are learning the program with a partner, or with two or three others, that's fine, as long as you all concentrate on what you are doing.

3. *You do have to take breaks between chapters.* I don't want you to overdo it, either. If you want to do more than one chapter a day, that's great, but be sure you take a five- to fifteen-minute break between each chapter.

4. *Maximum study time of Advanced Mega Memory should be about three hours per day.* Don't do any more. As with so many other things in life, I've found that breaking down the course into smaller bits is the best way to achieve results.

   I'm very emphatic about not overdoing. I've seen what happens to people in full-day seminars. Perhaps you've attended one. You invest a few hundred dollars. You also invest time and energy to get there. At first, you're eager to get going, full of energy and drive, as you absorb all the new information that is being thrown at you. But sooner or later, usually right after lunch, fatigue sets in. Number one, your body is busy digesting your meal. And number two, you can assimilate only so much information at one time. Follow the same rule they tell you to follow at the gym: Don't overstrain your muscles by putting a week's work into the first hour. Gradual improvement—assimilation—that's how you see results.

5. *Do the work on a daily basis.* As I said above, to make sure you reap the benefits of the advanced course, gradual but steady progress is the best way to go.

My main concern is that you try not to take a day off between chapters. Once you start, you can do as many each day as you want up to the three-hour limit, but do at least one. I'm emphasizing this because it's even more important here than in the first section. We're going to be plunging into some techniques in the first five chapters that really need to be done in a concentrated fashion. That's going to establish a solid foundation for the remaining material. Do this course properly.

6. *Be sure to say things out loud when I tell you to.* As you will see, it's even more important here than in Part I.

7. *Watch your food intake before you start your lessons.* You can go back and review the material in Chapter 8 if you like. The rules are the same here: Don't eat a heavy meal before a lesson, watch your sugar and white-flour intake, and of course no alcohol. And try to stay away from coffee.

You want to be as fresh and alert as you possibly can be, so watch your stress level as well. Remember, *you're having fun and working the program at the pace that suits you best.* So relax, and don't worry about anyone else. Competition, getting a good grade, and Mega Memory do not go with one another.

Your Teachability Index

I also want to say a few more words about your teachability index, which we discussed in the first chapter. Remember, it consists of two components:

1. willingness to learn
2. willingness to accept change

Obviously, since you've completed Part I, and you are continuing with the advanced section, we'll take it for granted that your willingness to learn is high. But that's the easy part. Please keep a watch on your willingness to accept change—that's really where it's at. If you thought we began to think differently in the first part of the book, wait until we get started here. We're really going to be stretching our minds.

And just as in learning how to type or ride a bicycle or drive that manual transmission for the first time, Advanced Mega Memory may not feel comfortable at first. As a matter of fact, I can guarantee right now the next few chapters are going to be rather uncomfortable. Be forewarned: In the beginning, the exercises you'll be doing may seem tedious, strenuous, and difficult. I want to encourage you, however, about the results. Not only will you have the tremendous recall ability if you continue with the program, but your mental functioning will be greatly advanced as well.

Willingness to accept change is the key here. Is it high enough to accept the challenge and benefits that Advanced Mega Memory offers you? Keep asking yourself that question throughout Part II. And keep saying yes, not letting yourself get discouraged if at first something doesn't work well. If you stay with it, your investment will pay off tremendously.

Review of Part I

I want to emphasize again that you must have full knowledge of the first section of the book before you go on to Part II. In the next few paragraphs, we will review what we learned in Part I, so you'll have a good checklist for yourself. If you feel at all rusty or have any doubts about anything in Part I—and you shouldn't at this point, unless you didn't do the work—go over whatever you feel unsure of. If you don't want to do that, give the book to someone else, because you can't go any further. You will not get any of the benefits from this section, because you won't understand the concepts underlying the exercises and techniques.

The first thing we learned in Mega Memory was the Tree List and basic word association. Basic word association is used by many memory training programs, and is defined as taking a piece of information you already know, a piece of information you don't know (i.e., something you are trying to remember), and putting both things together in a logical fashion. An example of basic association is using the mnemonic HOMES to remember the five Great Lakes. However, you rarely use basic association in real-life situations because mnemonics only work in certain cases, and you don't have the time to sit around and create mnemonics for everything, anyway. However, by learning a little about basic association, you used it to commit twenty items to memory, "tree" through "cigarettes." Those twenty items became a peg list, your Tree List, places in your mind to store information. More important, the exercises that you did in order to learn that list began to stimulate the brain's neurotransmitters, and set you on the road to releasing the powerful photographic memory—the instant recall memory—that you have right now.

The second thing we learned was chaining or linking. The definition of chaining is creating a vivid picture of one thing, creating a vivid picture of something else, and putting both vivid pictures together in your mind in an exaggerated, nonsensical way. That technique is the basis of all memory development because of one fundamental principle: We think in pictures. The important point here—and I will continue to emphasize it throughout the advanced section—is making sure your picture is vivid.

What is a vivid picture? It is a picture in your mind's eye that you see in color and in great detail. It's as crystal clear and specific as you can make it. You can smell smells, hear sounds, feel feelings, and experience things as though they are really happening. That's what we mean by vivid in Mega Memory.

We played Concentration to learn how to create pictures of abstract terms, concepts, and names. Breaking down the terms into syllables and creating sound-alike pictures for the syllables allowed us to start pegging. We learned how important action is in pegging—active action. The action has to be strong, clear, and as dynamic and animated as you can make it. We established two more peg lists for ourselves, the ten pegs of our Body List, and the twenty pegs of our House List.

Putting all our techniques together, we learned what we need to do in remembering just about anything. We call them the three basic steps of remembering:

1. place to put the information, which is a peg
2. the information itself turned into a mental picture
3. mental glue to hold the picture in place, which is action

By applying these three basic steps, we began practicing for situations that occur in our daily lives. We saw how Mega Memory helps us to become better readers, and to absorb more information in classes and lectures without taking notes. We began applying our Mega Memory techniques to vocabulary words, spelling, and remembering numbers, learning to trust our memories in the process.

In the first section, we also learned about the underlying foundation of Mega Memory. This foundation is built on five mental steps your mind performs when it processes information. The stages are: think, emote, look/search, create, know. Those stages are at work whether you are putting in, that is filing away, new information, or retrieving old information. The Mega Memory techniques help get us beyond that first stage, the think stage, which is limited to our conscious mind at work, which is so much less powerful than the deeper thought processes of the unconscious. The exercises and techniques in Mega Memory involve the unconscious mind, so that when we recall information we do it very quickly and efficiently.

Finally, in the first section we learned how important physical factors are in maintaining a good memory. We discussed nutrition, stress, and certain diseases that can affect memory in bewildering, insidious ways.

At this point, if there are any exercises and techniques mentioned in this brief review you aren't completely comfortable with—the Statue of Liberty story, the Body List, the House List, pegging, turning abstracts into pictures, using active action— go back and review them before you continue. As I said earlier, if you don't, there's no use in going ahead with Part II. There is one exception to this request, however. It concerns the Tree List. We're going to be using it less in Advanced Mega Memory. The Body List and the House List will be your two most powerful lists and you should know those like, well, like the back of your hand.

Chapter 17—Review

Review of Part I

The Body List—10 pegs
1. toes
2. knees
3. muscle
4. rear
5. love handles
6. shoulder
7. collar
8. face
9. point
10. ceiling

The Tree List—20 pegs
1. tree
2. light switch
3. stool
4. car
5. glove
6. gun
7. dice
8. skate
9. cat

10. bowling ball
11. goalpost
12. eggs
13. witch
14. ring
15. paycheck
16. candy
17. magazine
18. voting booth
19. golf club
20. cigarettes

The House List—20 pegs
1. Choose any four rooms in sequential order.
2. In each room, pick any five pieces of furniture in sequential order.

The Statue of Liberty Story
Statue of Liberty   torch   book   big fat man   electric power drill
bar of soap   purple pennies   padlock   house trailer   black
limousine   John Travolta   black Stetson hat   black vest   black boots
Cathy Lee Crosby   pink polka-dot bikini   letter to her agent
a big Saint Bernard   fur coat   diamond collar   ham bone   mountain
lion   palm tree   Statue of Liberty

Word Association
Linking together in logical fashion something you are trying to remember and something you know already.

Chaining
Creating a vivid mental picture for something you are trying to remember, creating another picture for something else you are trying to remember, and putting both pictures together using illogical, exaggerated action.

Pegging
Taking a vivid mental picture of a preestablished peg, creating a picture for something you are trying to remember, and linking (peg-

ging) the second picture to the first using illogical, exaggerated action.

Chapter 17—Required Mental Exercises

Exercise 1
Review all three of your peg lists to make sure you know them without hesitation and in both directions. If you're learning Mega Memory with a partner, have your partner call out a number or a word, and you call out its corresponding item. If you're doing this alone, cover up one side of the lists above, then the other side, and make sure you can call out the corresponding items immediately.

Exercise 2
Make sure you are clear on the differences among word association, chaining, and pegging. If not, go back to the particular chapters on each and review the material and the exercises.

18 Body List Phonetics

The first thing we're going to work with in Advanced Mega Memory is the Body List. The Body List is composed of ten items, or pegs: toes, knees, muscle, rear, love handles, shoulders, collar, face, point, and ceiling. When we learned the Body List, I mentioned that there was a reason for the name we gave each peg. For example, toes had to be called toes, not foot. Muscle wasn't thigh, it was muscle. Rear wasn't bottom or butt, it was rear. In a moment you'll see the reason for this.

Before we do anything, though, I'd like you to review the Body List to make sure you have it down pat. I'm going to ask you to stand up and repeat the Body List out loud while performing the actions associated with each peg, the pointing, tapping, and so forth. For example, number 1 is toes. Wiggle your toes and repeat out loud, "Number 1, toes." Then go on to the next peg, making sure you have the sequence correct.

Stand up, and do the exercise now. "Number 1, toes." Wiggle your toes. "Number 2, knees." And pat your knees. "Number 3, muscle." Pat your thigh muscle. "Number 4, rear." Pat your rear. "Number 5, love handles." Grab your love handles. "Number 6, shoulders." Tap your shoulders. "Number 7, collar." Touch your collar with your hand. "Number 8, face." Touch your face. "Number 9, point." Point with your finger to your point (i.e., the top of your head), and tap it. "Number 10, ceiling." Point to the ceiling.◆

Remain standing and do it twice more.◆

You're going to close the book in a moment and do it again to make sure it is second nature to you. If you have a partner, take turns checking each other until your recall of this list is instantaneous. If you are alone, make sure you know the sequence before you start the exercise. It's very important that you speak out loud and touch the pegs as instructed. Close the book and do the review drill now.◆

Okay. There's a specific reason why we have ten pegs on our Body List and why we call them what we do. It has to do with phonetics, which is the study of the sounds that make up our speech. We are going to establish our own phonetic alphabet, using ten basic phonetic sounds of the English language. Once you have committed these ten sounds to memory, we will establish a number for each one.

Why are we doing this? Just as phonetics, or sounds, are the basis of our language, the phonetic alphabet we develop will be the foundation of a powerful and complete Mega Memory. Think of it as an alphabet for your language of memory, the uses of which are as limitless as the alphabet you use now.

It is crucial that the phonetic exercises be done out loud. I will say this over and over. As you are learning the phonetic sounds, you will say each sound several times when you encounter it. If you remember, when I began telling you to repeat things out loud in Part I, I said that doing so would engage the memory in additional ways. I told you that one of those ways had to do with what is called neuromuscular memory. When you say something out loud, you not only think it, you get the vocal chords involved as well. That forces the neurotransmitters of the brain to fire away in yet another pattern, creating yet another memory pathway. For example, instead of just thinking, "Number 1, toes," your vocal chords have to say it. That further helps to make "Number 1, toes" part of your memory.

There's another reason for saying things out loud. Have you ever heard your voice on an audiocassette and said, "That's not me. I don't sound like that"? Well, for better or worse, that's exactly how you sound. You may think that you hear yourself talk every day and that you recognize your own voice. However, when you hear your voice on a cassette player, 100 percent of the sound arrives at your eardrum from the air. When you hear yourself speak, only 50 percent of the sound arriving at your brain has come through your ear; the other 50 percent is coming from your vocal chords, which makes its way back through connecting tissues to your brain. You sound different to yourself than you do to other people.

This difference has an impact on your memory. When you speak out loud, the sound passing through your vocal chords and bone hits more connecting fibers in the brain than it would if you were merely hearing the sound (that is, the sound was all coming to your brain through the eardrum). This, too, creates an additional memory pathway for whatever it is you were saying. In other words, it is yet another way to ingrain the information in your memory. Speaking out loud is vitally important to success and has a major influence on how well you pick up the Mega Memory techniques.

The Phonetic Alphabet

The first phonetic sound is the "t" sound, or "ta." Say "Ta." (Vowels don't count in our phonetic alphabet. Our phonetic alphabet is made up of consonants only. We're only adding the "a" sound to make pronunciation easier.) Say it again. "Ta, ta, ta." Notice that your tongue goes to the roof of your mouth when you say the "t" sound. "Ta." Now say the "d" sound. "Da, da, da." Notice where your tongue is—almost in the same exact position against the roof of your mouth as when you said the "t" sound.

Repeat both the "t" and "d" sounds out loud. "ta, da, ta, da." They are considered the same phonetic sound. Now, what's the first peg on your Body List? Toes. And what's the first phonetic sound? "Ta" (and "da"). "Ta" equals "toes." "Ta"—toes. So our first phonetic sound is "ta." Can you see why I said the naming of pegs on the Body List was done very purposefully? I was preparing you to learn the phonetic alphabet.

Let's go to the second peg on your Body List. Your knees. Knees. You may already know what our phonetic sound will be: the "n" sound. "Na." Now repeat, "Na, na, na. Number 2 is na—knees."

The third peg on your Body List is muscle, and our third phonetic is the "m" sound, or "ma." Repeat, "Ma, ma, ma. Number 3 is ma—muscle."

Our forth Body List peg is the rear, and our fourth phonetic is the "r" sound, or "ra." Repeat, "Ra, ra, ra. Number 4 is ra—rear."

Number 5 is love handles. The fifth phonetic is the "l" sound, or "la." Repeat, "La, la, la. Number 5 is la—love handles."

Number 6 is shoulders. The sixth phonetic is the "sh" sound, or "sha." Repeat "Sha, sha, sha. Number 6 is sha—shoulders." Just like the first phonetic, "sha" has a relative phonetic. In fact, it has two related sounds, "ch" and the hard "j" (pronounced "dzh"), or "cha," and "ja." You can feel the similarity of the sounds when you say them out loud. "Sha," "cha," and "ja." Your tongue is slightly curved, and just its tip is touching the roof of your mouth toward the front. Repeat all three phonetics again. "Sha, sha, sha. Cha, cha, cha. Ja, ja, ja."

Let's review one more time by saying it all out loud. "Sha, sha, sha; two other phonetic sounds are related to it, cha, cha, cha and ja, ja, ja. Number 6 is sha, cha, ja—shoulders."

Our seventh Body List peg is the collar. Our seventh phonetic is hard "c" sound, or "ca." Repeat, "Ca, ca, ca." It has a related phonetic as well, the "g" sound, or "ga." Repeat, "Ga, ga, ga. Ca, ca, ca, ga, ga, ga. Number 7 is ca, ga—collar."

Out eighth Body List peg is the face. Our eighth phonetic is the "f" sound, "fa." Repeat, "Fa, fa, fa." It, too, has a related phonetic, the "v" sound, or "va." Repeat, "Va, va, va." "Fa, fa, fa, va, va, va. Number 8 is fa, va—face."

Number 9 is our point. The ninth phonetic, the "p" sound, or "pa," also has a relative, the "b" sound or "ba." Repeat, "Pa, pa, pa.

Ba, ba, ba," and feel the similarity when you say them. Your lips close lightly and you let out a breath of air as you open them to make the sound. "Number 9 is pa, ba—point."

Number 10 is the ceiling. It is associated with the "s" sound, or "sa." "Sa, sa, sa." Its related sound is "z," or "za." Repeat, "Sa, sa, sa. Za, za, za." Here is a little twist: Number 10 on the Body List is 0 in our phonetic alphabet, not number 10. Say it out loud. "Zero is sa, za—ceiling."

You have just learned the complete set of phonetic sounds in Mega Memory's phonetic world. And we have established a number to go with each of them.

Here is the complete list once more:

1. "ta" (and "da")	6. "sha" (and "cha," "ja")
2. "na"	7. "ca" (and "ga")
3. "ma"	8. "fa" (and "va")
4. "ra"	9. "pa" (and "ba")
5. "la"	10. "sa" (and "za")

Now what I'd like you to do is practice recalling the phonetic sound that corresponds to each number. The way to do this is simply to think of the appropriate body peg. For example, if you ask yourself what is the phonetic sound for number 4? What's the fourth peg? Your rear. What's the phonetic sound? "Ra."

What's the phonetic sound for number 9? The ninth peg is what? Your point. And what's the phonetic sound? "Pa." Does it have another related phonetic? Yes, "ba." So number 9 is "pa" and "ba."

What's the phonetic sound for number 6? What's your sixth peg? Your shoulders, which gives you "sha." Does it have another related phonetic? Yes, two of them. "Cha" and "ja." Those are the three phonetics that go with number 6.

What's the phonetic sound for number 0? Remember, 0 in our phonetic alphabet is 10 on our Body List. What's your tenth peg? The ceiling, and its corresponding sound is what? "Sa," as well as "za." So number 0 is "sa" and "za."

Your goal now is to drill this relationship between the phonetics and the numbers. You want to have instant recall; that is, you want to be able to say a number and instantaneously recall the sound. To do this drill, ask yourself out loud what the phonetic sound is for a particular number. For example: "What's the phonetic sound for 4?" The first thing you do is think of the fourth peg on your Body List, which is your rear. What's the phonetic sound? "Ra."

As you do this drill, be deliberate and slow at first. Accuracy is more important than speed. The speed will come, believe me. Think of a steam locomotive, which needs time to get up to full throttle. That's you at this point, as far as the phonetic alphabet is concerned. If you have a partner, take turns calling out a number while the other person responds with the phonetic. But whether you're doing this with someone else or not, say everything out loud. Do the drill for five or ten minutes, or however long is necessary to get the sounds and their corresponding numbers right. And for now, don't be concerned with the sounds that are related to the ten basic ones. Just concentrate on the ten basics.

Once your feel comfortable with accuracy, pick up the pace. Ultimately, you should be able to do two sounds in about a second: "Two, na. One, ta." That gives you an idea of the pace needed in order to go on with the rest of the book. As I've been saying, though, don't overdo the speed. Walk before you run. Now close the book and do the exercise.◆

How are you doing? If you are having trouble reaching the two-per-second mark, that's normal. Just keep at it.

Drill once more, and if you are feeling comfortable with both your accuracy and speed, add the additional sounds. To make sure you incorporate the related sounds, let's review them once more: Number 1 is either "ta" or "da." Number 6 is either "ja," "sha," or "cha." Number 7 is "ca" or "ga." Number 8 is "fa" or "va." Number 9 is "pa" or "ba." Zero is the "s" and the "z" sound, "sa" or "za." If you do add the related sounds to your drill, don't call out all the sounds that belong to a particular number. Do one sound per number. For example, if you ask yourself, "What's the phonetic sound for number 7?" call out either "ca" or "ga," but not both. You can choose number 7 again and call out "ga" later. Close the book again and do that now.◆

You need to be able to recall in both directions. Repeat the drill, this time calling out the phonetic sound and asking yourself what number goes with it. Just stick with the basic ten sounds, and remember to do this all out loud, whether you are drilling with someone else or alone. Close the book and do it now.◆

Now I want you to drill back and forth, using both the basic and related sounds. Call out a number, and instantly come back with a corresponding phonetic sound. Call out a different phonetic sound, and instantly come back with the number. I want you to drill this for a good five or ten minutes, so that the relationships between the numbers and phonetics really become ingrained in your memory.

Remember, only one sound per number and vice versa. An example of ten choices might be as follows: "Ta, one. Two, na. Da, one. Six, sha. Six, ja. Cha, six. Nine, pa. Ba, nine. Ga, seven. Three, ma."

Your goal for this drill? Any run containing ten choices as in the paragraph above should be done in five seconds, or two per second. Since there are a total of seventeen sounds, the whole set should easily be done in ten seconds—with time to spare!

Are you ready? Accuracy and speed are important. Close the book and do this drill now.◆

Let's do it one more time, to make sure you're both accurate and fast. You can't go further in the book unless you can do two combinations per second, or ten in five seconds. Do a drill of ten sets now.◆

Before you go to the next lesson, take a five- to ten-minute break. Then review the phonetics and the numbers again in your head. The importance of having these committed to memory and available for instantaneous recall is vital for the rest of the book.

If you're still struggling, stop, relax. For a laugh, *not a drill,* imagine yourself touching all the pegs at this speed! Now try the drills again, or feel free to go back and reread the entire chapter from the beginning. Once you feel comfortable with this exercise, go on to the next chapter.

Chapter 18—Review

The Body List Phonetics

1. toes—ta, da
2. knee—na
3. muscle—ma
4. rear—ra
5. love handles—la
6. shoulders—sha, cha, ja
7. collar—ca, ga
8. face—fa, va
9. point—pa, ba
10. ceiling—sa, za

Chapter 18—Required Mental Exercise

Exercise

Make a copy of the Body List Phonetics chart on the previous page. Cut this chart up. After mixing up the pieces, reconstruct the chart from memory as quickly as possible. Time yourself. Continue practicing until you can reconstruct the chart in just a few seconds.

19 Picture Words 1–25

Now that we have assigned phonetic sounds to numbers, what good does that do us? You will find that much of Advanced Mega Memory is focused on numbers, because numbers give us a host of opportunities in which to apply our memory techniques. However, to take advantage of this, we must have what I call numbered pictures committed to memory. Those numbered pictures will serve as our Advanced Mega Memory vocabulary.

Numbers 0 through 9 now have phonetic sounds attached to them. Because we think—and remember—in pictures, phonetic sounds don't do us much good, but pictures, or more accurately picture words, do. Using our new phonetic alphabet and the numbers 1 through 100, we're going to create picture words that represent these numbers.

Creating a Picture Word Vocabulary

Before we start creating our vocabulary, one basic instruction: *Be sure to say things out loud when I tell you to.*

Now consider the word "tail." Say it out loud and determine its phonetic sounds in order. Remember, you are only concerned with consonants, not vowel sounds. The first is "ta," corresponding to number 1. Say it out loud. "Ta." The next phonetic in "tail" is "la" for the "l" sound, corresponding to number 5. Say it out loud. "La." Thus, in the word "tail" we have two phonetic sounds and two numbers, 1 and 5. So "tail" is number 15.

We'll do another one. Consider "nun." Say the word out loud. "Nun." Say the first phonetic out loud. "Na." What's the next phonetic in "nun"? "Na," as well. Repeat it out loud. "Na." "Na" is number 2, so "nun" is number 22. Simple.

Do the same thing for the following three words. Say the words and sounds out loud, and assign numbers for the words. Do it in your head, without writing anything down. Complete the exercise before reading on:◆

toad
dish
net

You should have the following results:

for "toad": "ta" and "da," which is 1 and 1, or 11
for "dish": "da" and "sha," which is 1 and 6, or 16
for "net": "na" and "ta," which is 2 and 1, or 21

Now let's do this exercise in reverse. What is a picture word for number 17? First you need to come up with the phonetics for numbers 1 and 7. The phonetic for number 1 is either the "t" sound, "ta," or the "d" sound, "da." The phonetics for 7 are "ca" or "ga." You can choose one for each number. But whatever you choose, the picture word you create from these two phonetics has to have only these two phonetic sounds in this same order. For number 17, I choose "ta" and "ca." And for "ta" and "ca," I selected the word "tack." "Tack—"ta" and "ca." Our picture word for number 17 is "tack." Follow?

As you can see, there can be many picture words for the same number. Other picture words for number 17 are "tic," referring to the parasite, or "tick," referring to the noise a clock makes. For the purposes of this book, I've already chosen the picture words for numbers 1 through 100. I want you to use these so that your learning of Advanced Mega Memory is as uncomplicated as possible. Ultimately, however, the purpose of this exercise is for you to be able to establish your own picture words for each number from 1 through 100.

A note of caution: During the exercises in this and the next few chapters, you're going to be mainly in the think stage, getting those neurotransmitters in the brain to fire away, consciously developing patterns of memory. It's another way of saying you'll be working hard. But if you approach this full of energy and vitality, and with complete commitment to the exercise, you will have established an extremely valuable knowledge bank. The return on your investment of energy will be a thousandfold.

There are a few guidelines I'd like to set down before we begin our exercises for turning numbers into picture words in earnest. The first guideline: We will eliminate all "h" and "w" sounds. If we were lucky enough to have attended a grammar school that taught phonetics, you would know that there are other phonetic sounds besides the seventeen we are using in Mega Memory. We will be working with only the sounds we've already gone over in the previous chapter.

Therefore, if in one of these exercises I ask you to consider the word "hail," for example, (you should have said it out loud by now—"hail"), what would you give me as the phonetic sounds? Not "ha," and not "a" because that's a vowel. These don't exist in our phonetic universe. It's the "l" sound, "la." "La" is number 5 on our phonetic alphabet list, so the picture word "hail" would be only one number, 5. You would treat the "w" sound the same way, so that "whale," for example, would give us number 5 also.

The second guideline is: When we are considering a picture word of more than three syllables, use only the first three phonetics. If we have a long word with four, five, or six phonetic sounds, we're going to work with only the first three to keep life simpler. That will give us more latitude in choosing picture words, too. When we get into bigger numbers, you'll see how this guideline becomes an advantage.

Creating Picture Words 1–25

Now, using our phonetic sounds, we are going to do an exercise establishing our first twenty-five picture words. The picture words will be committed to memory, recallable instantaneously. Remember, you are building a vocabulary, a mental tool needed to do other types of applications for which numbers will be required. When I give you the phonetic sound, repeat it out loud. Then go to the next line, where I give you the picture word we are establishing for that number. Make sure you create a vivid picture of that word, and then continue reading the line, saying the number, phonetic sound, and picture word out loud.

Let's start the exercise now.

Number 1 is what phonetic sound? I am choosing "ta." (If you were creating the list, you could also choose "da," but remember, we are using my choices for now.) Say it out loud. "Ta."

The picture word I am establishing from that phonetic is "tie." Vividly picture a tie. And repeat out loud, "One, ta, tie."

Number 2 is what phonetic sound? "Na." Repeat, "Na."

The picture word is "Noah." You can picture an old man with a bear or an ark. Repeat, "Two, na, Noah."

Let's review. Give me the phonetic and picture word for number 1. "Ta, tie." What's number 2? "Na, Noah." (Did you say everything in quotes out loud?)

Number 3 is what phonetic sound? "Ma." Repeat, "Ma."

Picture a lawn mower, but the word is going to be "mow." Repeat, "Three, ma, mow."

Number 4 is what phonetic sound? "Ra." Are you saying "ra" out loud? Remember, I'm sitting next to you, and I want to hear it loud and clear! "Ra!"

The picture word is "row." Repeat, "Four, ra, row."

Let's review. The first phonetic sound is "ta"; the word is "tie." Repeat, "One, ta, tie," three times.

The second phonetic sound is "na"; the word is "Noah." Repeat, "Two, na, Noah," three times.

The third phonetic sound is "ma"; the word is "mow." Repeat, "Three, ma, mow," three times.

The fourth phonetic sound is "ra"; the word is "row." Repeat, "Four, ra, row," three times.

Let's continue. From now on, I will only occasionally remind you to say things out loud, when I think a reminder is needed. Do it on your own whenever you see anything in quotes.

Number 5 is what phonetic sound? "La."

The picture word is "law." "Five, la, law." By the way, what's a good picture for "law"? A policeman, the scales of justice, a badge—remember, something concrete because "law" is an abstract.

For number 6 we will choose the phonetic "ja." "Ja." (I could have also chosen "sha" or "cha.")

Our picture word is "Joy," as in the dishwashing liquid. Yes, we can use proper names for our picture words. Repeat, "Six, ja, Joy."

For number 7 we choose "ca." "Ca."
Our picture word is "key." "Seven, ca, key."

Let's go back and review. Remember, say it out loud.
"One, ta, tie." Repeat, "One, ta, tie."
"Two, na, Noah." Repeat, "Two, na, Noah."
"Three, ma, mow." Repeat, "Three, ma, mow."
"Four, ra, row." Repeat, "Four, ra, row."
"Five, la, law." Repeat, "Five, la, law."
"Six, ja, Joy." Repeat. "Six, ja, Joy."
"Seven, ca, key." Repeat, "Seven, ca, key."

For number 8 we choose "fa." "Fa."
The picture word is "fee." You can picture "fee" as money on a counter or dollar bills exchanging hands. "Eight, fa, fee."

For number 9 we choose "pa." "Pa."
The picture word is "pie." "Nine, pa, pie."

Number 10 is what phonetic sound?

Number 10 is our first double-digit number. So we have to choose a phonetic for number 1, "ta," or "da," and a phonetic for number 0, "sa" or "za." Keep in mind that the phonetics have to go in order to match the order of the numbers.

I am choosing "ta," for number 1 and "sa" for number 0. Repeat "ta" and "sa." We are establishing the picture word "toes" from these phonetics. So for number 10 picture toes and repeat, "Ten, ta, sa, toes."

Number 11 consists of what phonetic sounds? Again, 11 is two numbers, 1 and 1. I have chosen "ta" for the first number 1 and "da" for the second number 1. Repeat, "Ta, da."

The picture word we are creating from these two phonetics, "ta" and "da," is "toad." Picture a toad for number 11 and repeat, "Eleven, ta, da, toad."

Let's review. Repeat after me. "Six, ja, Joy. Six, ja, Joy."
"Seven, ca, key. Seven, ca, key."
"Eight, fa, fee. Eight, fa, fee."
"Nine, pa, pie. Nine, pa pie."
"Ten, ta sa, toes. Ten, ta sa, toes." Repeat once more, "Ten, ta, sa, toes."
"Eleven, ta da, toad. Eleven, ta, da, toad." Repeat once more, "Eleven, ta, da, toad."

In a moment, I'll ask you to close the book and review all eleven numbers. Say each number out loud, say its corresponding phonetic or phonetics, and then say the picture word, visualizing it in your mind clearly. Then repeat all three items—number, phonetic, word—quickly. It would be helpful to have a partner for this exercise, but you can do it on your own, too. Take about five or ten minutes for the drill. Close the book and do them now.◆

Let's continue.

For number 12 we choose the phonetics "ta" and "na." "Ta, na." Our picture word is "tin." Vividly picture a tin can and repeat, "Twelve, ta, na, tin."

Number 13 will be "da" and "ma." "Da, ma." Our picture word is "dam." Repeat, "Thirteen, da, ma, dam."

Number 14 is "ta" and "ra." "Ta, ra." Our picture word is "tire." Repeat, "Fourteen, ta, ra, tire."

To review what we're doing, can you tell me why we chose "tire"? What's the first number in 14? Number 1. And what are the phonetics for number 1? "Ta" or "da." What's the next phonetic? "Ra" for number 4. "Tire" is our picture word. (Another acceptable word might be "dire," though I chose "tire" because it's easier to picture.)

Number 15 is "ta" and "la." "Ta, la." Our picture word is "tail." Repeat, "Fifteen, ta, la, tail."

Let's review:

"Twelve, ta, na." What's the picture word? "Tin." Say it again. "Twelve, ta, na, tin."

"Thirteen, da, ma, dam." Picture a dam. Say it again, making sure you are saying it out loud. "Thirteen, da, ma, dam."

"Fourteen, ta, ra, tire." "Fourteen, ta, ra, tire." "Fourteen, ta, ra, tire."

"Fifteen, ta, la, tail." "Fifteen, ta, la, tail." Picture a wagging tail vividly in your mind.

Number 16 is "da," and "sha." "Da, sha." Our picture word is "dish." Repeat, "Sixteen, da, sha, dish."

Number 17 is "ta," and "ca." "Ta, ca." Our picture word is "tack." Repeat, "Seventeen, ta, ca, tack."

In a moment, you will close the book again and drill numbers 1 through 17. Do exactly the same thing as you did in the previous drill, either with a partner or alone. Say the number out loud, say the phonetic, and then say the picture word, visualizing it in your mind clearly. Then repeat all three quickly. When you're finished, there should be no hesitation or doubt. And you should not be writing anything down. Close the book and review numbers 1 through 17 for about five to ten minutes, now.◆

Time to continue.

Number 18 is "ta" and "va." "Ta, va." Our picture word is "TV." Repeat, "Eighteen, ta, va, TV."

Number 19 is "ta" and pa." "Ta, pa." Our picture word is "tape." Repeat, "Nineteen, ta, pa, tape."

Number 20 is "na" and "sa." "Na, sa." Our picture word is "nose." Repeat, "Twenty, na, sa, nose."

Number 21 is "na" and "ta." "Na, ta." Our picture word is "net." Repeat, "Twenty-one, na, ta, net."

Number 22 is "na" and "na." "Na, na." Our picture word is "nun." Repeat, "Twenty-two, na, na, nun."

Number 23 is "na" and "ma." "Na, ma." Our picture word is "enema." Repeat, "Twenty-three, na, ma, enema."

Number 24 is "na" and "ra." "Na, ra." Our picture word is "Nero." Picture a slightly overweight man in a Roman toga playing the fiddle. Repeat, "Twenty-four, na, ra, Nero."

Number 25 is "na" and "la." "Na, la." Our picture word is "nail." Repeat, "Twenty-five, na, la, nail."

Now close the book and drill all the picture words, 1 through 25, exactly as you did before. Say the number out loud, say the phonetic, and then say the picture word, visualizing it in your mind clearly. Close the book and drill numbers 1 through 25 now.◆

Picture Words 1–25: Reverse Drill

Now we're going to reverse the drill. I'm going to call out a word and you're going to repeat the number out loud. If you slide a straight edge down the page, you won't see the number until you have given me your answer. An explanation for the answer will follow.

For example: "Dish." What number is "dish"? To come up with the number, first ask yourself what the first phonetic is. It's "da," which gives you number 1. What's the second phonetic? "Sha," which gives you number 6. So "dish" is 16.

Ready? Let's do the exercise now.

What is the number for pie?
9. The only phonetic is "pa," so pie is 9.

nun
22. "Nun" has two "na" phonetics: 2 and 2 is 22.

nail
25. "Na" is 2, "la" is 5. Nail is 25.

tire
14. "Ta" is 1, "ra" is 4. Tire is 14.

toad
11. "Ta" is 1, "da" is 1. Toad is 11.

law
5. "La" is 5. That's the only phonetic, so law is 5.

key
7. "Ca" is 7. There's no other phonetic, so key is 7.

TV
18. "Ta" is 1, "va" is 8. TV is 18.

nose
20. "Na" is 2, "sa" is 0. Nose is 20.

net
21. "Na" is 2, "ta" is 1. Net is 21.

enema
23. "Na" is 2, "ma" is 3. Enema is 23.

Joy

6. "Ja" is 6. That's the only phonetic, so "Joy" is 6.

tie

1. "Ta" is 1. That's the only phonetic, so tie is 1.

mow

3. "Ma" is 3. There's no other phonetic, so mow is 3.

toes

10. "Ta" is 1, "sa" is 0. Toes is 10.

tape

19. "Ta" is 1, "pa" is 9. Tape is 19.

In a moment you will close the book, and I will ask you to write numbers 1 through 25 in a column on a piece of paper. Then next to those numbers you will write first the phonetic sounds that correspond to the number, and second, the picture word we've created for that number. Leave some space between the columns. Close the book and do that now.◆

Check your list to see how many you got. If you missed any, don't worry; just make sure your written list is correct. Once you've done that, review it until you feel very sure of it. Then practice first covering one side, then the other, so that the number instantly gives you the word and the word instantly gives you the number. Close the book and do that now.◆

Picture Words 1–25: Test

Now I'm going to give you a test on the twenty-five words. I'm going to give you numbers and you're instantly going to call out the corresponding picture word. A partner can read the numbers out loud, while you call out the picture word. If you're working alone, slide a straight-edge down the page. Since you know the list accurately by now, you should work toward speed. Try to do one "set" (a number and its corresponding picture word) per second. And remember, OUT LOUD.

Ready? Let's take the test now.

8?

fee

19?

tape

14?

tire

25?

nail

21?

net

11?

toad

7?

key

13?

dam

18?

TV

22?

nun

15?

tail

16?

dish

17?

tack

4?

row

9?

pie

How did you do? If you got stuck on some of the items, you're not alone. On number 16, for example, you may think of both the "ta" and "da" phonetics for number 1, which may cause you to hesitate or go blank. If that happens, just keep drilling the numbers, phonetic sounds, and picture words. As before, say the number out loud, say the phonetic, and then say the picture word, visualizing it in your mind clearly. You can use your written list as a guide.

If you did well on the last test, you are ready for the next one! The same rules apply as in the previous test. I'm going to give you a number and you're instantly going to call out the picture word. Keep working toward speed, with a goal of doing one set per second. This is the last test before you go on to the next lesson.

Ready? Here's the second test.

1?

tie

2?

Noah

3?

mow

4?

row

5?

law

6?

Joy

7?

key

8?

fee

9?

pie

10?

toes

11?

toad

12?

can

13?

dam

14?

tire

15?

tail

16?

dish

17?

tack

18?

TV

19?

tape

20?

nose

21?

net

22?

nun

23?

enema

24?

Nero

25?
nail

If you're up to speed, congratulations! If you're still having trouble, just keep doing the drills in this chapter until the picture words come quickly to you. The more you do this, the faster you will become. Just stay with it. You have to be accurate and at top speed before you continue to the next lesson.

What you have started to do in this chapter is commit sounds and pictures to memory. Hearing sounds, and then turning them into pictures is the way your unconscious processes information. By learning to commit information to memory this way, you are giving your unconscious the software it needs to process what you want to commit to memory and give it back to you as quickly and efficiently as possible. In other words, you are creating an immense filing cabinet, and one that you can access at top speed.

Chapter 19—Review

Establishing phonetic-based picture words for numbers:

1. Eliminate all vowels.
2. Eliminate "h's" and "w's."
3. Use only the first three phonetics for any word.
4. Picture each word as vividly as possible.

Picture Words 1–25

1. tie
2. Noah
3. mow
4. row
5. law
6. Joy
7. key
8. fee

9. pie
10. toes
11. toad
12. tin
13. dam
14. tire
15. tail
16. dish
17. tack
18. TV
19. tape
20. nose
21. net
22. nun
23. enema
24. Nero
25. nail

Chapter 19—Required Mental Exercise

Exercise

Go down this column as fast as you can, and call out the corresponding number or picture word. It is vitally important that you say these words out loud. You will not remember them as quickly or as completely if they are not said aloud.

14
2
pie
TV
nail
23
6
dish
tie

nun

8

17

nose

key

net

3

24

toad

tin

dam

19

14

tail

law

toes

20   Picture Words 26–50

As usual, before we go on with this lesson, I want you to
test yourself on the previous lesson. You have to be certain that you
are at the proper speed, which means instantaneous recall of the
numbers and the picture words in our phonetic alphabet. The best
way to do this is with a partner calling out the numbers, while
you call out the corresponding picture words. Otherwise, slide a
straightedge down the page.

You should complete this list in about fifteen seconds, with complete accuracy and no hesitation on any item. Having this list down
pat is vitally important for your continued success with this chapter.

Ready? Take the test now.

19?

tape

22?

nun

6?

Joy

17?
tack

25?
nail

12?
pin

14?
tire

16?
dish

15?
tail

5?
law

9?
tie

11?
toad

21?
net

18?
TV

23?
enema

Okay. We're now going to continue assigning picture words to numbers 26 through 50. In this chapter, though, I'm going to teach it to you in reverse. I'm going to give you the picture word first, and you're going to identify the phonetic sounds and then decide what number they represent. Again, the best way to do this is to have a partner read the words, while you respond with the numbers.

Otherwise, use that straightedge. If your partner is studying the Mega Memory program also, take turns calling out words and finding the appropriate numbers.

Don't forget to create vivid pictures of the words. After I give you the word, say it out loud. Then, as indicated by the second line in each item, identify and repeat the phonetic sounds out loud, and call out the number they represent. This list is not in any particular order.

Ready? Here we go.

Rice? Say it out loud. "Rice, rice, rice."
Out loud. "Ra. Sa. Ra is 4. Sa is 0. Rice is 40."

Maid? "Maid, maid, maid."
"Ma. Da. Ma is 3. Da is 1. Maid is 31."

Roof? "Roof, roof, roof."
"Ra. Fa. Ra is 4. Fa is 8. Roof is 48."

Neck? "Neck, neck, neck."
"Na. Ca. Na is 2. Ca is 7. Neck is 27."

Moose? "Moose, moose, moose."
"Ma. Sa. Ma is 3. Sa is 0. Moose is 30."

Mail? "Mail, mail, mail."
"Ma. La. Ma is 3. La is 5. Mail is 35."

Mug? "Mug, mug, mug."
"Ma. Ga. Ma is 3. Ga is 7. Mug is 37."

Rat? "Rat, rat, rat."
"Ra. Ta. Ra is 4. Ta is 1. Rat is 41."

Hinge? "Hinge, hinge, hinge."
The "h" doesn't exist in our phonetic universe, as we pointed out in the previous chapter. The next phonetic sound is "na." And then "ja." "Na is 2. Ja is 6. Hinge is 26."

Knife? "Knife, knife, knife."
"Na. Fa. Na is 2. Fa is 8. Knife is 28."

Knob? "Knob, knob, knob."
"Na. Ba. Na is 2. Ba is 9. Knob is 29."

Man? "Man, man, man."
"Ma. Na. Ma is 3. Na is 2. Man is 32."

Mime? "Mime, mime, mime."
"Ma. Ma. Ma is 3. The second ma is 3 as well. Mime is 33."

Match? "Match, match, match."
"Ma. Cha. Ma is 3. Cha is 6. Match is 36."

Movie? "Movie, movie, movie."
"Ma. Va." Now, how are you going to picture a movie? You may want to picture a movie reel, or a movie projector, a theater, or a director with his bullhorn, sitting in his director's chair. Keep it as concrete at you can.

Let's continue with "movie." "Ma is 3. Va is 8. Movie is 38."

Mop? "Mop, mop, mop."
"Ma. Pa. Ma is 3. Pa is 9. Mop is 39."

Rhino? "Rhino, rhino, rhino."
"Ra. Na. Ra is 4. Na is 2. Rhino is 42."

Ram? "Ram, ram, ram."
"Ra. Ma. Ra is 4. Ma is 3. Ram is 43."

Rare? "Rare, rare, rare."
"Ra. Ra. Ra is 4, both times. Rare is 44."

Rail? "Rail, rail, rail."
"Ra. La. Ra is 4. La is 5. Rail is 45."

Roach? "Roach, roach, roach."
"Ra. Cha. Ra is 4. Cha is 6. Roach is 46."

Rake? "Rake, rake, rake."
"Ra. Ca. Ra is 4. Ca is 7. Rake is 47."

Lassie? "Lassie, Lassie, Lassie."
"La. Sa. La is 5. Sa is 0. Lassie is 50."

Ruby? "Ruby, ruby, ruby."
"Ra. Ba. Ra is 4. Ba is 9. Ruby is 49."

Mare. "Mare, mare, mare."
"Ma. Ra. Ma is 3. Ra is 4. Mare is 34."

Now I'm going to give you the numbers first, and you're going to come up with the picture word. After you see the number (or hear it, if you're doing this with a partner), repeat it out loud. Then identify the two phonetic sounds, say them out loud, and say the picture word. Don't forget to create a vivid image for your word and then repeat everything. If you're having trouble remembering the phonetics or the word, they're on the next line, which will give you the sequence in order. Make sure you read the second line out loud before you go to the next number.
Ready? Here we go.

26? Say it out loud. "Twenty-six." Now call out the phonetics and the word.
For 26 you should come up with "na, ja, hinge." Picture a hinge and repeat, "Twenty-six, na, ja, hinge." Do the following items in this exercise the same way.

27? "Twenty-seven."
"Na, ca, neck. Twenty-seven, na, ca, neck."

28? "Twenty-eight."
"Na, fa, knife. Twenty-eight, na, fa, knife."

29? "Twenty-nine."
"Na, ba, knob. Twenty-nine, na, ba, knob."

30? "Thirty."
"Ma, sa, moose. Thirty, ma, sa, moose."

31? "Thirty-one."
"Ma, da, maid. Thirty-one, ma, da, maid."

32? "Thirty-two."
"Ma, na, man. Thirty-two, ma, na, man."

33? "Thirty-three."

"Ma, ma, mime. Thirty-three, ma, ma, mime."

34? "Thirty-four."

"Ma, ra, mare. Thirty-four, ma, ra, mare."

35? "Thirty-five."

"Ma, la, mail. Thirty-five, ma, la, mail."

36? "Thirty-six."

"Ma, cha, match. Thirty-six, ma, cha, match."

37? "Thirty-seven."

"Ma, ga, mug. Thirty-seven, ma, ga, mug."

38? "Thirty-eight."

"Ma, va, movie. Thirty-eight, ma, va, movie."

39? "Thirty-nine."

"Ma, pa, mop. Thirty-nine, ma, pa, mop."

In a moment you will close the book and write down in order numbers 26 through 39 on a piece of paper. Then next to those numbers, write down the corresponding phonetic sounds followed by the picture word. Leave some space between the columns. Close the book and do that now.◆

Check your list and see how many you got. If you forgot a few that's okay; fill them in now. If your answers didn't match mine, you may have created a picture other than the one I chose for a particular number. For example, take number 31. Many people choose the word "mat," since 3 is "ma" and 1 can be "ta." Mat is a good picture. I chose "maid" only because I think it's a picture with which we can do more, and you'll see why later. Neither picture is wrong, but for now, as I've said, let's use my picture words. If any of your picture words are different from those in the list above, cross them out and use the given words. As you become more proficient with Mega Memory, however, let me reemphasize that you should use what works best for you.

Now take your corrected written list of numbers 26 through

39. Cover one side and then the other, drilling it until the number instantly gives you the picture word and the picture word instantly gives you the number. Close the book and do that now.◆

Let's continue with numbers 40 through 50. Remember, after you see the number, repeat it out loud. Then identify the two phonetic sounds, which will give you the picture word. Don't forget to create a vivid picture of your word and to repeat everything out loud.

40? "Forty."
"Ra, sa, rice. Forty, ra, sa, rice."

41? "Forty-one."
"Ra, ta, rat. Forty-one, ra, ta, rat."

42? "Forty-two."
"Ra, na, rhino. Forty-two, ra, na, rhino."

43? "Forty-three."
"Ra, ma, ram. Forty-three, ra, ma, ram."

44? "Forty-four."
"Ra, ra, rare." Now how are you going to picture rare? Maybe a rare gem or maybe a rare antique. A lot of people use a rare steak. All of these objects work well, as long as they remind you of something rare. Now repeat, "Forty-four, ra, ra, rare."

45? "Forty-five."
"Ra, la, rail. Forty-five, ra, la, rail."

46? "Forty-six."
"Ra, cha, roach. Forty-six, ra, cha, roach."

47? "Forty-seven."
"Ra, ca, rake. Forty-seven, ra, ca, rake."

48? "Forty-eight."
"Ra, fa, roof. Forty-eight, ra, fa, roof."

49? "Forty-nine."
"Ra, ba, ruby. Forty-nine, ra, ba, ruby."

50? "Fifty."
"La, sa, Lassie. Fifty, la, sa, Lassie."

Do the same thing now with numbers 40 through 50 that you did with Numbers 26 through 39. Number 40 through 50 down the left side of a piece of paper and next to those numbers write down the corresponding phonetic sounds followed by the picture word. Close the book and do that now.◆

Now check your list. If you missed some, don't worry, but correct them on your sheet. And as before, use the words I gave you, even though words that you thought of might be just as legitimate.

As you did before, go to your list and drill numbers 40 through 50 in both directions, so that the number instantly gives you the word, and the word instantly gives you the number. Say everything out loud, and create clear, vivid pictures for your words. Close the book and do the drill now.◆

We're now going to do a little speed drill on numbers 26 through 50. I'll give the number and you'll give me—out loud—the phonetic sounds and the word. If you're alone, use a straightedge; if you're doing this with a partner, have your partner call out the number while you call out the phonetics and the word. Your goal is to do one set in about two seconds.

Ready? Start the drill now.

27?
"Na, ca, neck."

29?
"Na, ba, knob."

32?
"Ma, na, man."

34?
"Ma, ra, mare."

37?
"Ma, ga, mug."

44?
"Ra, ra, rare."

48?
"Ra, fa, roof."

40?
"Ra, sa, rice."

50?
"La, sa, Lassie."

26?
"Na, ja, hinge."

28?
"Na, fa, knife."

30?
"Ma, sa, moose."

31?
"Ma, da, maid."

38?
"Ma, va, movie."

49?
"Ra, ba, ruby."

All right. That drill should have taken thirty seconds or less. Now close the book and go back to your written lists. Drill yourself for the next five to ten minutes with numbers 26 through 50. Cover up the left side of your list and make sure you come up with the picture words instantly. Then cover up the right side and make sure the numbers come to you. If you aren't up to speed, keep drilling. If you are, review the numbers once and then go on to the next drill. Do this now.◆

Now I'm going to give you words and you will say the numbers out loud. Use a straightedge or have your partner call out the word while you call out the number. Again, it's important that you're up to speed. This should go a little faster than the last drill because there is less to say. You should try to do one set in about a second. Since there are nineteen sets of items, this should take you about twenty seconds total.

Ready? Begin.

Mop?
39

Rat?
41

Ram?
43

Rake?
47

Man?
32

Knob?
29

Lassie?
50

Ruby?
49

Roach?
46

Rail?
45

Rhino?
42

Rice?
40

Match?
36

Mail?

35

Mime?

33

Maid?

31

Moose?

30

Neck?

27

Knife?

28

If you are not up to speed yet, close the book and continue to review, simply by saying out loud, in sequence, the number, the phonetic sounds, and the picture words.◆

If you are finding this process difficult, you're not alone. Getting the picture words and their corresponding numbers into your knowledge bank is the most difficult part of our Mega Memory program. It is the type of memory work that we ultimately want to be rid of. However, just like any athlete, you have to go through some tedious and repetitive exercises to get your muscles conditioned so that they perform at peak capacity. And just like any football or baseball player, once you're in the game, and your conditioning is supporting your every move, any distaste you have for these exercises will fade to nothing. In fact, that conditioning will become a source of pride. So take heart! The same principle applies here, except that the muscle you are conditioning is your brain.

Before you take the final test in this chapter, go back to your written lists and make sure you know the numbers and picture words instantaneously. Close the book and do that now.◆

In this final test, I'm going to give a number and you're instantly going to call out the picture word. Make sure you're at speed, about one combination per second, before you go on.

Ready. Take the test now.

42?
rhino

45?
rail

32?
man

28?
knife

38?
movie

39?
mop

34?
mare

33?
mime

50?
Lassie

49?
ruby

48?
roof

47?
rake

46?
roach

45?
rail

44?
rare

40?

rice

41?

rat

30?

moose

32?

man

26?

hinge

27?

neck

If you remember all fifty picture words and are doing the exercises up to speed, congratulations! You are making tremendous progress. If you're still unsure of the words, or your speed is a problem, do not go on to the next lesson. Continue to drill and review the numbers, the phonetic sounds, and the picture words, by reciting each in sequence. You can do this drill while you're driving your car, while you're taking a shower, or in just about any place where you can talk out loud and not be considered a public nuisance!

And don't be concerned. Many of my seminar participants have trouble absorbing all the picture words. If you keep drilling, I promise you the words will come.

Chapter 20—Review

Picture Words 26–50

26. hinge
27. neck
28. knife
29. knob

30. moose
31. maid
32. man
33. mime
34. mare
35. mail
36. match
37. mug
38. movie
39. mop
40. rice
41. rat
42. rhino
43. ram
44. rare
45. rail
46. roach
47. rake
48. roof
49. ruby
50. Lassie

Chapter 20—Required Mental Exercise

Exercise

Go down this column as fast as you can, and call out the corresponding number or picture word. Remember to say the words out loud.

44
36
neck
ruby
mop
26

50
mare
ram
knob
41
30
movie
rail
man
47
28
roof
maid
mug
33
40
mail
roach
rhino

21 Picture Words 51–75

Before we continue establishing picture words for our next group of numbers, let's review the numbers and picture words from the last chapter. In the drill that follows, I'm going to give you a number and you're going to say the picture word out loud. Your speed goal is one set of items per second.

Ready? Let's begin.

47?
rake

32?
man

27?
neck

41?
rat

37?
mug

39?

mop

31?

maid

42?

rhino

48?

roof

26?

hinge

You should have worked through that list in about ten seconds. If you hesitated or forgot any, go back and review drills in Chapter 20. At this point you should have instant recall of numbers 1 through 50, their corresponding phonetics, and their picture word.

Now we're going to establish picture words for numbers 51 to 75. First I will give you the number. You will repeat it out loud, and then go to the following line, reading it out loud. The line will give you the two phonetics I chose and the picture word that I chose using those two phonetics. Make sure you create a vivid, crystal clear image of the picture word in your mind's eye.

Let's establish picture words 51 through 60 now.

51? Say it out loud. "Fifty-one." Now go to the next line, reading it out loud.

"La, da, lid. Fifty-one, la, da, lid."

52? "Fifty-two."
"La, na, lion. Fifty-two, la na, lion."

53? "Fifty-three."
"La, ma, lamb. Fifty-three, la, ma, lamb."

54? "Fifty-four."
"La, ra, lure." Picture a lure, like a fishing lure. "Fifty-four, la, ra, lure."

55? "Fifty-five."
"La, la, lily. Fifty-five, la, la, lily."

56? "Fifty-six."
"La, sha, leash. Fifty-six, la, sha, leash."

57? "Fifty-seven."
"La, ca, lock. Fifty-seven, la, ca, lock."

58? "Fifty-eight."
"La, fa, leaf. Fifty-eight, la, fa, leaf."

59? "Fifty-nine."
"La, pa, leap. Fifty-nine, la, pa, leap."

60? "Sixty."
"Cha, sa, cheese. Sixty, cha, sa, cheese."

All right. Now I'm going to give you a picture word, and you're going to call out the phonetics and the number. Use the straightedge if you're alone, or have a partner read the word to you, while you call out the phonetics and the appropriate number.

Ready?

Lid?
"La, da, 51."

Lion?
"La, na, 52."

Lamb?
"La, ma, 53."

Lure?
"La, ra, 54."

Lily?
"La, la, 55."

Leash?
"La, sha, 56."

Lock?
"La, ca, 57."

Leaf?
"La, fa, 58."

Leap?
"La, pa, 59."

Cheese?
"Cha, sa, 60."

In a moment you will close the book and do some more drilling. You will repeat each number, in order 51 through 60. Then you will repeat the phonetics and the picture word that go with each one. Say everything out loud, and don't forget to create vivid pictures of the words when you recite them. If you have a partner, take turns prompting each other. Close the book and do that now.◆

How did you do? Were you able to get all ten? If you forgot any, review our list up above and do the drill once more.

Let's continue establishing picture words for numbers 61 through 69. I'll give you the number and you call out the phonetics and the word. And don't forget those vivid pictures!

61? "Sixty-one." Now go to the next line and read it out loud. "Cha, ta, cheetah. Sixty-one, cha, ta, cheetah."

62? "Sixty-two."
"Cha, na, chain. Sixty-two, cha, na, chain."

63? "Sixty-three."
"Ja, ma, gym. Sixty-three, ja, ma, gym."

64? "Sixty-four."
"Sha, ra, shower. Sixty-four, sha, ra, shower."

65? "Sixty-five."
"Sha, la, shell. Sixty-five, sha, la, shell."

66? "Sixty-six."
"Ja, ja, judge. Sixty-six, ja, ja, judge."

67? "Sixty-seven."
"Sha, ca, sheik. Sixty-seven, sha, ca, sheik."

68? "Sixty-eight."
"Sha, va, shave. Sixty-eight, sha, va, shave."

69? "Sixty-nine."
"Ja, pa, jeep. Sixty-nine, ja, pa, jeep."

All right, let's review. I'm going to give you the words, and you're going to call out the phonetics and the numbers, and then repeat everything. Use your straightedge, or have a partner read to you—and keep creating those vivid pictures!

Cheetah?
"Cha, ta, 61. Cheetah, cha, ta, 61."

Chain?
"Cha, na, 62. Chain, cha, na, 62."

Gym?
"Ja, ma, 63. Gym, ja, ma, 63."

Shower?
"Sha, ra, 64. Shower, sha, ra, 64."

Shell?
"Sha, la, 65. Shell, sha, la, 65."

Judge?
"Ja, ja, 66. Judge, ja, ja, 66."

Sheik?
"Sha, ca, 67. Sheik, sha, ca, 67."

Shave?
"Sha, va, 68. Shave, sha, va, 68."

Jeep?

"Ja, pa, 69. Jeep, ja, pa, 69."

In a moment you'll close the book and recite what you just learned. Repeat numbers 61 through 69, out loud in order, and then, just as you did in the previous recitation, repeat the phonetics and the picture word that go with each one. Close the book and do that now.◆

Now let's establish picture words for numbers 70 through 75. I'll give you the number, you repeat it, along with its phonetics. Then go to the line below and read it out loud, creating vivid pictures of each word.

70? "Seventy."
"Ca, sa, case. Seventy, ca, sa, case."

71? "Seventy-one."
"Ca, ta, cat. Seventy-one, ca, ta, cat."

72? "Seventy-two."
"Ca, na, coin. Seventy-two, ca, na, coin."

73? "Seventy-three."
"Ca, ma, comb. Seventy-three, ca, ma, comb."

74? "Seventy-four."
"Ca, ra, car. Seventy-four, ca, ra, car."

75? "Seventy-five."
"Ca, la, coal. Seventy-five, ca, la, coal."

Let's review. I give you the picture words, and you call out the phonetics and the number, and then repeat everything.

Case?
"Ca, sa, 70. Case, ca, sa, 70."

Cat?
"Ca, ta, 71. Cat, ca, ta, 71."

Coin?

"Ca, na, 72. Coin, ca, na, 72."

Comb?

"Ca, ma, 73. Comb, ca, ma, 73."

Car?

"Ca, ra, 74. Car, ca, ra, 74."

Coal?

"Ca, la, 75. Coal, ca, la, 75."

Coin?

"Ca, na, 72. Coin, ca, na, 72."

Case?

"Ca, sa, 70. Case, ca, sa, 70."

Coal?

"Ca, la, 75. Coal, ca, la, 75."

Comb?

"Ca, ma, 73. Comb, ca, ma, 73."

Car?

"Ca, ra, 74. Car, ca, ra, 74."

Cat?

"Ca, ta, 71. Cat, ca, ta, 71."

All right. In a moment, you'll close the book and review all of the picture words we've established in this chapter, 51–75. Create a written list as you've done in previous chapters, numbering 51 through 75 down the left side of a piece of paper. Next to each number, write down the phonetic and the picture word. Then cover up each side and test yourself. Close the book and do this exercise now.◆

Now we will drill with speed in mind. If you're working with someone, have your partner call out the number while you call out the phonetics and the word. If you're alone, call out all three items in sequence—the number, the phonetics, and the picture word. Keep increasing your speed until there's no hesitation between items. Take five, ten, or twenty minutes, however long it takes to have everything down pat. Close the book and do it now.◆

It's test time. I'm going to give you numbers, you're going to call out the corresponding phonetic sound and picture word. Your pace must be rapid-fire quick, your goal being about one set of items every two seconds. And, of course, you must be accurate. If you're still unsure of some of the combinations, do the drill above, then come back here. Use the straightedge, or, preferably, have a partner call out the numbers to you.

Ready? Begin.

52?
"La, na, lion."

66?
"Ja, ja, judge."

61?
"Cha, ta, cheetah."

60?
"Cha, sa, cheese."

58?
"La, fa, leaf."

57?
"La, ca, lock."

55?
"La, la, lily."

74?
"Ca, ra, car."

70?
"Ca, sa, case."

67?
"Sha, ca, sheik."

65?
"Sha, la, shell."

62?
"Cha, na, chain."

If you weren't at speed, continue to drill numbers 51 through 75. If you are up to speed, drill yourself in the opposite way, that is, by calling out the word and then coming up with the phonetics and the number. It's important that the number instantly gives you the word, and the word instantly gives you the number. Close the book and do the review drill now.◆

Okay. I'm now going to test you again, this time by giving you the picture word, while you call out the corresponding number. This is a test to make sure that you have access to the information at the proper speed.

Ready? One set per second.

Cat?
71

Coal?
75

Lily?
55

Cheetah?
61

Leap?
59

Leaf?
58

Lock?
57

Lure?
54

Shave?
68

Jeep?
69

Shell?
65

Coin?
72

Leap?
59

Cheese?
60

If you're accurate and at speed, congratulations. You have established seventy-five picture words for seventy-five numbers so far—almost to our goal of one hundred. Remember, to keep yourself from getting rusty, make it a habit to review these words and numbers wherever you are. Just call out a number at random, from 1 to 75, and then call out its phonetics and its picture word.

Chapter 21—Review

Picture Words 51–75

51. lid
52. lion
53. lamb
54. lure
55. lily
56. leash
57. lock
58. leaf
59. leap

60. cheese
61. cheetah
62. chain
63. gym
64. shower
65. shell
66. judge
67. sheik
68. shave
69. jeep
70. case
71. cat
72. coin
73. comb
74. car
75. coal

Chapter 21—Required Mental Exercise

Exercise

Go down this column as fast as you can, and call out the corresponding number or picture word. Remember to say the words out loud.

73
64
judge
lamb
car
56
69
chain
case
lure
61

51
coin
gym
lily
75
67
shave
leaf
cat
60
52
shell
leap
lock

22 Picture Words 76–100

We've established seventy-five picture words for seventy-five numbers so far. Before we continue with numbers 76 through 100, let's do a quick drill reviewing all our picture words. I'm going to call out a number and you're going to say the picture word out loud. Your response should be instantaneous.

Let's review:

39?
mop

14?
tire

50?
Lassie

66?
judge

5?
law

75?
coal

56?
leash

20?
nose

42?
rhino

29?
knob

Now let's continue with numbers 76 through 100. As before, I will give you the number, and I want you to repeat the number and then read the next line out loud. Make sure you say everything out loud, and that you create vivid pictures of the picture words. Let's begin.

76? "Seventy-six."
"Ca, ja, cage. Seventy-six, ca, ja, cage."

77? "Seventy-seven."
"Ca, ca, cake. Seventy-seven, ca, ca, cake."

78? "Seventy-eight."
"Ca, fa, coffee. Seventy-eight, ca, fa, coffee."

79? "Seventy-nine."
"Ca, pa, cap. Seventy-nine, ca, pa, cap."

80? "Eighty."
"Va, sa, vase. Eighty, va, sa, vase."

81? "Eighty-one."
"Fa, ta, fat. Eighty-one, fa, ta, fat."

82? "Eighty-two."
"Fa, na, fan. Eighty-two, fa, na, fan."

83? "Eighty-three."
"Fa, ma, foam. Eighty-three, fa, ma, foam."

84? "Eighty-four."
"Fa, ra, fry. Eighty-four, fa, ra, fry."

85? "Eighty-five."
"Fa, la, file. Eighty-five, fa, la, file."

In a moment, you will close the book and do an oral drill. For numbers 76 through 85, call out the number, the phonetic sounds, and the picture word. You are doing it all from memory—don't write anything down. If you have a partner, rehearse together. Speed isn't a factor yet; just make sure numbers 76 through 85 have been committed to memory. Close the book and do the exercise now.◆

Let's continue establishing picture words.

86? "Eighty-six."
"Fa, sha, fish. Eighty-six, fa, sha, fish."

87? "Eighty-seven."
"Fa, ga, fig. Eighty-seven, fa, ga, fig."

88? "Eighty-eight."
"Fa, fa, fife. Eighty-eight, fa, fa, fife."

89? "Eighty-nine."
"Va, pa, VP." I'm using the abbreviation VP for vice president, so you may picture the current Vice President if you'd like. Otherwise, any object that you associate with the current, or any other, Vice President is fine. "Eighty-nine, va, pa, VP."

90? "Ninety."
"Ba, sa, bus. Ninety, ba, sa, bus."

Now do an oral review of numbers 76 through 90. Say the numbers, the phonetic sounds, and the picture words, making sure you're speaking out loud and picturing each word. If you're doing this with someone else, take turns calling out the numbers. Close the book and do it now.◆

Let's continue with numbers 91 through 100.

91? "Ninety-one."
"Ba, ta, boat. Ninety-one, ba, ta, boat."

92? "Ninety-two."
"Ba, na, bone. Ninety-two, ba, na, bone."

93? "Ninety-three."
"Pa, ma, palm. Ninety-three, pa, ma, palm."

94? "Ninety-four."
"Ba, ra, beer. Ninety-four, ba, ra, beer."

95? "Ninety-five."
"Ba, la, ball. Ninety-five, ba, la, ball."

96? "Ninety-six."
"Pa, cha, peach. Ninety-six, pa, cha, peach."

97? "Ninety-seven."
"Pa, ga, pig. Ninety-seven, pa, ga, pig."

98? "Ninety-eight."
"Ba, va, beehive." Notice that there are only two phonetics in this word. Although it's a long word, the "h" doesn't exist in our phonetic universe, so we are left with the "ba" and "v" sounds, "ba" and "va." "Ninety-eight, ba, va, beehive."

99? "Ninety-nine."
"Pa, pa, pipe. Ninety-nine, pa, pa, pipe."

100? "One hundred."
"Da, sa, sa, daisies. One hundred, da, sa, sa, daisies." This is our only three-digit word.

Now do an oral review of numbers 91 through 100. Say the numbers, the phonetic sounds, and the picture words, making sure you speak out loud and vividly picture each word. Close the book and do it now.◆

Let's go back and review. I'm going to give you some of the picture words we've just established. You will see the word in your mind's eye, call out the phonetics, and come up with the number. Use a straightedge to cover the second line if you're alone; if you're doing this with someone, have your partner call out the word while you call out the phonetics and the corresponding number.

Let's begin.

Cake?
"Ca, ca, 77."

Fat?
"Fa, ta, 81."

Foam?
"Fa, ma, 83."

File?
"Fa, la, 85."

Fife?
"Fa, fa, 88."

Boat?
"Ba, ta, 91."

Palm?
"Pa, ma, 93."

Ball?
"Ba, la, 95."

Pig?
"Pa, ga, 97."

Pipe?
"Pa, pa, 99."

Cage?
"Ca, ja, 76."

Cap?
"Ca, pa, 79."

Coffee?
"Ca, fa, 78."

Fan?
"Fa, na, 82."

Fry?
"Fa, ra, 84."

Now do a written review of numbers 76 through 100. Number 76 through 100 down the left side of a piece of paper, and next to each number write the phonetics and our corresponding picture word. Then cover up the right side, making sure you are able to come up with the right phonetic and picture word for each number; and then cover up the left, making sure you know the correct number for each phonetic and picture word. Try to get to the point where you can recall each item without hesitation. Close the book and do it now.◆

Okay. Here's the first test in this chapter. I will give you the number and you will call out the phonetics and the picture word. Speed is important. As previously, try to get up to doing one set per second. If your accuracy is a problem, keep doing the oral drill above before you take this test.

Ready? Let's begin.

76?
"Ca, ja, cage."

77?
"Ca, ca, cake."

78?
"Ca, fa, coffee."

79?
"Ca, pa, cap."

80?
"Va, sa, vase."

81?
"Fa, ta, fat."

82?
"Fa, na, fan."

83?
"Fa, ma, foam."

84?
"Fa, ra, fry."

85?
"Fa, la, file."

86?
"Fa, sha, fish."

87?
"Fa, ga, fig."

88?
"Fa, fa, fife."

89?
"Va, pa, VP."

90?
"Ba, sa, bus."

91?
"Ba, ta, boat."

92?
"Ba, na, bone."

93?
"Pa, ma, palm."

94?
"Ba, ra, beer."

95?

"Ba, la, ball."

96?

"Pa, cha, peach."

97?

"Pa, ga, pig."

98?

"Ba, va, beehive."

99?

"Pa, pa, pipe."

100?

"Da, sa, sa, daisies."

Now I'd like you to work on your speed. It is most helpful to have a partner, but you can do it alone as well. Have your partner call out the number while you call out the phonetics and the picture words. If you're alone, call out all three items in sequence. Your speed goal is one set per second. Remember to do everything out loud. Close the book and do the exercises now.◆

If you're up to speed, congratulations! You have now committed to memory a picture word vocabulary for the numbers 1 through 100. In your unconscious, there is no more 22. Twenty-two is the sound "na-na," and it's a picture of a nun.

Before you start reading the next chapter, please go to the review section. There are different conversion exercises to do. Make sure you can do them up to speed. I can't overemphasize the importance of having the numbers and picture words come easily and immediately to you. You should, by this point, have them committed to memory.

You may know that when you completed "Mega Memory," Part I, you had achieved a level of recall ability that few people have in this country. Now, you're not only in the top 5 percent, but, in the top quarter of 1 percent! And we've only just begun with the basics of "Advanced Mega Memory." I want to congratulate you personally for achieving this level of memory excellence by learning the numbers, the phonetic alphabet, and picture words. I want you to know I'm proud that you've stayed on course, working through what was the hardest part of the Mega Memory program. And most of all, I hope you're looking forward to all of the benefits that this enhanced memory will reap for you.

Chapter 22—Review

Picture Words 76–100

76. cage
77. cake
78. coffee
79. cap
80. vase
81. fat
82. fan
83. foam
84. fry
85. file
86. fish
87. fig
88. fife
89. VP
90. bus
91. boat
92. bone
93. palm
94. beer
95. ball
96. peach
97. pig
98. beehive

99. pipe
100. daisies

Chapter 22—Required Mental Exercise

Exercise

Go down this column as fast as you can, and call out the corresponding number or picture word. Remember to say the words out loud.

85
93
fan
beer
pig
100
76
79
file
VP
94
98
77
beehive
daisies
cap
82
92
fig
fife
peach
cake
80
90
palm

23 Polishing Your Name Recognition

It's time to take a break from the phonetic alphabet and our hundred picture words. Let them percolate in your unconscious for a while. You've committed them to memory, and they will be there for you in the later chapters of Part II of this book.

In this chapter, we're going to return to one of my favorite subjects, remembering names. In Part I of this book, you learned the basic technique of remembering a name. It consisted of three steps: (1) You pick a see peg, which is the first thing you notice about a person. (2) After hearing it, you turn someone's name into a picture by breaking down the name into syllables, and imagining sound-alike pictures for the syllables. (3) Using exaggerated action, you put the sound-alike pictures on the see peg.

While these three steps are your basics, there are other things you can do to reinforce the pegging process described in the paragraph above. These are tips I want to pass on, things I have learned in my years of traveling and constantly meeting people. They are things you, too, can do with very little practice; all you need is an awareness of the different options you have in different situations.

The Four Rules for Meeting People

Here are four rules I would like you to follow whenever you are meeting people for the first time. If you follow them, they will help your name recall even more.

1. When shaking hands or otherwise greeting someone, always introduce yourself first.
2. When the person gives you his or her name, repeat it.
3. Ask questions and talk about a person's name.
4. Show a genuine interest in, and a concern for, the people you meet.

Let's review them.

Rule 1. When shaking hands or otherwise greeting someone, always introduce yourself first. It is very important when meeting someone to say hello and give them your name. That shows an openness on your part, a willingness to share something important about yourself. And make it your full name. You can only expect the other person to provide as much information as you have offered.

Generally—and this happens about nine times out of ten—when you give someone your name, the other person will feel obliged to give you his or her name in return. Because you've shown an openness, the other person is willing to do the same. What happens to your conversation from that point on depends on many factors, but at least you've both broken the ice in a very subtle, yet real way.

Sometimes, however, the person will not respond to your greeting. Quite frankly, I'm still taken aback when that happens. It's not like I'm walking up to them and saying, "Hey, give me fifty dollars." When people hold back, I usually suspect that it's because they're either shy or cautious, or need further prompting for whatever reason. My advice in situations like that is not to take it personally. Firmly but gently press on, and feel free to ask someone's name directly at this point. "And your name is . . . ?" Or, if you have exchanged a few words without the person revealing their name, you can say, "I'm sorry. I didn't catch your name." When prompted that directly, people will usually respond.

Rule 2. When the person gives you his or her name, repeat it. When you hear someone's name, make a point of repeating it. If the person gave you their full name—and they should, if you gave them your full name—repeat both names. "Hi, I'm Kevin Trudeau." "Hi, my name is Matt Gurke." "Matt Gurke, nice to meet you."

As we discussed in Part I, saying the name out loud reinforces it in your memory. A name, like any other word, is really nothing more than a conglomeration of sounds. The repetition of those sounds has a conditioning effect. Your vocal chords become involved in the process. When you repeat a name, your vocal cords get into the habit of pronouncing that conglomeration of sounds. Your neuromuscular memory is activated, as those neurotransmitters in the brain fire away, creating yet another memory pattern. I've been asking you to say things out loud throughout the Mega Memory program. It was especially important in learning the phonetics and picture words in order to reinforce that link between sound and picture. It's also important with things you hear infrequently, foreign languages, foreign names, or abstract concepts that you're trying to remember. Getting your vocal chords to reproduce the sounds helps ingrain them into your memory.

If you don't hear someone's name clearly the first time, don't be afraid to ask that it be repeated. When we don't hear someone's name, our tendency is to gloss over it because we are concentrating on other things that the person is saying. But keep in mind, in the long run the name is the single most important piece of information you can remember about anyone. And how can you remember something you don't know in the first place?

This problem is even greater with foreign names. You may hear the name clearly enough, but because it is so unfamiliar to you, you don't process the information quickly enough and the name doesn't stick. When that happens, you can not only ask for the name to be repeated, but you can specifically ask how to pronounce it. For example, on one of my business trips I met a man from India named Pardy Shaveik. He said his name very clearly when we were first introducing each other, and I heard it. But the unfamiliarity left some doubt in my mind. So I asked him, "Could you please repeat it?" And he said it again, "Pardy Shaveik." I repeated it out loud; then I asked, "Am I pronouncing your name correctly? I've never come across it before." I slowed down the entire process of our introduction to make sure I got his name right. In my experience, people are only too happy to oblige you in situations like that because you are showing interest in something that's very important to them. And they've learned from experience that very few people take the trouble to do it.

Rule 3. Ask questions and talk about a person's name. Asking someone about their name is a great way not only to reinforce the name in memory, but to show your interest in the person. In the above example, I asked Mr. Shaveik about the origin of the name, about the part of India he came from, and a whole host of other questions. It not only gave me a great opportunity to repeat his full name a number of times, it was also a segue into other topics of conversation.

When talking about someone's name, there are always some basic questions you can resort to. How do you spell the name? What ethnic background is the name? Does it have any literal translations, another meaning? Has it been shortened from a longer name? What was your maiden name? Is it a common name in a particular part of the country? When asking these questions, you're only really limited by your imagination and the time you have.

Here's a typical conversation you might have with someone. You've just been introduced to someone with a rather complex name, such as Harry Wysnoski. Ask him how to pronounce it. Repeat the name and say, "That's an interesting name. What background is that? Is it Polish?" Mr. Wysnoski responds, "Yes, it is." At this point you could either do a quick pegging exercise—"wiz-nose-ski" are the three syllables I'd use for my sound-alike pictures for his last name—or you could try to ask a few more questions. You might ask, "Does the name mean anything special in Polish?" or "Was it ever anything different?" and you have further topics to discuss.

Some people wonder whether asking such questions offends anybody. Of course not—remember, you are discussing someone's favorite subject, themselves. In all my travels, I have yet to come across someone who didn't like talking about his name.

Very simple names present a different challenge. For example, if you meet someone named Bill Smith, your range of questions is more limited. If you ask Bill Smith how to spell his name, he's going to think you've got one short oar. At most, you might say, "Smith. Is that with an *i* or a *y*?"

You can comment on the fact that the name is easy to remember, pronouncing it again. That works especially well if your own name is longer or more difficult. And of course, you can resort to our pegging technique. In the case of Bill Smith, I've established pictures for both names that I use over and over: dollar bills for the first name and a blacksmith bent over an anvil for Smith, which, needless to say, I come across often.

Throughout your conversation, use the name as many times as possible. For example, ask questions of the people with their name. "Are you from the area, Bill?" "Bill, it was nice to see you." "Bill, do you want to get a table over here?" "What type of work do you do, Bill?" "Do you have any children, Bill?" Don't go overboard on this, obviously; but if you do it, even a few times, it will sink in very quickly.

Rule 4. Show a genuine interest in, and a concern for, the people you meet. I've already discussed how important this is in Part I of the book. I want to share one marvelous story here that shows the effect it has on people. The story involves Dale Carnegie, regarded at the turn of the century as the greatest conversationalist in America. He was the author of the still-popular book *How to Win Friends and Influence People.* As someone who was sure to make any party a smash hit, Carnegie received many invitations to social events attended by dignitaries and socialites, although he declined most of them. On one particular occasion, he did accept an invitation.

The hostess was thrilled. Her party was packed with people in anticipation of meeting Mr. Carnegie. When he came in and was introduced, the hostess rushed to greet him. The conversation went something like this:

"Mr. Carnegie, it's such a pleasure to have you here. I've heard you're the world's greatest conversationalist!"

Mr. Carnegie nodded, taking it all in stride. "Well, thank you. I appreciate that comment."

"I understand that you travel around the world teaching seminars and lecturing on how to be a great conversationalist."

"Yes, I do."

"You must have wonderful stories to tell us about your travel adventures."

"Yes," Mr. Carnegie replied. "I have many interesting stories to share. But let me ask you a question. Someone told me that you went on a safari to Africa recently. Is that true?"

The hostess nodded. "Well, actually, it was over two and a half years ago, now, but yes I did."

"You know, of all the places I've traveled, I've never been to Africa," Mr. Carnegie told her. "What's it really like?"

And she began to tell them.

As she talked about her safari, the great conversationalist smiled, nodded, and asked a few questions. They parted ways and did not speak for the rest of the evening. The next day, *The New York Times* ran an article about this party in its Society column, and the hostess was quoted: "I had the opportunity last night to meet Dale Carnegie, reputed to be the world's greatest conversationalist. We talked for over forty-five minutes, and my guests and I agree— he is the world's greatest conversationalist!"

What did Carnegie do for forty-five minutes? He listened. He showed genuine interest, and he talked about her favorite subject, herself. It always works.

Other Aids in Remembering Names

The question often arises, "Kevin, what happens if I go over to a group and the host introduces me to four or five people at one time? What do I do then?"

There are two answers to the question. When you're proficient at using Mega Memory techniques, you will pick see pegs and come up with sound-alike pictures almost instantly. Let's say your host starts rattling off names: "This is Bill Johnson, this is Mary Smith, Harry Jaber . . ." As soon as you hear the first name, you already have a picture in your mind, because you have established a picture vocabulary. You can put the picture of the first name on the see peg in about two seconds. Sometimes, you can also peg the last name; other times you can't.

Your second option is to try to control the entire situation, so that it doesn't become too overwhelming. When I approach a group and the host says, "Let me introduce you to everybody," I say, "No, that's okay, I'll meet them one at a time." That usually gives me more time to orient myself.

What if the host just rushes up and starts introducing people to you? I have a trick for that situation as well. Let's say I'm first introduced to Mr. Bill Johnson. When I shake Mr. Johnson's hand, I try to turn my back to everyone else and I do not let go of Mr. Johnson's hand. I say, "Bill Johnson? Nice to meet you, Bill." I then try to say something else to give me those precious few extra seconds to lock myself into this person, as I call it. That gives me time to take in the person, and anything else I observe.

Many times I'll be sly. Even though I heard the name perfectly, I'll say, "I'm sorry, I didn't quite catch that. What was your name again?" "Bill Johnson." "Oh, Bill Johnson. Thank you." If you ask someone to repeat their name immediately on hearing it, it's different from asking, "I'm sorry, what was your name again?" a few minutes later. In this situation, you're telling the person you didn't hear the name clearly in the first place. When you ask them to repeat it a few minutes later, you tell them you've forgotten it. It makes a world of difference.

Don't be afraid to ask people for their business cards when the situation calls for it. Yes, it's a crutch, not a memory technique, but it's a good thing to have in case you forget the name.

Preloading

Another technique at your disposal is called preloading. It simply means familiarizing yourself with names before you actually greet people at any function, business meeting, or other social situation. At a social event or conference, spend a few minutes going over the register or guest list before walking into the room where the event is taking place. Cast your eye over any table holding place cards or name tags.

You can also preload in offices. Check the bulletin board. Look at desks for business cards. Notice sales charts on walls where the people's names are listed. The reception area might contain the office mailboxes with everyone's name listed. In some offices, they have pictures on the walls with the person's name under them. That's a wonderful luxury. If I have a scheduled appointment, I can take the name and say it to myself softly a few times before I actually meet the person, and I can turn the name into a picture. When I greet the person, I pick a see peg, and when they tell me their name, I'm already prepared. Watch for opportunities to preload during business calls and social functions—when you keep your eyes open, the opportunities will be there.

You can sometimes even preload at parties and meetings even if there's no list or register to scan. Just ask someone else, the host for example, what someone's name is. You can turn the name into a picture and pick a see peg in advance, so when you walk over and shake the person's hand, most of your work is already done.

Two other little tips. The first is, take a few minutes to hide if you feel you've reached the limit of your meet-and-greet quota. If I don't want to meet too many people too quickly, I'll run to the bathroom or to the coffeepot. I'll even make believe I'm busy reading a pamphlet or other material. What I'm really doing, of course, is thinking about the people that I've just met, going over their names, their see pegs, or any other information that I find valuable or interesting. And I will say the name softly to myself in order to build memory in my vocal cords and get acclimated to pronouncing someone's name.

The second tip: If you're going to a group event, such as a convention or meeting of some sort, you can often call ahead and get a list of attenders. I find that helps me tremendously. Then on the flight over, I have the names to work with, perhaps spending a half hour doing this. Since I have a picture vocabulary for almost every first name, it usually only takes me that long to go over a list of about fifty or a hundred, or even more, people. Last names are harder, of course, but I still try to play with them, pronouncing the name how I think it's pronounced, breaking it down, and turning it into pictures. And I don't put pressure on myself to make everything perfectly correct. As I've already said, if it's not fun, you'll never do it. So I stay relaxed, and make a game of it, as I've been stressing for you to do throughout the book. If I have a friend or colleague along, I get them involved, and we can have a great time doing it together.

All that remains when you arrive is to pick out see pegs. When someone tells you their name, just put the picture on the see peg— it literally takes seconds. Preloading is very effective when you're going to meet fifty, one hundred, or two hundred people. Very, very effective.

And let's not forget how important your greeting is. When you shake someone's hand, really shake it—don't be a dead fish. Touch the person lightly on the shoulder or upper arm with your other hand. Look them in the eye. This effort on your part will pay off later because it shows other people that you're interested enough to want to remember them. Never underestimate the power of remembering who people are. It's the kind of honest flattery that no one is immune to.

Chapter 23—Review

Reminder from Part I—Committing Names to Memory
1. Pick a see peg for the person whose name you want to remember.
2. Turn the name into syllables, and the syllables into pictures.
3. Peg the pictures to the see peg.

The Four Rules for Meeting People
1. When shaking hands or otherwise greeting someone, always introduce yourself first.

2. When the person gives you his or her name, repeat it.
3. Ask questions and talk about a person's name.
4. Show a genuine interest in, and a concern for, the people you meet.

Preloading

Familiarizing yourself with names before you actually greet the people at any function, business meeting, or other social situation.

Chapter 23—Required Mental Exercises

Exercise 1

To review what we learned in Part I, practice pegging the names of five people you meet today. Also integrate the tips discussed in this chapter.

Exercise 2

The next time you go to any function or conference, try to make yourself aware of how many different ways you can preload the names.

24 Remembering Longer Numbers

In this lesson, you will see all your hard work with phonetics and picture words pay off!

Before we go on, I want you to spend ten minutes reviewing numbers 1 through 100 as rapidly as you can. Close the book, call out a number, and then call out the phonetics and picture word we established for the number. For example: "Seventy-eight, ca, fa, coffee," or "Fifty-eight, la, fa, leaf." Number, sound, word, in that order. Picture the word vividly and don't forget to say everything out loud. Do the exercise now.◆

Converting Longer Numbers into Picture Words

Now that the hundred numbers are fresh in your mind, I want to tell you something that you probably won't be surprised to hear. The same system that we used to create picture words for the numbers 1 through 100 can be used for any size number. If something is big or long or complicated, you can remember it easily by breaking it down into smaller sections. This is a common thread running through the Mega Memory program. It's what we did with names by breaking them down into syllables, and what we can do with numbers by breaking them down into phonetics and picture words.

Consider the number 142, for example. Let's convert it into a picture by using our phonetic alphabet. What are the three phonetics you're looking for here? "Ta" or "da" for 1; "ra" for 4; "na" for 2. Repeat the phonetics out loud. "Ta-ra-na" or "da-ra-na." "Ta-ra-na. Da-ra-na." "T-r-n." "D-r-n." What vowel sounds can you add to create words here? How about "train" or "drain"? Do you see how easy this is? Let's do a few examples together to make sure you understand how it works. As you work on the example, be sure to repeat the quoted material out loud and picture each word as vividly as you can.

Number 347: Our first phonetic is "ma" for 3. The phonetic for 4 is "ra." For 7, it's either "ca" or "ga." So we have "ma," "ra," and "ca" or "ga." "Ma-ra-ca" or "ma-ra-ga." I can't think of something with the "m," "r," and "g" sounds, but for "ma-ra-ca" I choose "mark," as in a check mark or a scratch on furniture or a car. So "mark" equals 347.

Number 491: 4 is "ra," 9 is "pa" or "ba," and 1 is "ta" or "da." "Ra-pa-ta." "Ra-pa-da." "Ra-ba-ta." "Ra-pa-da." Repeat these combinations for a few seconds and what do you come up with? I come up with "rabbit," for the "r," "b" and "t" sounds. The number 491 can be represented by a fluffy white rabbit.

Number 915: 9 is "pa" or "ba," 1 is "ta" or "da," and 5 is "la." "Pa-ta-la." "Pa-da-la." "Ba-ta-la." "Ba-da-la." Repeat them and see what picture words come to you. How about "paddle" for the "p," "d," and "l" sounds? Or "battle" for the "b," "d," and "l" sounds? "Paddle" or "battle" can represent 915. For me, "paddle" is a little better because it's more concrete, easier to picture than "battle."

Now what do you do if the number is longer, having four, five, six, or more digits? What did I say earlier? You break it down into smaller sections. Let's take the number 7783. For 7783, I have a picture of a cake with foam all over it. Why? If you worked the earlier chapters of "Advanced Mega Memory" properly, you should know. I broke 7783 into 77 and 83. What's our picture word for 77? Cake. For 83? Foam. Break the number into smaller pieces—

however many pieces you need—and use your picture words for those smaller pieces.

Let's work on another four-digit number: 3063. Close the book and figure out how you would turn 3063 into picture words ◆

It's easy—how about a moose pressing barbells? How did I arrive at that picture? I would break it into 30, for which our picture word is "moose." For 63, our picture word is "gym." When I think of a gym, I think of barbells. So a moose pressing barbells would give me 3063.

For a longer number, you would link many pictures together, using the same chaining and pegging techniques we learned in Part I of the book.

Telephone Numbers

Things would be easier if you didn't have to look up phone numbers all the time, wouldn't they? Just practice turning whatever phone numbers you want to remember into picture words, then put them together, and shortly you'll start remembering the numbers instantly.

With a phone number, by the way, you usually want to remember a person's name with it. Let's work on an example together. You want to remember Bill Smith's phone number, which is 472-2252. How do you commit it to memory using our Mega Memory techniques?

What you do is peg the phone number to Bill Smith. What is our first rule in remembering anything? We need to establish a peg, a place to put the information. We know Bill Smith, so we can peg the phone number right on him, that is, a vivid picture of him, since we think in pictures. We need to turn the number into pictures, too. That's step two. Then using action, step three, we will be able to peg the number to Bill.

So let's peg 472-2252 to Bill. I'll first break the number down into smaller sections. For 472, I'm going to use the word "raccoon." The number 4 gives me the phonetic "ra," 7 gives me the phonetic "ca," and 2 gives me the phonetic "na." So for 472, I can use a picture of a raccoon.

Then I'll break the last four numbers into two sections. We already know the picture for 22 is "na-na"—"nun." And we know the picture for 52 is "la-na"—"lion." Now taking five minutes, we can commit Bill's phone number to memory. Close the book and try to do this yourself, and then I'll explain how I did it.◆

Were you able to come up with vivid pictures full of action? I pictured Bill Smith with raccoons all around him. He keeps picking them up and throws them at a nun, with whom he is playing catch. Then a lion comes and stands behind the nun. He roars so loudly he makes the nun nervous, so she starts throwing the raccoons back to Bill faster and faster. Faster and faster, as the lion roars louder and louder. That's it.

Run that little scene in your mind two, three, four, or five times. The next time you think, "What's Bill Smith's phone number?" that scene involving raccoons, the nun, and the lion will instantly pop up in your mind. You can decipher that in a matter of seconds, to be 4-7-2-2-2-5-2.

Now here's the exciting part of the system: By creating pictures and linking them together with action, you lock whatever information you are trying to remember into your memory. When you try to recall the information, you remember the pictures for the first two or three times. Then, you begin to recall the information without going through that interim step of remembering the pictures. In Bill Smith's case, his number would come to your instantly. The pictures would stay in your unconscious. When you think of Bill, you will know his telephone number. All the groundwork you have done before starts paying off.

Here's another telephone number, 648-7910. For 648, we can use the picture word "sheriff." "Sh-ra-fa" is 6-4-8. The number 7910 could be "Cupids." "Ca-pa-da-sa" gives us 7-9-1-0. So picture in your mind a sheriff shooting at a bunch of Cupids fluttering around him, and peg that picture to whatever person or organization has that number. The next time you ask yourself, "What was that phone number?" the sheriff shooting the Cupids will come to you. You'll decode "sheriff" into "sha-ra-fa" and "Cupids" into "ca-pa-da-sa," 648 and 7910, and you'll have your phone number.

When you become skilled at it, you can even use this pegging technique with longer numbers such as bank accounts and credit cards.

Let's say you want to remember your American Express card number, for example, which is fifteen digits. First picture your American Express card, huge and larger than life. It will be your peg. Then break the number down into smaller chunks and turn each chunk into a picture. Chain those pictures together. In your mind's eye, attach it to the credit card using exaggerated, nonsensical action. The number is now committed to memory.

The next time you ask yourself, "What's my card number?" a huge American Express card will pop into your mind, along with whatever pictures you pegged to it. Just as we did with "raccoon," "nun," and "lion," you'll be able to decode the pictures in a matter of seconds.

Converting Picture Words Back to Numbers

In order to be fluid with these techniques, you need to be able to convert back and forth instantly. We've practiced converting numbers into pictures, now I want us to practice converting words back into numbers.

For example, let's take the word "casino." What number is "casino"? Say it out loud a few times: "Casino, casino, ca-si-no." "Casino" gives us the "c," "s," and "n" sounds, "ca-sa-na." "Ca" is 7, "sa" is 0, and "na" is 2. "Casino" is the number 702. (If by any chance you forget what numbers go with each phonetic, just go back to your Body List. In this case, "ca" is "collar," which is our seventh peg. "Sa" is "ceiling," our last peg, which is zero. "Na," is "knees," which is our second peg. All of which gives us the same result, 702.)

Isn't it interesting that 702 is the area code for the state of Nevada? And isn't that a great way to remember the area code for Las Vegas, Reno, and the rest of the state? Simply think of a casino. For area codes for the rest of the country, use the pegging technique for remembering telephone numbers or credit cards. To do that, in your mind's eye, create a picture of an object that reminds you of a part of the country. That picture will be your peg. Then take the area code, turn it into a picture word, and peg the two pictures together.

Let's take a few more words and turn them back into numbers. "Rainbow." Say it out loud: "Rainbow, rainbow, ra-na-ba." "Ra" is 4, "na" is 2, and "ba" is 9. So "rainbow," "ra-na-ba," is 429.

"Mint." Say it out loud: "Mint, mint, ma-na-ta." "Ma," is 3, "na" is 2, and "ta" is 1. "Mint" is 321.

Now that we know how to convert pictures and words into numbers and numbers into pictures, we have an easy way to recall any number. To remember any number—a price, a code, an account—take a few seconds to turn it into pictures and either peg those pictures to something else or chain them together. The next time you need to remember that number—when you ask yourself, "What is the price/code/account number?"—these pictures will pop into your mind. It will then take you a few more seconds to decipher them, and you'll have your answer.

Knowing the Day of the Week, for Any Date

Now I'm going to teach you something that's a lot of fun. You are going to be able to figure out the day of week for any date in history, past and future! You'll do this by using a mathematical formula. When you commit the formula to memory, you'll be able to tell on what day of the week you, a friend, or a loved one was born. You'll know on what day of the week a historical event took place. You'll know on what day of the week your parents or your Aunt Matilda and Uncle Mortimer were married. It's a fun little skill to have, a neat little parlor trick for parties, outings, and get-together when you're searching for an interesting way to entertain your friends or pass the time.

The mathematical formula has eleven steps, so please pay close attention to my explanation. In summary, it is as follows:

1. Convert the month into its numerical equivalent.
2. For the day of the month, subtract the multiple of 7 that is closest to it.

3. Save the remainder.
4. Turn the first two numbers of the year (the centuries) into their numerical equivalent.
5. Subtract the multiple of 7 that is closest to the last two digits of the year.
6. Save the remainder.
7. Divide the last two numbers of the year by 4.
8. Discard the remainder.
9. Add lines 1, 3, 4, 6, and 7.
10. Subtract the multiple of 7 closest to the answer to line 9.
11. Convert the remainder to its daily equivalent.

To make this mathematical formula work, what you essentially do is assign numbers to the four items that form a date: the month, the day, the century, and the last two digits of the year. For March 13, 1891, which will be our example, you will assign a number to March; a number to the day, which in this example is 13; a number to the century, which is the 1800s; and then a number to the year, which is 91.

Months. Your first step is to commit to memory the numbers you assign to each of these items. We start with the month. I'm going to give you the numbers, and then help you commit them to memory by using a combination of our Mega Memory techniques. There are duplicate numbers, so please don't be thrown off by that.

January is 2. For January, picture a brand-new baby in your mind. It's a baby born on New Year's Eve, wearing a party hat, and it has two huge buck teeth. January's number is 2, for the buck teeth.

February is 5. The first thing that comes to mind about February is winter and Valentine's Day. Picture giving your valentine one brand-new glove. Glove is number 5 on our Tree List, which should make it easier to remember that February's number is 5.

March is 4. The first thing I associate with March is Saint Patrick's Day, and the first thing I associate with Saint Patrick's Day is a four-leaf clover. So picture a giant four-leaf clover to better remember that the number for March is 4.

April is 0. I think of showers when I think of April, but in this case, instead of rain it's showering Cheerios. Picture big, crunchy Cheerios coming down from the sky to better remember that April's number is 0.

May is 2. We're going to picture a maypole in your mind's eye. Imagine two lovers running around the maypole, laughing and trying to catch each other. That will help you to remember that the number for May is 2.

June is 5. I think of weddings when I think of June. And when I think of weddings I think of two people in love, dancing up a storm in their wedding regalia, holding each other by their love handles. Picturing a couple holding on to their love handles at a wedding should help remind you that the number for June is 5 (just as it was for February).

July is 0. I want you to picture a giant firecracker, so that you will think of the Fourth of July. Now in your mind's eye, take some Hula Hoops and throw them over this huge firecracker. Hoop after hoop is being thrown onto the firecracker to help you remember that the number for July is 0.

August is 3. I think of summer when I think of August. Picture yourself sitting on a stool in the backyard, trying to hose yourself down. Make sure the stool is vivid; stool is number 3 on our Tree List, which will remind you that the number for August is 3.

September is 6. I think of kids going back to school in September. And I think of the joy on their parents' faces as they look forward to some peace and quiet once their kids are out of the house. Make sure you vividly see the joy on the parents' faces. Joy is our sixth picture word, which should help you remember that the number for September is 6.

October is 1. I associate Halloween with October, and I associate a jack-o'-lantern with Halloween. Picture a glowing jack-o'-lantern, which has only one tooth in its gaping mouth. That should help you remember that the number for October is 1.

November is 4. Most of us think of Thanksgiving when we think of November. Picture a big, juicy turkey running down the highway as you chase it in your car. The turkey's fast and you're fast because you really want him for your Thanksgiving dinner. Picture yourself in that car going after the turkey. Since "car" is number 4 on our Tree List, that should help you remember that the number for November is 4.

December is 6. December is Christmas. Imagine your happiness and sense of expectation standing in the living room, waiting for Santa Claus to come down the chimney. And when he does, he opens his bag and starts throwing out big bottles of Joy to everyone. This will help you remember that the number for December is 6.

Now I'd like you to review the twelve images. Each month is listed below; on the line underneath is its number and the image we created for it. So review; simply read through the list and vividly picture the image.

January?
January is 2, because you think of a January baby with two
    huge buck teeth.

February?
February is 5, because you think of giving a glove to your
    Valentine.

March?
March is 4, because you think of a four-leaf clover and Saint
    Patrick's Day.

April?
April is 0, because you imagine it raining Cheerios.

May?
May is 2, because you think of two people running around
    a maypole.

June?
June is 5, because you think of a newly married couple holding
    on to each other's love handles.

July?
July is 0, because you think of a giant firecracker on the Fourth of
    July, and you're throwing Hula Hoops over this firecracker.

August?

August is 3, because you picture yourself sitting on a stool, wearing a swimsuit, and hosing yourself down to keep cool.

September?

September is 6, because you think of the joy on parents' faces when they send the kids off to school.

October?

October is 1, because you think of a giant jack-o'-lantern with one tooth in its gaping, glowing mouth.

November?

November is 4, because you think of yourself driving a car as fast as you can, trying to run down a big juicy turkey for dinner.

December?

December is 6, because you think of Santa Claus coming down the chimney, handing out big bottles of Joy.

Now I want you to close the book and test yourself on these associations. Use a straightedge or have a partner call out the month, while you call out the number and picture the image we've created vividly. Keep going over this list until you have instant recall of the months and their numbers. Close the book and do it now.◆

Day of the month. To derive the number for the day of the month, we subtract the closest multiple of 7 from that number. Using our example of March 13, 1891, we subtract 7 from 13 and get 6. So the number assigned to the thirteenth day of the month is 13. If the date is a number less than 7, use that number from which to subtract 7. In this case, your remainder, step 3, will be zero, since we don't use negative numbers in this formula.

Centuries. Assigning numbers to centuries follows another easy formula. There are only four numbers, 6, 4, 2, and 0, and they are assigned in sequence every four centuries. We start with the 1600s.

Because it ends in the number 6, it's easy to remember, and I don't think we need to create a picture for it.

The 1700s is number 4. To create pictures, let's use our Tree List. Number 17 on our Tree List is "magazine," and 4 is a "car," so I picture myself in a car reading a magazine. Don't forget, you can create a picture using any technique you want; we could also use our list of phonetics to turn numbers 17 and 4 into pictures.

The 1800s is 2. My picture here is of a voting booth, and in the voting booth I picture a giant light switch, which I'm flicking on and off. I used the Tree List again. "Voting booth" is number 18, and "light switch" is number 2.

The 1900s is 0. I picture in my mind the nineteenth hole, and I take my golf clubs and score a 0. That's impossible (though I come close!), but remember, a nonsensical picture is always good. It will help you remember that the number for the 1900s is 0.

To review the list above, in your mind's eye, link the number with the century, using my pictures or ones that you created. Link the 1600s with 6. Link the 1700s with 4. Link the 1800s with 2. And link the 1900s with 0. Close the book and do it now.◆

As I mentioned, the numbers assigned to centuries repeat every four years. So for any date beginning in the year 2000, the number 6 is assigned again. For the 2100s, we assign 4, and so on. Going back in time before the 1600s, you do the reverse. The 1500s is number 0. The 1400s is 2. The 1300s is 4. The 1200s is 6 again, and so on. Get the picture? Take a few minutes to review this concept. The most important centuries are the last four, the 1600s, 1700s, 1800s, and 1900s. If you remember that their numbers are 6, 4, 2, and 0, everything else will fall into place. Close the book and review these numbers now.◆

Last two digits of the year. In our example of March 13, 1891, we have assigned a 2 for the 1800s. Now we have to assign numbers for the actual years, steps 5 through 8. To do this, we'll be converting numbers into other numbers, something that we haven't yet done. Let's continue with 91.

For step 5, we have to find the closest multiple of 7 to our number (91) without going over, and subtract it from the number. In the case of 91, the closest multiple is 91 because 7 times 13 is 91. Subtracting 91 from 91 gives us 0. You will be using the 0 in a minute, which is step 6.

In step 7, we have to account for leap years. Divide the last two digits by 4 and discard any remainder, step 8. Number 91 divided by 4 is 22, with a remainder of 3. So our two numbers for 91 are 0 and 22.

Now on to steps 9 through 11, to finish up our formula.

For step 9, we have to add the month, the day, the century, and our two numbers for the last two digits of the year. Let's do it for March 13, 1891. The numbers we found for each of the 5 steps are as follows: March is 4; the thirteenth day is 6; the 1800s is 2; for 91 we got 0 and 22. Add 4, 6, 2, 0 and 22 and you get 34.

Step 10: Subtract the closest multiple of 7 from 34. The closest multiple is 28; 34 minus 28 is 6. Our final step, 11, is to convert the number to the day of the week.

Days of the week. Converting days of the week to numbers is very easy. We start with 1 for Sunday, and continue in sequence, ending with 7 for Saturday.

So for our final step, 11, we have to convert 6 to the day of the week. And that's Friday. You now know that March 13, 1891, was a Friday.

To make sure you understand the formula, I want you to use it to tell me what day of week December 7, 1941, fell on. I will then give you the answer. You can keep the book open for reference. Do it now.◆

All right. December is what number? (Santa is handing out bottles of Joy.) It's number 6.

The day of the month is 7. To come up with our assigned number, we subtract the closest multiple of 7, which is of course 7. Our assigned number is 0.

The number we assign to the 1900s is also 0.

Now the last two digits of the year, 41: What's the nearest multiple of 7? It's 35. Subtracting 35 from 41 we get 6. That's our first number for the year. To calculate the second, we divide the year by 4 and discard the remainder. The number 41 divided by 4 is 10, which is our second number.

Now add the month (6 for December), the day (0 for the seventh), the number assigned to the century (0 for the 1900s), and the two numbers assigned to the last two digits of the year (6 and 10). Adding up 6, 0, 0, 6, and 10, we get 22. Subtract the multiple of 7 closest to this sum. In this case it's 21, so 22 minus 21 is 1. Converting our number to the day of the week, we get Sunday. And if you haven't figured it out by now, December 7, 1941, was the date of the Japanese attack on Pearl Harbor. Anyone in the United States who was alive then remembers it was on a Sunday morning.

You may be wondering what you do if the last two digits of the year add up to a number less than 7, as in October 1, 1906. In cases like that, as with days of the month that are less than 7, subtracting 7 would give you a negative number for a remainder. So you would use a zero.

To see how this would work, let's use the formula with October 1, 1906.

For the number of the month, step 1, we get 1 (we visualized the jack-o'-lantern with one tooth). The day is 1 (step 2), and the remainder after we subtract 7 is 0 (step 3), since we don't use negative numbers. For the 1900s (step 4), we assign a 0. The last two digits of the year are 06 (step 5), and subtracting 7 from 6 leaves us with a remainder of 0 again (step 6), because we don't use negative numbers. Dividing 06 by 4, we get 1 (step 7), with a remainder of 2 (step 8).

Now we add steps 1, 3, 4, 6, and 7, or 1, 0, 0, 0, and 1. Our sum is 2. Since the sum is less than 7, we can't subtract any multiple of 7 (step 10) or we would end up with a negative number again. So we convert this 2 directly into the day of the week, which is a Monday.

Chapter 24—Review

Converting Longer Numbers into Pictures
1. Break any long number into smaller sections.
2. Choose picture words for each section.
3. Chain the pictures together.

Committing Telephone Numbers to Memory
1. Create a vivid picture of the person whose phone number you want to remember. That is your peg.
2. Break the telephone number into smaller sections and create pictures for each section.
3. Put the pictures together and peg them to your picture of the person.

Knowing the Day of Week, for Any Date
1. Convert the month into its numerical equivalent.
2. For the day of the month, subtract the multiple of 7 that is closest to it.
3. Save the remainder.
4. Turn the first two numbers of the year (the centuries) into their numerical equivalent.
5. Subtract the multiple of 7 that is closest to the last two digits of the year.
6. Save the remainder.
7. Divide the last two numbers of the year by 4.
8. Discard the remainder.
9. Add lines 1, 3, 4, 6, and 7.
10. Subtract the multiple of 7 closest to the answer to step 9.
11. Convert the remainder to its daily equivalent.

Months

January	2	July	0
February	5	August	3
March	4	September	6

April	0	October	1
May	2	November	4
June	5	December	6

Days of the Month

Numerical equivalent: Subtract multiple of 7 closest to the day, without going over. If the date is 1 through 7, use that number.

Centuries

1600s	6
1700s	4
1800s	2
1900s	0

Daily Equivalents

Sunday	1
Monday	2
Tuesday	3
Wednesday	4
Thursday	5
Friday	6
Saturday	7

Chapter 24—Required Mental Exercises

Exercise I

Next to each number, write the phonetic sounds corresponding to each number, and think of a picture word.

173
314
339
116
818
919
596

720
500
261
287
494
672
946
789

1061
7458
8199
3276
5523
6600

244-3922
713-7281
$21,932
$512,215
561-0098
922-9063
$8,607
$333,499

Exercise 2

Provide the corresponding three-digit number for the list of words given.

1. terror
2. margin
3. castle
4. loudly
5. passionate
6. bombs
7. topic
8. wrist

9. panic
10. laughter
11. fashion
12. enlarge
13. vacuum
14. fallacy
15. caffeine
16. ravioli
17. manage
18. chopper
19. native
20. dazzle

(Answers: terror—144; margin—346; castle—705; loudly—515; passionate—962; bombs—930; topic—197; wrist—401; panic—927; laughter—581; fashion—862; enlarge—256; vacuum—873; fallacy—850; caffeine—782; ravioli—485; manage—326; chopper—694; native—218; dazzle—105)

25　Remembering Playing Cards

I held a workshop in Las Vegas once, with several thousand people in the auditorium. I said to the crowd, "This is Mega Memory class. How many people are interested in learning how to remember playing cards?" All hands shot up. "That's great," I said, excited, "but once you learn this, please don't use it as an unfair advantage against your friends to make money." A guy in the back of the room yelled out, "Why not?"

How you use your skills is up to you, but I guarantee that once you have become proficient with the techniques taught in this chapter, you're going to have a big advantage over your fellow card players. Those techniques are particularly suited for any game for which it's important to remember what cards were played by whom, and when, such as bridge. Such a game will change from one of pure luck to a game of skill, i.e., memory, and you will have a distinct edge.

As we've been saying throughout the book, to remember anything, you need three things: (1) a place to put the information, which is a peg; (2) the information turned to a vivid picture; and (3) the mental glue to hold it in place, which is action. We've already had a lot of practice with steps one and three, creating pegs and putting pictures together using action. Those steps will work the same way with playing cards. The only new aspect of this process as far as playing cards are concerned, is step two, converting the playing cards into pictures. We'll spend the bulk of this chapter learning how to do that—using our picture words and the Body List. Then I'll give you some examples of how you can use this skill when you're actually playing.

Have a pack of cards handy for some of the exercises in this chapter.

Establishing Pictures for Playing Cards

We're going to establish a picture vocabulary for all fifty-two playing cards. It's not going to be that difficult. As a matter of fact, in the next few minutes, you're going to have a picture for every single playing card committed to memory, because you're already halfway there, having created picture words for the numbers 1 through 100. Now we're going to assign a number for every playing card. Once we do that, our work is done, because we already have pictures for all the numbers.

There's a simple way to do this. Playing cards have four basic suits: spades, diamonds, clubs, and hearts. We will assign certain key numbers to each of the four suits.

Spades. Imagine that you have a small shovel—a "spade"—in your hands. In your mind's eye, take that spade and chop your toes off with it! "Ouch!" Now, what number is "toes" on our picture word list? It's number 10: "ta," which is 1, and "sa," which is 0, so "toes" is number 10. We're going to start the process of establishing pictures by assigning the number 10 to spades.

Diamonds. Let's continue with diamonds. Picture a big moose in your mind. And all over that moose are hundreds of diamonds. He's draped in diamonds, shimmering and glistening in the light. Everything about this moose is sparkling, his ears, his toes, his back, and his antlers—brilliant diamonds are hanging everywhere. See that in your mind's eye as vividly as you can. Now what number is "moose" on our picture word list? Number 30? So the key number for diamonds is 30.

Clubs. Picture Lassie in your mind's eye, everybody's favorite collie. Now picture a club, a big fat club, the kind that we think of cavemen using. In your mind's eye, imagine taking the club and swinging it at Lassie, while she bravely barks back, "Arf, arf, arf!" avoiding your blows as you continue to swing that club. "Lassie" is number 50 on our picture word list, so the suit of clubs will be assigned the number 50.

Hearts. Now picture in your mind a vase, a white porcelain vase in front of a sunlit window. The vase is encrusted with ruby-red hearts. The hearts are of all shapes, brilliantly reflecting the sunlight. Vase is number 80 on our picture word list, so the suit of hearts is assigned the number 80.

Let's review the four key numbers above by answering the following question. What number goes with spades? A picture of a spade cutting off your toes should pop into your mind. The number is 10. What number goes with diamonds? There's the diamond moose, which is number 30. What number goes with clubs? You're trying to beat Lassie with the club, and Lassie is number 50. How about hearts? They're on a beautiful white vase, reflecting sunlight. Vase is number 80.

Make sure you have these four key numbers firmly in your mind. Review them, by covering up one side of the list below, and then the other, to make sure that when you call out the suit you get the right number, and when you call out a number, you get the right suit. Do it now.◆

Spades	10
Diamonds	30
Clubs	50
Hearts	80

Now, how do we establish a number for each card within the suit? There are thirteen cards in every suit; we simply assign a number to each card, 1 through 13, and add it to the key number we've established for the suit.

In Mega Memory, we start with the ace, then continue with 2, 3, 4, 5, 6, 7, 8, 9, 10, jack, queen, king. The jack is 11; the queen, 12; and the king, 13.

Spades. The suit of spades is number 10. To establish a number for the ace of spades, which is 1, add it to 10, which equals 11. So the ace of spades will be number 11. The 2 of spades is 12, because 10 plus 2 is 12. The 3 of spades is 13, the 4 of spades is 14, and so on. The jack of spades is 21 (add 11 to 10), the queen is 22 (add 12 to 10), and the king is 23 (add 13 to 10). We now have a number for each of the spades.

Let's recap by doing a review drill. Give me the numbers associated with the cards, calling the numbers out loud. Use a straightedge to cover up the answers or do this with a partner.

What is the number for the 7 of spades?
17

What is the number for the 10 of spades?
20

What's the number for the ace of spades?
11

What's the number for the jack of spades?
21

What's the number for the king of spades?
23

What's the number for the queen of spades?
22

What's the number for the jack of spades?
21

What's the number for the 2 of spades?
12

What's the number for the ace of spades?
11

What's the number for the 8 of spades?
18

What's the number for the 9 of spades?
19

What's the number for the 5 of spades?
15

How quickly were you able to come up with the answers? In the drill below, I want you to work on speed, i.e., instant recall. Cover one side of the list, then the other. When you call out one item, its corresponding number or card should pop into your mind immediately. You must have it cold in both directions. I want you to drill for five to ten minutes, either alone or with a partner, so you have instant recall from number to card and card to number. Say everything out loud. Do the drill now.◆

7 of spades	17
10 of spades	20
jack of spades	21
king of spades	23
queen of spades	22
2 of spades	12
ace of spades	11
8 of spades	18
9 of spades	19
5 of spades	15
6 of spades	16
3 of spades	13
4 of spades	14

We're going to drill once more, mixing it all up, to make sure we're at speed before we go on to the next suit. I'm going to give you a number or a card, and you're going to instantly say its opposite. Use a straightedge or do it with a partner. Remember, say it out loud, and it must be done in a rapid-fire manner.

Ready? Let's begin.

19?
9 of spades

23?
king of spades

20?
10 of spades

11?
ace of spades

5 of spades?
15

8 of spades?
18

king of spades?
23

jack of spades?
21

10 of spades?
20

7 of spades?
17

11?
ace of spades

16?
6 of spades

22?
queen of spades

21?
jack of spades

12?
2 of spades

ace of spades?
11

Were you up to speed? Go back to your two-column list above and drill all the spades for five to ten minutes more to make sure it's firmly ingrained in your memory.◆

Diamonds. Let's continue with diamonds. What is the key number for diamonds? The diamonds were draped all over a moose, number 30. Our key number for diamonds is 30.

Drill the two columns below until both numbers and cards are instantly recallable in both directions. Say the name of the card on the left, instantly calling out the number; or say the number, then call out the name of the card. Do this back and forth for about five or ten mintues before continuing.◆

7 of diamonds	37
10 of diamonds	40
jack of diamonds	41
king of diamonds	43
queen of diamonds	42
2 of diamonds	32
ace of diamonds	31
8 of diamonds	38
9 of diamonds	39
5 of diamonds	35
6 of diamonds	36
3 of diamonds	33
4 of diamonds	34

I'm going to drill you one more time to make sure you're at speed before we go to clubs. I'm going to give you a number or a card, and you're going to instantly call out loud the opposite. As before, use a straightedge or do it with a partner. Rapid-fire, please—and out loud.

Ready? Begin.

31?
ace of diamonds

36?
6 of diamonds

40?
10 of diamonds

queen of diamonds?
42

king of diamonds?
43

jack of diamonds?
41

3 of diamonds?
33

5 of diamonds?
35

9 of diamonds?
39

10 of diamonds?
40

jack of diamonds?
41

queen of diamonds?
42

king of diamonds?
43

jack of diamonds?
41

queen of diamonds?
42

king of diamonds?
43

Now I want you to take your pack of cards. Pick out the diamonds and the spades, and shuffle them well. Holding the deck in your hand facedown, flip each card over one at a time. As soon as you see what the card is, instantly call out its corresponding number. Do that as fast as you can. After you go through the stack, reshuffle and do it again. Repeat this for about ten to fifteen minutes—I want your recall to be absolutely instantaneous. Close the book, and do the exercise now.◆

Clubs. Now we're going to continue with the clubs. What were you doing with the club? Trying to beat up on Lassie, who is number 50? So our key number for clubs is 50.

As you did with diamonds, drill the two columns below in both directions. Say the name of the card on the left, instantly calling out the number; or say the number, then call out the name of the card. Do this back and forth for about five or ten minutes before continuing.◆

7 of clubs	57
10 of clubs	60
jack of clubs	61
king of clubs	63
queen of clubs	62
2 of clubs	52
ace of clubs	51
8 of clubs	58
9 of clubs	59
5 of clubs	55

6 of clubs	56
3 of clubs	53
4 of clubs	54

Now let's do our first test to make sure we're up to speed. After I give you the number or the card, instantly call out its opposite. Use a straightedge or do it with a partner. Rapid-fire and out loud.

Ready? Begin.

51?
ace of clubs

55?
5 of clubs

59?
9 of clubs

60?
10 of clubs

63?
king of clubs

12?
Aha! It's the 2 of spades.

5 of clubs?
55

63?
king of clubs

60?
10 of clubs

58?
8 of clubs

36?
6 of diamonds

19?
9 of spades

Go back to your double-column list and drill clubs for five to ten minutes. Make sure you know the number and the card in either direction. Do it now.◆

Hearts. Now on to hearts. What's your picture of hearts? They're all over that beautiful vase, which gives you number 80 as our key number.

Drill the two columns below as you've been doing. Say the name of the card on the left, instantly calling out the number; then call out the number, giving its corresponding card. Do this back and forth for about five or ten minutes before continuing.◆

7 of hearts	87
10 of hearts	90
jack of hearts	91
king of hearts	93
queen of hearts	92
2 of hearts	82
ace of hearts	81
8 of hearts	88
9 of hearts	89
5 of hearts	85
6 of hearts	86
3 of hearts	83
4 of hearts	84

Now let's do our drill to make sure we're at speed. I'm going to give you a number or a card and you give me its opposite. Remember, speed is important, and do it out loud.

Ready? Begin.

89?
9 of hearts

83?
3 of hearts

93?
king of hearts

81?
ace of hearts

90?
10 of hearts

88?
8 of hearts

84?
4 of hearts

How about the 3 of hearts?
83

jack of hearts?
91

queen of hearts?
92

king of hearts?
93

Now take five or ten minutes to review the double-column list of hearts above, to make sure the numbers are fully ingrained in your memory.◆

Let's take your pack of cards again, and do the same thing with the clubs and hearts that we did with the spades and diamonds. Shuffle the clubs and hearts, hold the deck facedown, and flip over the cards, calling out their corresponding number as rapidly as you can. Spend the next fifteen minutes with these two suits. It's a great way to review. Close the book and do that now.◆

Now repeat the exercise with the entire deck of cards. Shuffle it well and spend fifteen to twenty minutes flipping the cards over and calling out their numbers. Do it now.◆

If you are an avid card player, I would recommend that you practice this exercise off and on for the next few days. The more you rehearse, the faster your memory will work, and the better you'll be at remembering what you need to remember when you are actually playing.

For the last exercise in this lesson, we will do a further variation on the drill with the deck of cards. We have practiced calling out the number when we flip over the card and seeing its face. Now, since we have mastered that, I want you to practice calling out the picture word for the number represented by each card. For example, you flip a card over and see that it's the 4 of hearts. What is the picture word for the 4 of hearts?

Let's figure it out. The number for the 4 of hearts is 84 (80 plus 4). And what's the picture word that we learned for number 84 a few chapters ago? A picture of a frying pan should have popped into your mind. So the picture word for the 4 of hearts is "fry."

Let's do one more. What's the picture word for the ace of diamonds?

The ace of diamonds is number 31 (30 plus 1). And what's the picture that pops into your mind for 31—a picture of a maid. "Maid" is the answer.

So now I want you to start flipping those cards over. When you see each card, think of the number, but call out the picture word that the number represents. You are using the phonetic alphabet you've already learned, and seeing each picture clearly in your mind's eye.

Close the book and start flipping now.◆

Techniques for Playing

You have now committed to memory the numbers and pictures for all fifty-two playing cards. Now, if you see someone play a 4 of hearts, for example, you'll know it's 84, which is the picture of a frying pan. That will be a great advantage when you are actually playing.

How do you use these pictures? There are two basic ways: The first is in knowing what person played what card when a group of you are playing.

Let's assume you are playing a game with three other people, bridge, for example. In bridge, it's very important to try to follow what cards have been played by what person. Keep in mind our three steps in remembering any piece of information, and that you now have pictures for every card. To use those pictures you'll need what?—a place to peg them on. You can use any of your peg lists for that purpose. When a person throws away a card or wins a particular card, simply create a picture of that card, and put it on a peg.

The House List works best for me in card games. Assign one room to each player, so that everyone has a room. We've established five pegs in each room, so player A, for example, has room 1, your living room, with its sofa, stereo, bookcase, lounge chair, and television. Player 2 might have your dining room, with its own five pegs. Of course, you can make these peg lists as long as you want, depending on your level of proficiency with Mega Memory.

When you want to remember a particular card a player throws away, take the picture of that card and put it on the first peg in the first room. If player A threw away the 4 of hearts for example, you would peg the frying pan to the sofa, perhaps imagining a delicious little sofa cooking in a huge frying pan. You could do this for however many cards you wanted to. It's like having a filing cabinet right there above each player's head. You can look anytime you want to, and remember what cards have been played by whom. Your great advantage, of course, is that you're the only one who has access to this information.

Your Mega Memory techniques can also come in handy where someone is going to test you by calling out cards or flipping them over, and you need to remember the exact order. When a card is flipped over, you will instantly know the picture for it. Use the same pegging technique you used above. You might prefer your other lists, the Body List or the Tree List, for this purpose. That's fine. The important thing is just putting the next card called out or flipped over onto a peg.

Some people prefer chaining when playing cards. They take the picture of each card played and create a ludicrous story with it. It's just like our Statue of Liberty story, getting crazier and crazier as it goes along. But by reviewing it in their mind, these players can remember the exact order in which the cards were played or given out.

Even if you have no special interest in cards, the memory exercises in this chapter are excellent for improving your memory skills in general and speed in particular. Just get a deck of cards and spend the time to establish the numbers and pictures for all fifty-two cards. And once you have them, they'll be yours to use as you wish.

Chapter 25—Review

Numerical Equivalents for Playing Cards

Spades 10

ace of spades	11
2 of spades	12
3 of spades	13
4 of spades	14
5 of spades	15
6 of spades	16
7 of spades	17
8 of spades	18
9 of spades	19
10 of spades	20
jack of spades	21
queen of spades	22
king of spades	23

Diamonds 30

ace of diamonds	31
2 of diamonds	32
3 of diamonds	33
4 of diamonds	34
5 of diamonds	35
6 of diamonds	36

7 of diamonds	37
8 of diamonds	38
9 of diamonds	39
10 of diamonds	40
jack of diamonds	41
queen of diamonds	42
king of diamonds	43

Clubs 50

ace of clubs	51
2 of clubs	52
3 of clubs	53
4 of clubs	54
5 of clubs	55
6 of clubs	56
7 of clubs	57
8 of clubs	58
9 of clubs	59
10 of clubs	60
jack of clubs	61
queen of clubs	62
king of clubs	63

Hearts 80

ace of hearts	81
2 of hearts	82
3 of hearts	83
4 of hearts	84
5 of hearts	85
6 of hearts	86
7 of hearts	87
8 of hearts	88
9 of hearts	89
10 of hearts	90
jack of hearts	91
queen of hearts	92
king of hearts	93

Chapter 25—Required Mental Exercise

Exercise
Write two responses for each card: the number corresponding to the card and the picture word corresponding to each number.

Number	**Picture Word**
1. 7 of clubs	
2. jack of spades	
3. 2 of spades	
4. 3 of clubs	
5. queen of clubs	
6. 10 of hearts	
7. ace of diamonds	
8. 10 of diamonds	
9. 6 of hearts	
10. 5 of diamonds	
11. king of diamonds	
12. 9 of clubs	
13. king of hearts	
14. 4 of spades	
15. 8 of hearts	

Answers

1.	7 of clubs	57	lock
2.	jack of spades	21	net
3.	2 of spades	12	tin
4.	3 of clubs	53	lamb
5.	queen of clubs	62	chain
6.	10 of hearts	90	bus
7.	ace of diamonds	31	maid
8.	10 of diamonds	40	rice
9.	6 of hearts	86	fish
10.	5 of diamonds	35	mail
11.	king of diamonds	43	ram

12.	9 of clubs	59	leap
13.	king of hearts	93	palm
14.	4 of spades	14	tire
15.	8 of hearts	88	fife

26 Day-to-day Reminders: From Birthdays to Presidents

In this chapter, I am going to give you more examples of how you can apply the Mega Memory techniques to everyday problems and tasks, like remembering birthdays and anniversaries, knowing where you parked the car, and not forgetting specific chores you set yourself at bedtime for the following day. Many involve numbers and the picture words you learned in the beginning of Part II. Using these techniques will make your life easier and a little more orderly, and you won't be dependent on paper and pencil.

Always keep in mind that Mega Memory is a process of filing information in a particular way for retrieval at a later date. Once you begin applying these techniques to release the photographic memory you already have, the techniques become second nature to you. Your unconscious gets into the habit of operating this way, and the techniques are applied without your making a conscious decision to use them. It all happens automatically, somewhat like breathing.

And keep this in mind, too. The examples I will give you in this chapter should be regarded as starters, jumping-off points to help you create your own techniques for situations that particularly apply to you. Other memory specialists are very detailed and specific on how to apply each and every technique. That's vastly different from the theory I've developed at the American Memory Institute, which is to give you as much free rein as possible. Yes, as you've seen, there are certainly specific rules to follow, but I also hope you've heard me say enough times that Mega Memory is tailored to your needs in particular. You proceed at your own pace. Use what works best for you. This has to do with the five stages of thought that I discussed in Part I: think, emote, look/search, create, know. These are the five stages your mind goes through when processing information, either for the first time or when recalling it later. And it's this process you will be working with as you file away information in the following exercises and techniques.

I also stressed that when you create something, you know it. Mega Memory allows, in fact, it begs for, the individual to be creative. I've been telling you that once you have mastered the techniques, it's not so much a question of right and wrong, as one of "good, better, best." Something might work for me, but something else may work better for you. As long as you understand the basics of each technique, feel free to use it however you want to. I hope you read this chapter with that principle very much in mind. Ultimately, Mega Memory is what you make it.

You now have absorbed about 90 percent of the Mega Memory system. If you've done the work, you've exercised your mind, and your recall ability is good. You've been stretching your imagination, too. At this point, it's simply a matter of wanting to remember, staying within the parameters you've learned, and taking the simple steps required to plug information properly into new situations. We're now putting the icing on the cake.

Remembering Birthdays and Anniversaries

Remembering someone's birthday or an anniversary is almost as important as remembering their name. We all like to be remembered, especially by the people we love. I think that's why the ritual of celebrating birthdays and anniversaries is so universally followed. Our birthdays and anniversaries are one of those small but very important things that make us who we are. When others remember these dates, they tell us they care.

To remember birthdays, we use our old three-step rule of remembering anything: a place to put the information, which is the peg; the information turned into a picture; and action putting the picture to the peg. A birthday falls under the same parameters. Your biggest question will probably be, how do you turn a birthday into pictures? To find your answer, think of it in this way: A birthday is a series of numbers. What you have to do is turn the numbers into pictures, which you have been practicing in the last few chapters. Once you've done that, the rest will be very easy.

Let's say your wife's birthday is November 20. How do you remember it? Well, November is the eleventh month, and we know the picture word for number 11 is what? "Ta-da"—"toad." What about number 20? Number 2 is "na," and 0 is "sa." "Na-sa"— "nose." November 20 is "nose" and "toad." In your mind's eye, I want you to see your wife opening a birthday present, and when she opens it, a giant toad jumps out right onto her and starts kissing her, really smooching, right on her nose. It kisses her so hard, her nose turns red. Picture that in your mind's eye, as clearly as you can.

Why do we include the birthday present? It's our peg, our reference point. You'll know "toad" and "nose," numbers 11 and 20, are associated with your wife's birthday. And when you ask yourself what her birthday is, that picture will flash into your mind, and you'll be able to decode it in a few seconds. Your reference point can be anything associated with that date. You also might have used a birthday cake, for example, having the toad jump out of it.

We can apply the same technique to remembering anniversaries or any other important date. Just think of an obvious thing associated with that date, something already in your knowledge bank, and make it your reference point. For a wedding anniversary, you can choose a wedding ring, a wedding gown, the couple walking down an aisle, any picture that reminds you of a wedding anniversary. And don't forget to include the person or persons in your picture.

That will tell you whose birth or anniversary or any other date you are remembering.

Let's say you were trying to remember June 19, the wedding anniversary of your Aunt Martha and Uncle George. June is the sixth month, and the picture word for number 6 is Joy. (Remember, I asked you to picture the dishwashing liquid.) Our picture word for number 19 is "tape." So in your mind's eye, picture Aunt Martha and Uncle George kissing each other right after the ceremony. Suddenly, Martha produces a big, yellow bottle of Joy and whacks George over the head with it. To stop her, he takes out a big roll of Scotch tape and starts taping her up.

Later when you think, "When's Aunt Martha and Uncle George's anniversary?" in your mind's eye you'll see them at the altar, Martha whacking George with Joy and George taping her up with Scotch tape. The wedding regalia will be your peg, while the Joy and the tape will be your dates, which you will be able to decode as being June 19.

If you want to include the year, just use the techniques we learned in Chapter 24, on numbers. Let's say George and Martha were married in 1960. Break 1960 into two sections. We have number 19 again—more tape!—and "cheese," which was our picture word for number 60. Just continue the scene, adding more tape and cheese. Perhaps coming to Martha's defense, the maid of honor takes a big piece of cheese, and starts hitting George with it. Coming to George's defense, the best man takes out an even bigger roll of Scotch tape, and starts taping both Martha and the maid of honor together.

Run the entire scene through your mind a couple of times: George and Martha kissing, Martha hitting George with Joy, George taping up Martha, the maid of honor hitting George with cheese, the best man taping up both Martha and the maid of honor. Can you see how you can have fun building on this as far as you want to go? The next time you ask yourself when is George and Martha's anniversary, this scene will pop into your mind. And as I've said before, eventually, just the dates will come to you, as the pictures remain in your unconscious.

Remembering Hobbies and Other Personal Data

Other personal information falls under the same parameters as birthdays and anniversaries, except that there are no numbers involved. Let's assume, for example, that a colleague, or someone you've just met at a party, told you they enjoy operating a hand radio as a hobby. You want to make a quick mental note to remember this information.

I would first create a detailed picture of the radio itself, or anything that represents the radio to me: the antenna, the box, the microphone, the earphone. I might then think of the person sitting on a park bench or at home, as she listens to the radio. But that's too logical. I need to add nonsensical action. I could exaggerate the size and color of the radio; I could give it a magnetic field of some kind, which causes it to push away from my friend, while she has to struggle to hold on to it. Or perhaps her whole house is a hand radio, and I see her walking from room to room, listening to the sound.

The information will be locked in after a few seconds. Later in the party or that week, or weeks and even months down the road, when I see this woman I'll have a general idea of what her hobby is. I can use it to start a conversation, bringing up what I know is one of her favorite topics.

The same thing can be done for someone's job, where someone likes to go on vacation, what someone likes to eat, virtually any piece of information you want to remember about a person. Simply turn that information into a picture, and using action, put both pictures together in a ludicrous, nonsensical way. Those few seconds of work will pay great dividends later.

And remember, you can now commit to memory any piece of information that has numbers in it. You know how to convert numbers into pictures by using our phonetic alphabet and our hundred picture words. And you can convert pictures back into numbers, too. Because you worked so hard drilling them in the beginning of this section, numbers, phonetics, and picture words are all now at your mental fingertips, instantly recallable, in whatever way you need them.

Where's My Car?

You parked your car in a big garage downtown, enjoyed a wonderful dinner with old friends laughing and telling stories till all hours of the night. You return to the garage, ready to drive home, and suddenly you realize you've forgotten where you parked your car.

I don't think there's anyone who hasn't been in that situation. Like everything else, the key to remembering where you parked the car, is in filing away the information when you park it. Use any of your peg lists for that purpose.

Let's say you parked the car in level 5. What's number 5 on the Tree List? Glove. As you walk away from the car, in your mind's eye picture a big, black glove sliding over the car for protection. When you're back and ask yourself where the car is, that picture will pop into your mind. You'll know "glove" is number 5 on the Tree List, and you'll have your level.

You can remember more complex information. Let's say the car is in 5D. I'd cover the car with the glove and add a mnemonic: a whole bunch of barking dogs. When I come back, and the picture of the glove covering the car with the barking dogs inside pops into my mind, I know I'm at 5D.

Once your mind is thoroughly trained, this is all so easy. You'll be creating pictures and putting them together almost automatically, wherever you are. Not only does it take just a few seconds, you don't have to rely on pen and paper.

Mental Reminders

How many times have you tried to remind yourself to ask someone a particular question when you see them next, or to do a particular task, and when the time comes to carry out the action, you forget to do it? Your Mega Memory can come in handy in these situations as well.

Let's say you tell yourself, "You know, the next time I see my friend John I want to ask him how his mother is doing, because I heard she was in the hospital." To remind yourself to do it, in your mind's eye simply create a picture of John and a picture of something that reminds you of the hospital, perhaps a hospital bed or a masked surgeon. Then put the two pictures together in a nonsensical way, perhaps the surgeon operating on John's stomach while John gives him instructions or argues with him. You've just gone through your three steps: picking a peg (John), creating pictures, and putting them together.

The next time you see John, what will pop into your mind? That picture, and it will remind you of what you wanted to ask John. This might happen immediately, or after you've exchanged a few words. "Yes, John, I'm doing great. Oh, by the way how's your mom? I heard she was in the hospital."

You can use this technique any time you either want to say something to someone or ask a question. Perhaps I want to see a particular movie, and I know that Mary sees a lot of movies. The next time I see her, I want to remind myself to ask her about it. In your mind's eye, picture lots of celluloid unwinding from a huge reel and wrapping around Mary. Or perhaps Mary is zooming through the air, holding a movie camera and filming everything she sees. And the next time you see Mary, one of these pictures will pop into your mind as you are talking to her. And you'll say to yourself, "Oh, I remember. I wanted to ask her about such and such a movie."

Another thing we tend to forget is the great idea we have before going to bed or the task we set ourselves for the next day. A good way to remember this piece of information is to use whatever objects are around you—maybe it's a book, a pen, something on the bed stand—take it from its normal place, and put it where you will have to see it in the morning. Just throw a book, let's say, on the floor in the middle of the room, and in your mind's eye, peg the information you want to remember to it. Use action and create a ludicrous scene; that's all you have to do.

The first thing you're going to see in the morning is this book lying in the middle of the room. As you pick it up you'll think, "Oh, yeah. I had to do such and such," or, "I had a great idea for my next book."

That is a very effective technique that can be used in a lot of situations, such as your den or office. In Part I, I talked about creating a Reach List in your office, as an additional peg list. You can take any item from this Reach List and make an even stronger peg out of it by moving it to a place it does not belong. For example, my office at the American Memory Institute is a hectic place, with people walking in asking questions, people saying things to each other loudly so that they can be heard over the din, phones ringing. I'm often on the phone myself. Many times, when I'm in the middle of a conversation, I'll remember something I have to do before I leave the office. I'll just take something off my desk, throw it by the door, and peg it. Twenty minutes later, as I'm rushing out to an appointment, I look down, I see what's on the floor, and I remember what I pegged to it. I know exactly what I have to do before I leave. And it's easier and quicker than jotting down a note.

Presidents, State Capitals, and Other Lists

You can also use Mega Memory techniques to help remember lists of Presidents, state capitals, or any other information that used to be taught by rote. I think the Mega Memory techniques are a quicker and more interesting way to learn these things. And because they're so much fun, they're much better motivators.

Let's say, for example, you are trying to memorize the list of our Presidents. One way to do it is to sit there and read through the list, and do it over and over again, until some of it penetrates your memory. Using Mega Memory, you break the information down into smaller pieces, and then chain it together or peg it to something you already know.

You are trying to remember the twenty-first President, Chester Arthur, and the fact that he was inaugurated in 1881. Here's how I would remember all the information. The smaller pieces I have to picture are: 21, Chester Arthur, and 1881. Number 21 can be turned into phonetics, "na" and "ta," which give me the picture word "net." I picture in my mind a big butterfly net. In this net is a treasure chest. I picture myself opening the treasure chest, and seeing beautiful paintings. I take one of those pieces of great art, and notice that it's not really art but a TV. I smash the TV over the head of a big fat man. That's it. If I run this scene in my mind a couple of times, I will have committed our twenty-first President, Chester Arthur, to memory. Now let's decode the picture. "Net" is our picture word for number 21. The two mnemonics, "chest" and "art," give me "Chester" and "Arthur." The TV gives me number 18, and the fat man, "fa-ta," gives me number 8 and number 1, 1881.

If I were teaching school, for example, I'd use this method to have the kids learn all our Presidents. Not only is the information important to know, by doing it in this way, which makes them more motivated, we would be providing more of a sense of accomplishment and self-esteem.

Learning states and their capitals, another list now done by repetition, can be memorized by using Mega Memory in the same way as the list of Presidents. Consider Arkansas, whose capital is Little Rock. Break it down into smaller pieces: "Ark-can-sas" and "Little Rock." Because it's an abstract term, we need to convert Arkansas into sound-alike syllables. The first syllable is "ark." Picture a big boat, like Noah's ark. The next syllable is "kan." How about a picture of a tin can—"can"? And "saw" for the last syllable. "Little Rock" is an automatic picture—a little rock. So I want you to picture yourself stepping onto a little rock, seeing an ark on one side and a tin can on the other. You then produce a huge saw, trying to decide which object to saw in half. You have your pictures: "a little rock, ark-can-saw." Little Rock, Arkansas.

If you wanted to remember the state capitals in alphabetical order, you would use a peg list, like your House List for example, and put all the pictures you created on consecutive pegs. Or peg them to the first fifty picture words we created for our numbers. I guarantee you'll have more fun doing it than if you used simple repetition.

Any information, no matter how advanced, can be committed to memory as long as you use the same basic principles. Break the information into smaller chunks, turn each chunk into a picture, and then put everything together by chaining or pegging.

The chemical elements of the periodic table are a good example of this. Let's say you are trying to remember the basic facts about carbon. Its atomic number is 6. Its atomic weight is 12.01. How do we commit this information to memory so that it's there for us later? Very simple. First of all, break the information into smaller chunks. You want to remember carbon, number 6, and number 12.01, and create pictures for them.

How do you picture carbon? Some people picture a piece of charcoal, which they know is carbon. I prefer to picture a pencil, because of the lead inside, which is carbon. If that doesn't work for you, you can break "carbon" into syllables, "car" and "bon." For the first syllable you can picture a car; for the second, "bon," "bun" is close enough. Picture buns all over a car. Or better yet, cars all over a bun, which is more nonsensical. For the rest of the example, though, I'm going to use a pencil because that's how I picture carbon.

Now you have to create pictures for the numbers. If you use the Tree List, number 6 is a gun. If you use our picture words, it's Joy, the dishwashing liquid. Let's use Joy. In your minds eye, picture a giant pencil. Think of it as a giant javelin, and hurl it into a big bottle of Joy. The pencil pierces the bottle and Joy soap leaks out. Walk over to the bottle, hoping to pull the pencil out of the bottle. But because of all the soap, you slip and slide, and you think, "Oh, this is no good," and you walk away and put on a tin suit to protect yourself. Run this scene in your mind a few times, and you will have committed carbon and its atomic number and weight to memory.

Let's decode the pictures. We've already discussed carbon. We know Joy is number 6 on our picture words list. And the tin suit? "Tin" is "ta," number 1, and "na," number 2. "Suit" is "sa," number 0, and "ta," number 1, which gives us 12.01.

You can also easily remember the elements by using mnemonics, that is, using letters that are associated with each element. For example, silver is "Ag." How do you remember that silver is "Ag"? Picture in your mind a giant, shiny silver spoon. Picture yourself sitting by a river shining this silver spoon. Picture an alligator coming by, trying to eat the silver spoon. Take the silver spoon and try to pull it away from the alligator. All of a sudden, a goat comes out of nowhere and bites you on the rear end. "Owww!" That's it. You've committed the symbol Ag and silver to memory. "Alligator" gave you "a," "goat" gave you "g." "Ag." It took approximately eight seconds, and it can be done with every single element. Simply turn it into a picture, review it three, four, or five times when you first create the pictures, and you have it committed to memory.

I hope I've given you enough examples in this chapter to show how you can use these techniques for just about any situation you are in. They're quick, they're fun, and they're very useful, coming in handy often. Whatever the situation, though, the concept is always the same. Break the information down into smaller chunks. Then create vivid pictures of each chunk, and put everything together using as much action as you can.

Chapter 26—Review

Remembering Birthdays and Anniversaries

1. Pick a peg (such as a present for a birthday, a ring for an anniversary).
2. Change the month to a number and visualize the corresponding picture word.
3. Turn the day of the month into a picture word.
4. Peg the pictures to the peg you have chosen.
5. Include the person in your pictures.
6. If you want to include the year, break the year down into smaller sections, create picture words for it, and include those pictures in your scene.

Remembering Hobbies, Jobs, and Other Personal Information

1. Create a picture of an object representing someone's hobby.
2. Create a picture of the person whose hobby it is.
3. Put the two pictures together using nonsensical, exaggerated action.

Remembering Where You Parked the Car
1. Notice whatever section or level you've parked your car in.
2. Create picture words for each letter and number.
3. Put the pictures together, including your car in the scene.

Mental Reminders
1. Create a picture of an object for any task you want to accomplish.
2. If the task includes another person, picture the person.
3. Put the two pictures together in a nonsensical way.

Using a Reach List
1. Take an object close to you, take it from its normal place, and put it somewhere else.
2. Peg the information you want to remember to this object, using nonsensical, exaggerated action.

Remembering Presidents, State Capitals, Other Lists
1. Break whatever information you are trying to remember into smaller sections.
2. Create pictures for each section.
3. Chain the pictures together or peg them to something you already know.

Chapter 26—Required Mental Exercise

Exercise
Describe out loud, whether to a partner or yourself, the vivid pictures you would use to remember the following information:

> Birthdays
>> August 28
>> December 4
> Anniversaries
>> June 12
>> October 19

Presidents
Thomas Jefferson, third President
Harry Truman, thirty-third President
States and Their Capitals
Cheyenne, Wyoming
Columbia, South Carolina

27 Using Acronyms and Remembering Written Passages

In the very beginning of the book, we spent some time discussing mnemonics, which is the favored way of teaching memory exercises by most experts. I told you that while mnemonics do have their place in helping us remember things, like the mnemonic HOMES for remembering the five Great Lakes, their use was limited, especially when compared with what you can do with a Mega Memory.

Now that you've completed most of the Mega Memory program and can appreciate its strengths, I'd like to spend a little more time discussing some of the uses of mnemonics. When you apply them in combination with Mega Memory techniques, you're not only adding another workout technique to your mental calisthenics, you're also increasing that ever-expanding bag of tricks you have for recalling information. We already did some of this in the last chapter.

Let's review the technique by going back to our discussion of the HOMES acronym. You take the word "homes," which you already know, and link each of the Great Lakes to one of the letters. To put it another way, we use the first letter of the name of each lake to create a word we already know. The letters H-O-M-E-S work like a peg because they're a place on which you put information you are trying to remember. But with acronyms, you aren't pegging. Pegging requires the use of vivid pictures and lots of nonsensical, exaggerated action. With acronyms, you are linking the information together *logically,* without necessarily using pictures.

After all you've learned in this book, I hope you can see why this kind of linking of information is so much less effective than using pictures and action. When we use pictures and action to commit things to memory, we are doing it the same way the mind works, with pictures. When you create a picture of something, it tends to stay in your memory longer and more clearly. And it comes back to you immediately. Also, you've seen how we can remember even more complex information by breaking it down into smaller pieces and turning it into pictures. Acronyms don't tap into this deeper, more immediate power of your unconscious; they merely scratch the surface. They're easy to use, but they also tend to be more superficial—you can forget them more easily.

For this very reason, they are useful in certain situations, especially when you are going to use the information repeatedly over a short period of time. Repetition is the alternative way of ingraining information into your memory. When you combine repetition with an acronym, which pulls all the information together, you have an effective memory technique at your disposal. That's why it's popular in schools. You start a new geography lesson, say on the Great Lakes, which you will be discussing for the next week or so. If you give the students an acronym as a memory aid, you are helping them manage all that information in a more understandable way.

Using Acronyms

I call the technique of using acronyms "initialing," since it covers a broader range of options. When you are initialing, you take the first letter of the words that you are trying to remember, and create another word from them, like HOMES. Initialing also works very well when you can take the information you want to commit to memory and turn it into a phrase or complete sentence. The initial letters of each word in that sentence will serve as your acronym, while the sentence itself can be used as a point of reference pulling all the information together.

For example, consider, "Kings play chess on fine green silk," which many of us learned in school. This sentence is used to remember the classification system used in biology. What are the first letters in this sentence?: KPCOFGS. In biology, the order of classifying any living thing is as follows: first the *k*ingdom it belongs to; then the *p*hylum; then the *c*lass; then *o*rder; then *f*amily; then *g*enus; and finally *s*pecies. KPCOFGS—Kings play chess on fine green silk. The sentence is easy to remember because it makes sense. Then, by looking at the first letter of every word, we can more easily remember the biological classification system. This sentence helps pull all the information together, providing a great reference point.

Initialing is commonly used to remember notation in music as well. How are we normally told to remember the names of the notes of the treble staff (G clef)? The spaces are noted F, A, C, and E, from which you can derive the acronym FACE. The lines are E, G, B, D, F. You can think of a sentence for these initials: "*E*very *g*ood *b*oy *d*oes *f*ine"—EGBDF.

The spaces on the bass staff (F clef) are notated, A, C, E, G. We can think of a sentence for these letters as well: "*A*ll *c*ows *e*at *g*rass"—ACEG. The lines of the bass staff are G, B, D, F, A. Our sentence: "*G*reat *b*ig *d*ogs *f*ight *a*nimals." There's an element of fun in inventing a sentence and creating an acronym that fits the information you are trying to remember. If you can, by all means feel free to use this technique.

You can also combine acronyms with other Mega Memory techniques. Let's use two other examples from music. When you follow a score for playing an instrument, such as a piano, the letter *P* indicates that you have to play that particular passage softly. The letter *F* is the opposite, indicating that you should play loudly. P and F stand for the Italian terms, *pianissimo* and *fortissimo,* which mean "softly" and "loudly."

If you don't know Italian, there's an easy way to remember what P and F represent. Create pictures for each. For P, picture a powder puff. For F, picture a firecracker. Notice how each picture works with both the visual and phonetic (sound-based) language of our unconscious. Once you commit those two pictures to memory, you'll always remember what P and F mean in music notation.

If you are learning to play a musical instrument, you can even use our picturing techniques for remembering certain simple passages of music. You first must create pictures for the notes, let's say the whole note, the half note, and the quarter note. The picture can be anything that reminds you of the note. I would choose a doughnut, for example. For a whole note, I would use a whole doughnut; for a half note, half a doughnut, and so forth. Then you can put these pictures together by chaining, which as you remember, is a series of scenes linked by nonsensical, exaggerated action.

Remembering Written Passages

Sometimes we need to commit material to memory verbatim: passages from the Bible, poetry, or parts of a play. To remember material verbatim, you use the same techniques we have been using all along. Break the material down into manageable pieces and then convert it into pictures, using lots of nonsensical action in the process.

Take scripture, for example. We need to remember different passages and quotations from the Bible for a multitude of uses. We also need to know where in scripture various passages are located. There are 27 books in the New Testament, 260 chapters, and 7,957 verses. How can we help ourselves remember this information?

Picture in your mind's eye your family Bible. Make it very big. Now in your mind's eye, go over to it and knock on the front cover, as though you were knocking on someone's front door. Why did we do that? What is "knock" phonetically? "Na" and "ca," which are numbers 2 and 7, for the 27 books. Now picture the huge Bible opening up to let you in to the New Testament. Put little nicks, or niches, over certain pages because they contain important information you want to remember. Why niches? Phonetically, "niches" gives us number 260. "Na" is 2; "cha" is 6; and "sa" is 0—260.

Now for the verse number, in case you ever need to know this information. As you leave the Bible, picture a baseball cap on top of it. I want you to be locking that cap to the Bible with a huge lock. "Cap" and "lock" are picture words for what numbers: 79 and 57.

Run that scene in your mind a few times: You knock, you put little niches on the pages, you lock a cap to the Bible. Twenty-seven books, 260 chapters, and 7,957 verses. You've committed the information to memory.

When you want to remember where something is in the Bible, you can create pictures for the particular book, chapter, or verse you want to remember. Let's say you want to remember the following, often quoted passage: ". . . because if you confess with your lips that Jesus is Lord, and believe in your heart that God raised him from the dead, you will be saved." This quote comes from the Book of Romans, Chapter 10, Verse 9. To remember where it is, first convert Romans to a picture. I picture the traditional Roman gladiator.

How would you convert 10 into a picture? You can use either number 10 from the Tree List, which is a bowling ball, or you can use the phonetic alphabet, creating a picture word from "ta" or "da" for number 1, and "sa" or "za" for number 0. Either one would work. Similarly, for Verse 9, you can use "cat," from our Tree List or create a word with the "pa" or "ba" phonetic for number 9. For this exercise, I'm going to use the bowling ball and the cat from our Tree List.

Now in your mind's eye, put all the pictures together in a chain: the Roman gladiator, the bowling ball, and the cat. I picture the gladiator bowling, with cats at the end of the alley meowing and howling indignantly because they're being used as the pins. The next time I ask myself where this passage is located, this picture will pop into my mind, and I can decode it accordingly in a few seconds. That's simply all you have to do, and that's how you remember specifically that Romans, Chapter 10, Verse 9 is that scripture.

If you want to go on and memorize the passage verbatim, you can continue using our techniques. Break the text of the passage down into smaller sections, or chunks, create pictures for all of them, and then chain them together, like you did for one of the exercises involving the Statue of Liberty story in Part I. Any type of verbatim information can be treated that way, whether it's a poem, lines from a play, or anything else. To create pictures for a sizeable amount of material, first ask yourself whether you can put yourself in the picture. That's most important because it makes it more personal, generating emotions, as we've already said. Then pick as many key words or phrases as you think there are in the material, and turn them into pictures. Once they're in pictures, just build an exaggerated, nonsensical chain out of them.

To commit the passage to memory, run through the pictures in your mind, and as you are doing this, repeat the passage *verbatim, out loud.* As you've already learned, this is a surefire way to reinforce in your memory whatever you are trying to put there.

Here's another example, using Abraham Lincoln's Gettysburg Address. Let's assume you need to memorize the first line of the address: "Four score and seven years ago our fathers brought forth on this continent, a new nation, conceived in liberty and dedicated to the proposition that all men are created equal."

After chunking the line, it may look like this (the remainder of the chunk represented appears in parentheses):

1. Four score (. . . and seven years ago)
2. our fathers (. . . brought forth)
3. continent (on this continent)
4. nation (a new nation)
5. liberty (conceived in liberty)
6. proposition (and dedicated to the proposition that)
7. created (all men are created equal)

Converting the key word or phrase of each chunk into pictures, you could then either chain them together or peg them to the pegs of one of your lists—while repeating the passage out loud verbatim.

Chapter 27—Review

Initialing
Taking the first letters of several items you want to remember and making one word from them (as in HOMES for the five Great Lakes).

Or, creating phrases or sentences in which the initial letters of the words are the same as the initial letters of the material you are trying to remember ("Kings play chess on fine green silk").

Remembering Text Verbatim—Chunking
1. Break the text to be memorized into "chunks" (paragraphs, sentences, phrases, concepts, or words).
2. Read the text aloud, paying special attention to the key word in each chunk. It will represent all of that chunk.
3. Convert the beginning of each chunk into pictures.
4. Peg those pictures to one of your peg lists or chain all the pictures together.
5. Run through the pictures in your mind while repeating the passage verbatim—and out loud.

Chapter 27—Required Mental Exercises

Exercise 1
By initialing, create ways to remember the seven continents: Asia, Africa, Antarctica, Australia, North America, South America, Europe.

Exercise 2
Memorize the following quotes using the methods we just reviewed:

1. "The moon could not go on shining if it paid attention to the little dogs that bark at it."—Anonymous
2. "The rung of a ladder was never meant to rest upon, but

only to hold a man's foot long enough to enable him to put the other somewhat higher."—Thomas Huxley

3. "To be, or not to be: that is the question: /Whether 'tis nobler in the mind to suffer /The slings and arrows of outrageous fortune, /Or to take arms against a sea of troubles, /And by opposing end them?"—William Shakespeare

28 Breaking Bad Habits and Retrieving Lost Memories

In this last chapter of of our Mega Memory program, I want to discuss two applications of Mega Memory techniques that hold much promise for the future. One has to do with breaking bad habits, such as overeating or smoking, and the other has to do with recalling "lost" memories.

Research on both these topics in ongoing. What I'll share in this chapter are my experiences with these two exciting, developing areas of Mega Memory. Hopefully they will inspire you to take your trained Mega Memory to new dimensions.

Breaking Bad Habits

Our unconscious mind is an associating computer, as I've been pointing out throughout the book. As information is processed by the brain, one thing reminds you of another, which reminds you of something else. And on and on. This complex, lightning-fast network of associations is the foundation of our Mega Memory techniques. By training ourselves to think in particular ways, we have learned to make some order out of all these linked bits of information, so we can retrieve whatever bits we need, whenever we need them.

Some of the associations our unconscious makes, however, don't help us very much. As a matter of fact, they can be very harmful when they turn into long-standing habits, such as smoking or over-eating. Because in the past we learned to respond to certain situations—usually stressful ones—in a particular way, these habits are now part of our memory circuits just as much as anything else in our knowledge bank. When we want to break these habits, we have a very hard time. Depending on the situation, some of the difficulty in breaking bad habits stems from physical factors (such as nicotine or alcohol addiction), and some from mental and emotional conditioning.

To begin this chapter, I want to discuss one of my own bad habits, and tell you how I used Mega Memory techniques to over-come something that was threatening to get out of control. While I can't claim that Mega Memory techniques will solve every bad habit you have, I do believe that the vast power you tap into when you acquire a Mega Memory gives you a powerful tool with which to help yourself. Just as you have taught yourself to link amazing amounts of information (and information is nothing more than pat-terns of thought), you can teach yourself to "de-link" patterns of thought, too.

My problem was eating—or more specifically overeating. I grew up in an Italian household, and we loved to eat. To us, as to many people, eating was a very important part of our life. If we were happy, we ate. If we were sad, we ate. If someone got a raise or was promoted, we ate. If someone was married, or christened, or died, we ate. Whatever happened, good or bad, eating always helped us feel better.

This linking of food and feeling is fine, unless, of course, you overdo it. Then, this association becomes so powerful and compel-ling, you need to do it even when you don't want to. Unconsciously, you are convinced you want to. It can create a situation where we are not in control of our eating habits. That is what happened to me.

I decided to try my own Mega Memory techniques to see if I

could come to grips with the situation. The first thing to do was to change my association of food with pleasurable feelings. As we discussed way back in Chapter 2, the body can't tell the difference between that which you imagine and that which is real. So I decided to create another reality for myself, replacing old associations with new ones. I began to associate cake, cookies, candy, and other sweets with pain. I pictured myself fat and miserable. In my images, no one liked me. I was crying and depressed—and eating ice cream and cake. At the same time, I began to link things like fruits, vegetables, and exercise with pleasure. I saw myself smiling, walking down the street slim and trim, feeling as though I had the world at my feet. I did these mental exercises every day, spending about ten minutes on them.

The results were amazing. In two months, I lost forty-eight pounds. I was never hungry, yet I would wake up full of energy. The more I lost, the more I would do this exercise in my mind. And today, as the saying goes, I'm a new man. I've completely changed the memories in my mind.

Now when I go to a restaurant, it's unbelievable—I actually get excited when they bring the dessert cart by and I say, "No, I'm fine." I get excited because my mind goes onto autopilot and says, "No, that's going to give you pain," (as opposed to, "Not eating that will give you pleasure." I chose to link my thoughts to pain because pain is a higher motivator than pleasure. Associating eating with pain will work better than associating *not* eating with pleasure.)

There are many different technologies for conditioning your mind to react to pain and pleasure. And many of them are fantastic. My technique is very simple: Create vivid, exaggerated mental pictures with emotion, and attach them in your mind's eye using action—that will change your memory, and it will change your behavior.

Recalling Your Past

I was a guest on a radio show several years ago, and a woman called up and said, "Kevin, I've seen you on television. I have your Mega

Memory tapes and it's fantastic. But I have a problem that's not covered in the course." I asked her what her problem was.

"Well, several years ago my husband and I went to Europe for a three-month vacation," she explained. "I hid my jewelry box where no one could find it, and no one ever has, including me!"

She and I laughed, the host laughed, and probably a lot of listeners laughed, too. But I told her I couldn't help her. I explained that the Mega Memory program teaches you how to organize and process *new* information, so it will be available for recall later. The location of the jewelry box had not been committed to this woman's memory in an orderly way, so our Mega Memory techniques wouldn't work in her case. She was out of luck.

However, I left the studio thinking about this woman's dilemma. How many people have lost something because their memory wasn't engaged at the moment they put it away or put it down, I wondered. How much other information is considered lost and not retrievable, while it in fact is somewhere in some deep recess of our minds? I had learned that everything we have ever experienced—seen, heard, smelled, touched, tasted, felt, thought about—remains with us, locked away somewhere in memory. Was there any way to use Mega Memory techniques to recall such information?

In the remainder of this book, I'm going to share with you two techniques that deal with this situation. I have been researching them for years and by now thousands of people have used them. The results are absolutely astounding. Letters arrive on a regular basis from people who use the particular techniques you're about to learn. They write because there's so much emotion associated with being able to find a precious object they had lost, getting back in touch with a long-lost friend, or recalling something they learned but thought they had long forgotten.

The two techniques are very, very simple. As a matter of fact, if I receive one comment more than any other, it's that they seem too simple to work. Of course, some of the greatest truths in life are simple. And just like the simple truth, these techniques don't have to be difficult to work.

I have to admit, however, that the techniques are not foolproof.

We don't know why yet but they don't work 100 percent of the time. If applied in a consistent and persistent manner, though, they do work the majority of the time. Each technique takes about ten minutes to apply, each day, every day. If you have no success the first day, try it again tomorrow. Whatever information you are seeking to retrieve may not come back tomorrow, either, so continue to apply the technique on an ongoing basis until it does come to you. In most cases, the information comes back after only a few sessions; occasionally it can take months. Some people have been unsuccessful (at least so far) in finding what they are looking for.

When I discussed the effect your body and your memory have on each other in Chapter 8, I told you how much stress affects recall. That is true both in situations where the stress is short-term (you are under a lot of pressure at work for a few days or weeks) or long-term. Long-term blockage can be caused by emotional pain. If there are painful memories associated with an event, and unconsciously you don't want to experience the pain, the memories associated with that event are suppressed. Sometimes, physical pain is associated with the event as well. Many different therapies have been developed to try to help people free themselves of these blocks. An analogy used to explain how many of those therapies work is the peeling away of the layers of an onion to get at the suppressed memories.

The Mega Memory techniques work similarly. You know that the information you want to recall is somewhere in your memory. But it is held back by other information surrounding it. The techniques are not a substitute for therapy and do not claim to resolve the complex emotional problems for which one goes to therapy, of course. But applied persistently and consistently, they can bring back pieces of information that you may have thought had been lost for good.

Technique I
The first technique has three steps:

1. Decide specifically what you want to remember and write it down.

2. As best you can, try to pinpoint the moment when you first realized that something was missing.
3. Try to relive that moment by asking yourself "backdrop" and "feeling" questions.

You must first decide exactly what you want to recall, and write it down. And you must do so in a positive, affirmative manner. If you lost a pair of sunglasses, for example, don't just write: "I lost my sunglasses." Write: "I want to remember where I put my sunglasses."

After you have decided exactly what it is that you want to recall and have written it down, you then try to relive the moment when you first realized an object was missing. If you are trying to remember "lost" information, you try to relive, as best you can, the circumstances of your first learning information.

You do this by taking step three, asking yourself what I call backdrop and feeling questions. You have to ask yourself those questions out loud. Throughout the book, I have put major emphasis on speaking out loud because it has a greater impact on memory. It's just as important with this technique; you want those neural passages in the brain to be processing the information in as many different ways as possible.

Using the example of lost sunglasses, let's go through the questions you would ask yourself. As best you can, go back to the moment when you first realized your sunglasses were lost. Let's say it was while you were watching television one night. Picture yourself watching television. See it vividly. Now start asking specific questions about that night—the more specific the better. Here are some of the questions you might ask yourself: "Why was the television on? What was I watching? Was I doing anything else? Where was I sitting? What did the couch or chair look like? Was I cooking anything at the same time? Was I eating (snacking)? Were there any sounds I remember from that night? Who else was in the room with me? Were we talking about anything? What was I doing the moment before I discovered the sunglasses were lost? What did I do after? What kind of mail did I get that day?"

Continue to ask yourself such questions, being as specific as you can. Don't forget to ask yourself about colors, sounds, smells, and other sensations you may have experienced at that time. And keep in mind that your questions are not about the object you are trying to remember but about the circumstances surrounding the moment you realized the object was lost. That's why I call them backdrop questions.

After spending a few minutes on backdrop questions, proceed to the next type of question, the feeling question. That is extremely important. "How did I feel that night? Was I in a good mood? Was I in a bad mood? Was I having fun? Was I stressed? Why was I feeling this way? Did I feel hurt that day for any reason? Did I experience any physical pain, a backache, a headache? Did I have a spat with my spouse? Did I receive any good news? Bad news?"

Keep the questions coming, out loud and nonstop for about five or ten minutes. And as you are asking yourself these questions, try to picture the scene as well.

Let me explain what's happening during the questioning. As I said in the beginning of this chapter, your mind is an associating computer. Every bit of information is linked to some other bit of information. You need to find the "something" that is linked to the object you are trying to recall. By asking all these questions, we're trying to find that special link. At the same time, we're also trying to unblock any emotional pain that might be preventing the information from surfacing, peeling the onion, so to speak. We're trying to isolate and neutralize the power that any hurt, discomfort, fear, anger, or other emotion has over the information. Once we do this, the information begins to be released.

In trying to decide how long to keep asking yourself questions, notice when you begin to feel bored. Paradoxically, getting bored is a good sign. When you're bored, you're not concentrating very hard on what you are doing. There's a greater chance you will get beyond the think stage and into the look/search stage of the unconscious. So try to continue if you're bored; you're increasing the chances of success. Although the time involved varies from person to person and situation to situation, on average, I recommend about fifteen minutes of questioning.

To end the questioning session, you need to give yourself a command to recall the information. Hopefully, now that all the data is closer to the surface, a positive command to release the information will do just that. Be specific, treating your mind as you would a subordinate. "Mind, let me recall where my sunglasses are." "Memory, let me remember easily and effortlessly, right now, what I did with Aunt Josephine's tie."

Once you've made this command, go about your daily business. Try to forget about what you've just been doing; information has a tendency to bubble up to consciousness when you're not thinking about it.

Sometimes it takes just one session of questioning; more often, however, it takes a few days and longer. But all of a sudden, when you're not thinking about it, perhaps while you're doing something at work or driving the car, you have a flash, "Oh, that's where the sunglasses are!" Your ten to fifteen minutes have paid off! For a simple mind exercise, it's incredibly effective.

At a seminar I was once conducting, a woman approached me in the hallway, describing to me what happened when she had used this technique to recover a lost ring. At some point about three years before, the ring had slipped off her finger without her being aware of it. But her body had felt the ring come off, and the knowledge of it was in her memory.

She faithfully went through the technique I just taught you for a ten-day period. Then, as she told me, "on the eleventh day, I was in the grocery store walking down the aisle with all the paper and tissue products. All of a sudden, boom! It dawned on me that the ring fell off as I was putting towels away in the bathroom cabinet, which also has all the tissue paper in it. When I put the towels in, the ring came off my hand. I rushed back home, took the towels off the shelf, and there was the ring!"

Everything is linked to something else. Three years before, when this woman had opened the cabinet to put the towels in, she saw tissue paper. Her mind registered seeing tissue paper, while her body felt the ring come off. There was the special link. But this information was locked away in her unconscious and she was unable to bring it back. Using our technique, she conditioned her mind into making the connection—when she wasn't consciously thinking about it, in the aisle of the grocery store. This is a wonderful example of how the technique works retrieving data that seems forever lost. For me, it's very gratifying to see such results.

Let me quickly tell you one other success story. Remember the woman who couldn't find her jewelry box after coming back from her three-month vacation? I got in touch with her and convinced her to try my technique. And, she found it! It was in a dog food container under the sink. What had suppressed the information in this case was the death of her dog, which occurred while she was away. The dog was old and had been rather sickly for some time. Sending it to the vet, as they had done before the trip, didn't seem like a big deal at the time. But because it died while they were away, this caused the woman to have some feelings of remorse and sadness. Therefore, the food container became a slight emotional block, and she couldn't remember where she had put the jewelry. After using these techniques, she was cleaning her house one day, when all of a sudden it dawned on her. In her mind's eye, she saw the dog and the dog food container with the jewelry box in it.

Practicing this technique has an added benefit. The longer and more persistently you use it for recall of specific things, the more you begin to "loosen up" other information as well. That is very beneficial, because it helps stimulate your imagination and your overall mental functioning. It's like a good house cleaning or tune-up for the car. When I began researching these techniques and using them, I found all of a sudden I was remembering things I hadn't consciously tried to remember.

Let's quickly review the technique. (1) Decide specifically what you want to remember and write it down. (2) As best you can, try to pinpoint the moment when you first realized that something was missing. (3) Try to relive that moment by asking yourself "backdrop" and "feeling" questions. Do it in vivid detail. Picture colors, smells, sounds, and other sensations. Try to picture exactly where you were.

Who was with you? What were you talking about? Then focus on your feelings to try and unlock any emotional blocks. By asking yourself these questions, you are retelling the story of what happened. Make sure you do it out loud to maximize its effectiveness. And finally, program yourself with a positive command to your memory to release the information.

Technique 2

There is a second technique, which, if used concurrently with the first, helps the first to work better and much more quickly. It can be used alone, though I don't find that alone it produces nearly the same great results.

The second technique is a visualization/relaxation technique. It is designed to harmonize the functioning of the left and right hemispheres of your brain so that it enters into a state of brain wave production known as the alpha state. Being in this state helps the unconscious mind to work with you to produce whatever information you are trying to recall more quickly and effortlessly.

This technique works as follows: Lie down on any flat comfortable surface, and close your eyes. It is helpful to be in low light or in the dark. With eyes closed, look straight up, moving your eyes as far as they can go toward your forehead. But don't strain. Continue to do this throughout the technique, and keep your eyes closed.

Picture yourself at the top of a very long escalator. See yourself slowly going down that escalator, and as you do, count down out loud from fifty. When you reach "one," step off the escalator into the most beautiful, perfect, peaceful place you can imagine. For some people, that may be next to a tree. For others, it's a beach. But it must be beautiful and peaceful—and completely relaxing. Once you are tuned in to this picture, give yourself a positive self-suggestion out loud, as you did before. Command your mind, by speaking out loud, to recall all the information you need, and tell yourself, "Memory, give me back easily and effortlessly all the information I want." This moves you toward the autopilot mode in which your unconscious begins to work for you.

If you are doing this in combination with Technique 1, do it after you've asked yourself the backdrop and feeling questions. That will put you in as relaxed a mode as possible as you command your mind to release whatever information you are looking for.

As I mentioned in the very first chapter of the book, I love receiving letters from people telling me the results they've experienced from studying Mega Memory. I also enjoy live appearances whether on television, radio, or in person, when people call in or come up to me and tell me what they like or don't like about the program. The mind and memory are fascinating topics, and I'm always happy to hear new ideas, critiques, and feedback. Now that you've finished the entire Mega Memory program, I want to say to you, "Feel free to write me. Let me know what you liked about the book. Tell me how it's helped you." Use the address and phone number on page 352.

The techniques I've taught you are universal. You can apply them to any area, in any situation. I hope the examples I've given you inspire you to think of other ways to use your newly trained memory. Be creative and practical at the same time. And above all— have fun!

Chapter 28—Review

Breaking Bad Habits
1. Create vivid pictures of yourself engaging in the habit you are trying to break.
2. Include negative emotions with those pictures—as many negative emotions as you can.
3. Chain the pictures together, using exaggerated, nonsensical action.
4. Create pictures with positive emotions where you are not engaged in the habit.
5. Chain the pictures together, using exaggerated, nonsensical action.

6. Run both sets of pictures through your mind for about ten to fifteen minutes a day, for as long as you need to.

Recalling Past Information

Technique 1

1. Decide specifically what you want to remember and write it down.
2. As best you can, try to pinpoint the moment when you first realized that something was missing.
3. Try to relive that moment by asking yourself "backdrop" and "feeling" questions.

Technique 2

1. Lie down on a flat surface.
2. Close your eyes.
3. With eyes closed, look straight up, moving your eyes as far as they can go toward your forehead.
4. Picture yourself going down an escalator.
5. Count out loud backward from 50 to 1.
6. Picture yourself stepping off the escalator into the most beautiful, perfect place you can.
7. By speaking out loud, command your mind to remember whatever information you are trying to recall.

Name Guide

The following is a list of suggested pictures and picture words for male and female given names and surnames.

Male Names

Aaron—air gun

Abe—ape

Abel—able Abe (Abraham Lincoln)

Abner—apple with fur on it

Abraham—ape eating ham

Abram—ape ramming a camera

Adam—a dam

Adolf—a dolphin

Adrian—a dream

Al—allergy

Alan—a lion

Albert—albatross

Aldous—adulterer

Alec—almanac

Alex—alchemist

Alexander—a leg sander

Alphonse—a pine hose

Alf—an elf

Alfred—a red elf

Alger—algae

Alistair—ailing stairs

Alonzo—a long zoo

Alvin—ailing vintage (liquor)

Ambrose—amber rose

Amos—American moss

Anatole—lower anatomy (use your imagination)

Andrew—ants' shoe(s)

Andy—android feet

Angelo—angel eating Jell-O, angel cow

Angus—angry bus

Anlos—ant lost

Anselm—ant psalm

Anthony—ants in a tree

Archibald—arched bald (head)

Archie—arched feet

Armand—almond

Arnold—arm hold

Art—artist, artwork
Arthur—author
Artie—artist wearing a tie
Ashley—ashes and leaves
Aubrey—auburn key
August—a gust (of wind)
Augustine—august stein (brown leaves on it)
Austin—august tin (brown tin)
Axel—axle
Baldwin—bald twin
Barnaby—barn of bees
Barney—barn on knee, bar on knee
Barrett—a baretta gun
Barry—berry, bury
Bart—barn
Bartholomew—barn on a pew
Barton—bar weighing a ton
Benedict—bean duct (duct that carries beans)
Ben—bench
Benny—bench feet
Benjamin—bent pajama
Bennett—bend a net
Bentley—Rolls-Royce, Bentley, bend a knee
Bernard—Saint Bernard, barnyard
Bernie—burn a knee
Bert—bird
Bertram—bird and ram
Bertrand—bird ran
Bill—duck's bill, dollar bill
Billy—billy goat
Bob—bobbing for apples, bobcat, bobsled
Bobby—bobby pin
Boris—bore us
Boyd—boy doll
Brad—bread
Bradford—bread in a Ford

Bradley—bread with leaves
Brandon—branding
Brian—brine
Brock—brick
Broderick—broad crook
Bruce—bruise
Bud—rosebud, Budweiser beer
Buddy—bee on a rosebud
Burt—bad burn, burnt steak
Burton—bird of tin
Byron—brine
Caesar—Julius Caesar's seal
Calvin—cave in, Calvin Klein jeans
Cameron—Camaro
Carl—curl
Carlos—car nose, car on the loose
Carroll—Christmas carol, rolling
Carter—car in a tree, charter boat
Cary—carry
Caspar—cast a (fishing) line, cantor (in a synagogue)
Cecil—seal
Cedric—seed on a brick
Chad—chat (verb or noun)
Charles—charcoal
Charlie—Charlie the Tuna, charcoal lighter
Charlton—charcoal by the ton
Chester—chest of drawers, jester
Chet—jet chest
Chris—cross, kiss, Christ
Christian—kiss tin, cross of tin
Christopher—kiss a fur
Chuck—ground chuck (hamburger)
Clarence—clarinet dance
Clark—clock, Clark Kent, Clark bar (candy)
Claude—cloud, clawed
Clayton—clay that weighs a ton

Clem—clam
Clement—cement
Cliff—cliff
Clifford—cliff with a Ford going over it
Clifton—cliff that weighs a ton
Clint—canned lint
Clinton—ton a lint
Clive—clove
Clyde—Clydesdale horse, collide with a horse
Cole—coal
Colin—coal falling in
Conrad—con(vict) rat
Corey—core, coral
Cornel—corn elk
Cornelius—corn ears
Craig—crack
Curtis—curfew, current list (things to do)
Cyris—cereal
Cyrus—siren on a (jack)ass
Damon—demon
Dan—den, dam
Daniel—den with a bell in it
Danny—den on a knee
Darren—dagger, dart (hitting a wren)
Darryl—rolling dart
Dave—dive, divine cave
David—Star of David, dive, divot
Davy—Davy Crockett, day to see
Dean—dean (of school)
Dennis—dentist
Derek—derelict (noun), derrick (large crane)
Dexter—deck stir
Dick—deck
Dirk—dark, dirt
Dom—domino

Dominick—dominoes
Don—Mafia don, down (goose down)
Donald—Donald Duck, bald dawn
Donny—geese down
Dorian—door ant
Doug—dug
Douglas—dug a glass
Drew—drew, brew
Duane—dug a vein, dug a vane
Dudley—deadly, dead leaves
Duke—duke, duck
Duncan—dunking, Dunkin' Donuts
Dustin—dusting
Dwight—dead weight, Dwight Eisenhower
Earl—earl (feudal), elephant with a curled tusk
Ebenezer—Ebenezer Scrooge, sneezer
Ed—Mister Ed, Eden
Eddie—eddy (back current in a river)
Edgar—headgear, Ed's car
Edmund—eddy mound (many eddies)
Edward—head ward, toward Eden
Edwin—head wind, Eden wind
Egbert—egg and bird
Elbert—elk with a bird
Eli—eel eye
Elias—eel highest, eel heist
Ellery—celery, electric eel
Elliot—eel yacht
Ellis—eel ass
Elmer—Elmer Fudd, elk with a mermaid
Emanuel—easy manual (noun)
Emery—emery board

Emmet—enemy

Emil—electric mill

Enoch—eunuch

Erasmus—erase most (of it),
  earmuffs

Eric—earache

Ernest—ear nest (birds in your
  ear)

Ernie—ear and knee

Errol—Errol Flynn, ear roll (rolling ears)

Erwin—ear and wind, ear blowing
  in the wind

Ethan—eat ham, eating, Ethan
  Allen (furniture)

Eugene—ewe in jeans

Evan—evening in a van

Everett—evergreen tree

Felix—feel an X, feel eggs

Ferdinand—fur in hand

Fletcher—fetcher, fetch her

Floyd—flood

Foster—fester (festering wound)

Fran—frown

Francis—Francis the Mule, fan kiss

Frank—frankfurter

Franklin—Benjamin Franklin,
  frankfurter standing in line

Franny—frown with knee in it,
  cut-off hot dog with knee

Fred—frayed, fried

Freddy—fried, frayed

Frederick—fried or frayed feet

Fritz—Fritz the Cat, freeze

Gabriel—grab a reel

Garrett—glare at a net

Gary—gear free (no gears)

Gaston—gas by the ton

Gavin—judge's gavel, gravel

Gaylord—a gay lord

Gene—blue jeans

Geoffrey—chef who is free, chef in
  a tree

George—gorge

Gerald—jeer that is old

Gideon—guiding beacon

Gifford—give a Ford

Gil—fish gill

Gilbert—gills on a bird

Glenn—glen (meadow)

Godfrey—God is free, God in a
  tree

Godwin—God in the wind

Gordie—gourd of a tree

Gordon—gourd that weighs a ton

Graham—graham crackers

Grant—granite, Ulysses S. Grant

Greg—gray keg

Gregory—gray gory (gray blood),
  gray glory

Griff—graph

Griffin—grip a fin, graph of a fin

Grover—lion roaring in a grove

Gunther—gunner, a gun store

Gus—gas, gust (of wind)

Gustave—gas stove, gas cove

Guy—guide (noun)

Hadley—head on knee

Hal—hall, hail

Hank—handkerchief

Hans—hands, hens

Harlan—hollering, Harley (motor-
  cycle) on land

Harold—hair that is old

Harry—hair

Harvey—hard carving (carving in
  stone)

Hector—heckler, hick store

Henry—Oh Henry! candy bar, a
  hen with a ray gun

Herb—herb
Herbert—herb and bird
Herman—her man, Hercules
Hiram—hire a man
Hobart—hobo bird, hobnobbing
   with art
Homer—homer (in baseball)
Horace—horse
Horatio—horse at you
Howard—hoe forward (as in
   farming)
Howie—hoeing to plant beet, hoe
   one's feet
Hoyt—hoist
Hubert—huge bird
Hugh—huge heart
Hugo—huge glow
Humphrey—hump a tree
Hyman—high man
Ian—ion, Ian Fleming
Ichabod—ink on a bud
Ignace—ignore taste
Ignatius—ignore nauseousness
Igor—ignore, eye gore
Ingram—ink gram
Ira—Iran, IRA (retirement)
Irv—irate nerve
Irving—ivy nerves
Irwin—irked wind
Isaac—eye sack, eye sick
Isadore—eyes on a door
Israel—eyes on a rail
Ivan—eye on a van
Ivor—eye and oar, ivy and oar
Izzy—iffy tizzy (is the anger
   righteous?)
Jack—car jack, jack-in-the-box,
   jumping jack
Jacob—Jacob's ladder, jack up
Jake—jock who is fake

James—jams
Jamie—jam on your knee
Jared—red jar, broken jagged
   glass jar
Jarvis—jar fizz, jar whiz
Jason—jay(bird) in the sun
Jasper—exasperated with a jar (it
   won't open)
Jay—jay(bird), jail
Jed—jester
Jeff—jiffy, falling jet
Jeffrey—jet in a tree
Jeremiah—jet mired
Jeremy—fleeing jet, my jet
Jerome—roaming jet, jet room
   (where jets are kept)
Jerry—jar a cherry (off a bush)
Jess—jazz
Jesse—jazzy jet (wings jagged)
Jim—gym, jungle gym
Jimmy—my gym, jimmy a door
Joe—sloppy joe, G.I. Joe
Joel—jewel, jowl
Joey—eating a sloppy joe
John—john (toilet)
Johnny—toilet on a knee
Jonah—man saying "ah" while
   using the john (relief)
Jonas—using the john with one's
   ass
Jonathan—john (toilet) that is thin
Jordan—jaw of tin
Jose—hose
Joseph—syphoning a sloppy joe
   through a hose
Joshua—job for department of
   water and power
Juan—wand
Jud—jug
Judson—jug in the sun

Jules—jewels

Julian—julienne chef salad, jewel and ant

Julio—jewel that's low

Julius—jewel on an ass

Justin—a justice, gust of wind

Keith—key, key in teeth, teeth

Ken—can

Kenneth—can on a net

Kent—canned, tent with big K

Kevin—cave in, heaven

Kimball—can of balls, can on a ball

King—king

Kirk—kick a bird

Kyle—baby crying for a ball

Laird—layered, lard

Lance—lance, lands

Lancelot—Sir Lancelot, lance a cot

Larry—lariat

Lawrence—law for ants, law of France

Lee—Lee jeans, Robert E. Lee

Lem—lamb

Len—lend, lens (eye or camera)

Lenny—lend a knee, lens on a knee

Leo—lion

Leon—lean on

Leonard—lean hard, a lean yard

Leroy—leaves toll, leaves on a toy

Les—less

Leslie—less leaves

Lester—less tear

Linus—Linus (and Lucy), blanket, lined paper

Lionel—Lionel train, lion lying on a field

Lloyd—Lloyd's of London, light turned on by a boy

Lon—Lone Ranger

Lonney—low knee, Lone Ranger on his knee

Lou—low blue (color)

Louis—louvers, loose goose

Lowell—low well, low L

Lucas—low kiss, look kiss

Lucian—loose shin

Ludwig—load wig, lug and wig

Luke—lukewarm water, look, Cool Hand Luke

Luther—Lex Luther, loose floor

Lyle—lily on a tile

Lynn—linament, line

Mac—Mack truck, Big Mac (hamburger)

Mal—mail

Malcolm—mail come, mail comb

Manny—man with big feet

Marcus—mark (jack)ass

Mario—mark an Oreo cookie

Mark—marker, marking pen

Marshall—marshal (sheriff), mark a shell

Martin—Martian (man from Mars)

Marty—mar tea, mark tea

Marv—mar or mark on a vampire

Marvin—mar or mark a vintage (liquor)

Mason—mason, mason jar, my son

Matt—doormat

Matthew—mat and ewe, mat pew

Maurice—more rice, more ice

Maury—moray eel, more leeway, more keys, more feet

Max—mix, maximum

Maximilian—makes a million

Maxwell—mix in a well

Maynard—main yard, mane (horse) yard

Mel—melt, melon

Melvin—melt, melon, melt van, melon van

Meredith—mare in a ditch

Merv—make love, marvel, mercury

Mervin—morbid van

Michael—microphone

Mickey—Mickey Mouse

Mike—microphone

Miles—miles

Milton—melt a ton

Mitch—match, mulch, mitt

Mitchell—mitt shell

Monroe—man row (a boat)

Montague—man playing tag

Montgomery—mound of gum in your hair

Monty—Mountie (Canadian police), mound of tea

Morgan—morgue can, mortgage in a can

Morris—more rice, Morris the Cat

Mortimer—morgue timer

Morton—morgue tin

Moses—Moses (Bible)

Murray—more ray

Nat—gnat

Nathan—gnat in your hand

Nathaniel—gnat tanning and yelling

Ned—kneeling in front of a bed

Neil—kneel

Nelson—kneel in the sun

Nero—knee row, hero with a big N

Newton—Fig Newton, newtons (measurement), Isaac Newton

Nicholas—nickel and (jack)ass

Nick—nickel, neck

Noah—Noah's ark, no air

Noel—Christmas, Noel

Norbert—north bird, sherbet

Norman—Norseman, horseman

Norton—north ton, north tin

Ogden—otter's den

Olaf—laughing otter

Oliver—olive

Orson—oar in the sun

Oscar—orange car, (jack)ass car, Academy award

Oswald—(jack)ass, old wall

Otto—auto, a toe

Owen—win an otter

Pat—pat of butter, lily pad

Patrick—pat of butter on a brick

Paul—pole

Pedro—paid row

Percival—purse fall

Percy—purse with a big C, purse sea

Perry—pear with a big E, Perrier (water)

Pete—peat (moss), pleat (in a skirt)

Peter—peter out, pedestrian

Phil—fill

Phillip—gas pump, filled cup, pill in a tux

Phineas—fin on an (jack)ass

Pierce—pierce (ears)

Pierre—pea air, pea hair

Prescott—press and cot

Preston—press and ton

Quentin—quotient of tin

Quincy—wind and sea, quotient of the sea (part of the sea)

Ralph—raft

Randall—ram and doll

Randolph—ram and dolphin

Randy—ram and tea, ram and a big D

Raphael—raft fill, raft fall

Ray—ray of light, ray fish

Raymond—ray and mound, ray and man

Reggie—red G, regiment (army)

Reginald—red gold, red wall

Reuben—Reuben (sandwich)

Rex—wrecks, racks

Reynolds—wren old, Reynold's Wrap

Rich—lots of money, sugar bowl, Ritz cracker

Richard—rich heart, rich yard

Richie—rich feet

Rick—brick, rock

Rob—robe

Robbie—bee stuck in a robe

Robert—robber, robe and bird

Robin—robin (red breast)

Rod—rod

Roddy—rowdy

Roderick—rod and brick, rob a brick

Rodney—rod and knee, rot knee

Roger—rod and chair

Roland—roll and land, row and land

Rollo—roll with an O, polo (water or horse)

Rolph—roll off

Ron—run, rum

Ronald—Ronald McDonald, run old

Ronnie—run and knee

Rory—roaring bees

Roscoe—Bosco (chocolate syrup), rescue

Ross—rust, boss

Roy—Roy Rogers (TV cowboy)

Rudolph—reindeer, Valentino

Rufus—roof fuzz

Rupert—roof bird

Russ—rush, rust

Russell—rustle

Sal—a salad

Salvatore—salamander, door with a salve on it, salad

Sam—Uncle Sam

Sammy—Uncle Sam on your knee

Samson—Uncle Sam in the sun

Samuel—Uncle Sam on a mule

Sandy—sand

Saul—soul, sole

Scott—Scotch, Scott towel

Sean—sauna

Sebastian—sea bass in the sun

Seth—a stethoscope

Seymour—sea moor

Sheldon—shell down

Shelley—shell with feet

Sherman—German, shirt and man

Sid—sit

Sidney—sit on a knee

Silas—silo, silence

Simeon—cinnamon

Simon—sign and man, Simon says

Sinclair—Sinclair gasoline (dinosaur), sink and lair

Sol—sole

Solomon—silo man, wise man

Spencer—Spencer Tracy, spend sore

Stan—stand (noun), stem

Stanley—stand on leaves

Stephen—stove and hen

Steve—stove, sleeve

Steven—steel van

Stewart—steward (airline), stew and art

Stu—stew

Sylvester—silver in a vest

Tad—tadpole

Ted—half a teddy bear

Teddy—teddy bear

Terrence—tear ants

Terry—terry cloth

Tex—Texas, tax, tacks

Theo—the Oval Office

Theodore—the door

Thomas—thermos

Thurston—thirsty ton

Tim—timer, Tiny Tim

Timmy—tinny

Timothy—tin tea

Titus—tide and (jack)ass

Tobias—toe buy (jack)ass

Toby—toe and bee

Tod—toad

Tom—tom-tom drum, turkey, thumb

Tommy—tummy

Tonio—toe and knee with a big O

Tony—Tony the Tiger, toe and knee

Tracy—trace feet

Ty—tie (noun)

Tyler—tire

Tyrone—tie rowing

Ulysses—you lifting with ease

Upton—uptown, Lipton (tea bags)

Valentine—heart, valentine card

Van—van

Vance—vans

Vergil—the Virgin Mary

Vern—Venus

Vernon—Venus on (glowing)

Vic—Vicks (cough syrup)

Victor—Viking

Vince—vine

Vincent—mint vine

Vinnie—vine with bees on it

Wade—wade (in a pool)

Waldo—wail and dough

Wallace—wall and lace, walrus

Wally—wall with bees on it

Walt—welt, waltz

Walter—wall tear, waiter

Ward—ward

Warren—warden

Wayne—John Wayne, weigh in (for a boxing match)

Will—wilted flower, well, last will and testament

William—yam on a wilted flower, yam in a well

Willis—will on an (jack)ass

Willy—wire, wilted feet (tired feet)

Zach—zebra with a crack in its back

Female Names

Abbey—a bee

Abigail—a bee in a pail, a big ale

Ada—Band-Aid

Addy—abbey

Adele—a bell

Adeline—a dandelion

Adelle—a dell, a dill pickle, a ladle

Adrianne—a dry ant

Agatha—a gate tore

Aggy—a guy, aggravated bees

Agnes—aggravated nest of bees

Alberta—albatross, Albany tan

Alexandra—a pair of legs made of sand

Alexis—a leg, person with one leg running for the exit

Alice—a lice, a lace

Alison—a list of lice

Alixe—ax, live by the ax

Amanda—a man with panda

Ambrose—amber rose, ambrosia

Amelia—airplane, a mealy banana, a meal

Amy—aim, amiable

Andrea—Andromeda, dreary anathema

Angela—angel and Jell-O

Angelica—angel, triangle

Angie—ant key

Anita—anteater

Ann(e)—ant

Anna—ant, apple, annihilate, anathema

Annabel—ants on a bell

Annette—a net

Annie—a knee

Antoinette—a torn net

April—ape roll

Arabel(la)—air in a bell

Arlene—leaning aria (good exercise—making one lean)

Audrey—airing laundry (hanging it out to dry)

Augusta—a gust of wind

Aurelia—aria of August

Ava—Avon lady ringing doorbell

Aveline—a jar of Vaseline

Avis—a wiz

Babette—bad bet

Barbara—barber, barbed wire

Bea—bee

Beatrice—beat rice

Beckie—bad key, peck a key

Belinda—bell in a window

Bella—bell

Belle—bell

Bernadette—burn a debt, burn a net

Bernadine—iodine bottle, match bottle

Bernice—burn a noose, burn, burn your knee

Bertha—bath

Beryl—bear that's ill

Bess—bass

Bessie—bees in the sea

Beth—bath, bet

Bethel—bath with an L

Bittina—ballerina

Betty—betting

Beulah—bugle

Bev—bevel, beaver, beverage can

Beverly—beaver with leaves, beverage

Bianca—breath spray, bee on a car, banker

Billie—billy goat, billy club

Blanche—ranch with bees

Bobbie—bobby pin, London policeman

Bonnie—bony, bonnet

Brenda—broom, branding iron

Bridget—bridge

Camille—camel

Candice—candy with aces, can with aces

Candida—can full of deeds

Candy—candy

Cara—car ah-chooing (sneezing)

Carla—car with lace

Carlotta—car lot

Carlotte—car in a lot

Carmel—caramel

Carmelita—caramel with leaves

Carmen—car and man

Carol—Christmas carol, coral

Caroline—carry a line, Christmas carolers drinking wine

Carrie—carry (verb)

Cass—kiss

Cassandra—cot with sand on it

Catherine—cat, cat with orange rind, queen

Ceal—seal envelope, beach ball

Cecilia—ceiling

Celeste—cedar chest

Celina—seal that is lean or leaning

Charlene—charcoal-covered jeans

Charlotte—cherry in a lot

Charmaine—charred mane, charcoal, toilet paper

Cherry—cherry

Cheryl—chair

Chiquita—Chiquita banana, chicken with a key

Chloe—clover with bees around it

Chris—cross, Christ on cross

Chrissie—cross in the sea

Christina—crucifix or Christmas tree with apple

Christine—Christmas tree

Cicely—sis being silly

Claire—eclair, bucket clear water, Lady Clairol

Clara—clarinet

Claudette—clawed at, claw a debt, claw a bed

Claudia—cloud

Claudine—cloud raining dimes

Clementine—clam on a valentine

Cleo—Cleopatra, cling on to a cliff

Cloris—chorus

Colette—collie in a bed or tangled in a net

Colleen—collie leaning

Connie—cone on knee

Constance—con(vict) dancing

Cora—coral

Corinne—apple cores raining

Cornelia—corn with nails

Crystal—crystal

Cynthia—cinders in tux, adult theater, sin theater

Dagmar—dagger with Magic Marker

Dale—dally, doll

Daphne—dolphin

Darlene—door with beans

Dawn—dawn, down

Debbie—dead bee, deputy, debutante

Deborah—dead boar

Delia—deal you some cards

Denise—dead bee, deputy, debutante

Desiree—heart's desire, desert, dessert

Diana—dying ants

Diane—dying ants, tie hand

Dinah—dying

Dixie—Dixie cups

Dolly—Dolly Parton, doll

Dolores—resting doll

Dominique—dominoes

Donna—Donald Duck, doughnut

Dora—door with an ax in it

Doreen—door wearing jeans

Doris—doors

Dorothy—door with tea on it

Dot—dots

Dottie—fleet of dots, teasing dots

Edie—eddy

Edith—frothy eddy

Edna—natural eddy, nocturnal eddy

Effie—effortless tease (can tease effortlessly)

Eileen—eye leaning

Elaine—chocolate éclair, Plains Indians, eels that complain

Eleanor—eel in a bowling lane

Elise—a lease, eel cold as ice

Elizabeth—eels are best in bed, eels and lizards in a bath

Ellen—eel island, lending an ear

Ellie—eels lying or leaving

Eloise—eels squeezing or making noise

Elsie—eels in the sea

Elva—vaccinating eels

Emily—empty family

Emma—empty ma (mother)

Erica—ear with a card

Erma—urn

Ernestine—urn and a stein

Essie—elf (elflike)

Estelle—elfy (elflike), eastern belle (southern belle) or bell

Esther—Easter Bunny

Ethel—ethel gasoline

Eunice—unicycle, united

Eva—Eve with apple

Eve—Christmas Eve, evoke evil

Evelyn—evening lynch

Faith—furious wraith

Fanny—fan or tan one's feet

Fay—falling into hay

Felicia—fleece

Fern—fern plant

Fifi—French poodle

Flora—flowers

Florence—floor dance

Flossie—dental floss

Frances—France, frantic seizure

Francesca—Fresca (soda), fanning a fresco

Freida—fried egg

Fritzi—Fritz the Cat

Gabrielle—a gabby (talking) bell

Gail—gill (fish)

Genevieve—a genie in leaves

Georgiana—gorge with ants

Georgina—gorge with genie

Geraldine—dining with a jerk

Gertrude—green bird interrupting (being rude)

Gina—ash-colored jeans

Ginger—gingerbread man, ginger snaps

Ginny—bottle of gin on your knee

Gisele—gazelle

Gladys—glad to tease

Glenda—dining in a glen

Gloria—glow, glory

Grace—grass

Gretchen—groveling in the kitchen

Hannah—hand

Harriet—hairy chest

Hattie—hat with bees in it

Hazel—hazy elephants

Heather—helter-skelter, lying on the heath

Heidi—someone hiding

Helen—lend hell, Helen of Troy

Helena—hell in a nutshell

Hilda—a hill

Hildegarde—hill full of guards

Holly—boughs of holly, holey (full of holes)

Honey—honey

Hope—Bob Hope, hopping over a rope

Hortense—horse that is tense, horse
in a tent

Ida—eye with polka dots

Irene—irate scene

Iris—fist in an eye

Irma—infirm arm

Isabel—a bell, Istanbul, island of
bells

Ivy—ivy on a wall

Jackie—car jack

Jacqueline—car jack leaning

Jamie—jam on your knee

Jan—jam

Jane—jam a game

Janet—jam in a net

Janice—jeans in a noose

Jean—jeans

Jeanette—jeans in a net

Jeannie—jeans, genie

Jennifer—janitor

Jenny—gentry, giraffe's enemy

Jessica—jester for a king

Jewel—jewels

Jill—jail

Jo—G.I. Joe, sloppy joe

Joan—Joan of Arc, ant on a
sloppy joe

Joanna—ant's jugular vein

Jocelyn—jostling a sloppy joe

Josephine—G.I. Joe in a latrine

Joy—jamming a buoy, joke in a toy

Joyce—juice

Juanita—one knee and toe

Judith—ditch full of juveniles,
judge in a ditch

Judy—judo

Julia—jewels with apples

Juliet—jewels in a net

June—June bug

Justine—justice scales, tin man

Kara—Karo syrup, care package
with doughnut

Karen—care for a wren, carton

Kate—kite

Katherine—cat in a latrine, cat run

Kathleen—cat with big feet

Kathy—cat

Katie—kite on a golf tee

Katrina—cat running to the latrine

Kay—key

Kim—kimono, kimchi

Kirsten—curfew at ten

Kit—cat kiss, kilt

Kitty—kitten

Krista—crucifix with apple, crystal

Kristin—tin crucifix, crystal

Laura—laurel (evergreen tree), lard

Lauren—loud wren, lore of the dis-
tant shore

Laurie—laurel with big leaves

Laverne—burning lashes, love an
urn

Leigh—leaf

Leona—a lioness

Leonora—Leo the Lion snoring

Leslie—Lassie (the collie)

Libby—lip with a bee on it

Lillian—lily with ants on it

Lily—lily

Linda—lint or window

Lisa—lease a Nova (car)

Lois—low (flying) saucer

Loretta—lower it, low red

Lorna—Lorna Doone (cookies)

Lorraine—low rain

Lottie—lottery

Louise—low easel

Lucia—loose shawl

Lucille—loose sail

Lucinda—loose cinder

Lucy—loose, Lucite
Luisa—loose ax
Lula—lukewarm lute
Lydia—lady, ladle
Lynne—liniment
Mabel—maple syrup
Madeline—mad at the line
Madge—maid's job
Madonna—mad onslaught
Maggie—magpie, mad key
Maisie—maze through daisies
Mandy—mandolin, dying man
Marcella—ma's cellar
Marcy—marching
Margaret—market, margarine
Marge—marring the job, march
Margie—march with sore feet
Marguerite—margarita
Maria—marriage
Marian—mare with ants
Marie—mare with big feet
Marietta—marry a teddy (bear)
Marilyn—marry at an inn
Marjorie—my jury
Marlene—a marlin on a fishing
    hook
Marsha—marsh or marshmallow
Martha—marvels of thyme
Mary—merry-go-round, bride
Mary Ellen—marry a melon
Mattie—doormat
Maud—mud
Maureen—marine
Maxine—Mack truck scene, Mack
    truck in a latrine
Meg—megabyte, megaton, magma
Melanie—melon on your knee
Melissa—molasses
Mercedes—Mercedes-Benz
Meredith—mare in a dish

Michelle—microphone in a shell
Mildred—a million dead
Millicent—a million cents
Millie—a mill of wheat
Mimi—mime with big feet
Minnie—Minnie Mouse, minnows
Miranda—mired in sand
Miriam—a mirror ham
Mitzi—a mitt that can see or in
    the sea
Molly—a mole on your knee
Mona—Mona Lisa, mole, monster
Muriel—mural
Myrtle—myrrh on a turtle
Nan—nanny, run
Nancy—ants that can see
Nannette—nuts in a net
Naomi—nine oats in a meal
Natalie—gnat on leaves, gnat on
    your knees
Nellie—kneel on one's knee
Netta—tennis net with apple
Nicole—nickel
Nicolette—nickel on a net
Nina—three ships (*Niña, Pinta* and
    Santa Maria), ant on a knee
Nora—Norse legends, north pole
Noreen—no rain
Norma—normal
Octavia—octopus in a cave
Odette—owe a debt
Olga—ogre
Olive—olives
Olivia—Oliver Twist, old liver
Opal—opal stone
Pam—pan, Spam
Pamela—paneling
Pandora—pan on a door, Pandora's
    box, pan pipes
Pat—pat of butter

Patricia—roof patches, rich pastor

Patty—met patty, patty melt
sandwich

Paula—pull her falling pole

Pauline—leaning pole

Pearl—pearls, pearl necklace

Peg—peg or Miss Piggy (Muppets)

Peggy—elephant with pegs on it,
Miss Piggy

Penelope—antelope with a pen
(draw on the antelope)

Penny—penny (coin)

Phoebe—free bee

Phyllis—fill us, filled with dust

Polly—pulley, parrot

Priscilla—press the cellar, pass the
Jell-O

Prudence—prune dancing

Rachel—ratchet, ray shining on
shell, rocket

Ramona—ram Mona (Lisa), ram a
mountain

Rebecca—reach for a deck (of
cards), rub a deck of cards

Regina—reach in, reach for a genie

Renee—rain on a knee

Rhoda—road

Rita—rotten pita pocket

Roberta—robed bird

Robin—robin (bird)

Rochelle—row of shells

Ronnie—run of shells

Rosa—flawed rose

Rosalie—rose on your knee

Rosalind—rose on land

Rosalyn—rosin (bag)

Rose—rose

Roseanne—a rose with an ant on
it, rose in sangria

Rosemarie—rose marriage

Rosie—rose with elephant

Rosita—a rose eater

Roxanne—rocks with ants, rocks
in hand

Ruby—ruby, rude bee

Ruth—Baby Ruth candy bar, raft,
Babe Ruth, roof

Sabina—save a bee on your knee

Sadie—saddle

Sally—salad, sail

Samantha—saw a man

Sandra—a sander

Sandy—sand

Sarah—Sara Lee (coffee cake)

Sasha—a sash

Selma—sell ma

Shari—sheared fleece

Sharon—share an iron

Shawn—shawl on lawn

Sheila—shield

Sherry—sherry (wine)

Sheryl—sherry tilting the brain

Shirley—free shirt, surly

Sidney—sit on knee

Sonia—Sony Walkman

Sophia—bee on a sofa

Stacy—bee on a stage

Stella—stellar, celestial

Stephanie—stuff a knee

Sue—suit

Sue Ann—suit with ants

Susan—sew a fan

Susannah—sustain an ant

Susie—Sioux Indian tribe, sue for
a xylophone

Sylvia—silverware

Tammy—tan men, tame a knee

Teresa—trees

Terry—terry cloth towel (or robe)

Tess—test (noun)

Tessie—test your knee

Theodora—ethereal door, the door to the castle

Theresa—trees, Mother Teresa

Tillie—till the fields, tiles with pictures of lilies on them

Tina—teeny-weeny

Toby—toe with a bee on it

Toni—toe and knee, hair perm (by Toni)

Tracey—trachea, trace around one's feet

Tricia—tree shawl

Trixie—tricks

Trudy—trudging with cold feet through the snow

Ursula—urn cellar

Vanessa—van wearing a dress

Vera—veer, beer

Veronica—veering on ice (easy to slip, change direction)

Vicky—Vicks cough drops, Viking ship

Victoria—victory

Viola—violet (flower), violent

Virginia—virgin

Vivian—vibrant-colored van

Wanda—wand

Wendy—windy, Wendy's hamburgers

Wilma—ma's will (legal document)

Winnie—Winnie the Pooh

Yvette—yellow Corvette

Yvonne—yellow van

Zoe—zebra, zoo

Surnames

Aaron—air run, heir—the son

Abbott—robot, a vault

Abel—a bell

Abelson—a bell in the sun

Abramowitz—ape ramming a witch

Abrams—ape and rams

Abramson—ape and rams in the sun

Acheson—ax a son

Ackerman—hacker man, acre of men

Adams—a dam

Addison—add a son

Adler—adultery

Albert—Albany bird

Albright—a long kit

Alcott—a long cot

Aldrich—a long ditch

Alexander—a leg in the sander

Allen—Allen wrench, alley

Altman—a long, tan man

Alvares—a lot of wares

Ambrose—amber rose

Amsterdam—hamster in a dam

Anders—antlers

Anderson—antlers in the sun

Andrews—ant drew, ant drool

Anthony—ant on a knee

Applebaum—apple with a bomb

Archer—archer (bow and arrow)

Armstrong—strong arm

Arnold—old arm

Aronowitz—a runner's wits, a running witch

Arthur—author

Ashburn—ashes burning

Atkins—a tough skin (on an animal)

Atkinson—a tough skin in the sun

Atwater—a tall waterfall

Auerbach—our back, hour back

Axelrod—axle and rod

Babcock—bad cook, bad cock (rooster)

Bailey—bay leaf, Beetle Bailey

Baird—bear with a beard

Baker—baker, bakery

Baldwin—Baldwin organ, bald one

Ballard—ballad, mallard (duck) with a B

Ballinger—ball and gear

Bancroft—bank and loft, bank and craft

Bankhead—bank and head

Barley—bard on a tree

Barnett—bar with a net

Barrett—barrette, beret

Barry—berry

Bartlett—bar and lettuce

Bartley—bar and tea

Barton—bar and ton, bar and tin

Bassett—basset hound

Bauer—bow-wower (dog)

Baum—bomb, burn

Baxter—back stir, backs tear

Beck—back, peck

Begley—bag with leaves

Benham—bend a ham

Bennett—bonnet, bend a net

Benson—bend a sun

Bentley—bend leaves, Rolls-Royce Bentley

Bergman—(ice)berg and man, bird man

Berkowitz—(ice)berg and witch, bird witch

Berman—barman (bartender)

Bernard—burn yard, Saint Bernard (dog)

Bernstein—burn a stein (of beer)

Berrigan—bury a can

Betancourt—betting a court

Birnbaum—burn a bomb, burn a bum

Black—blackboard, blackjack

Blair—baby (small) flare

Blake—lake with a bee in it

Blum—plum with a bee in it

Borden—boarding, border

Boswell—boss in the well

Bowen—bowling

Boyd—boy with a duck

Braddock—brand a dock

Bradley—bread and leaves

Bradshaw—bread and shawl

Brady—braid a bee, Brady Bunch (TV)

Brandt—brand

Brennan—brand a nun

Brent—bent

Brewster—brew or brewery

Brock—rock with a bee on it

Broderick—broad brick

Brody—broke a tree, broad bee

Brophy—trophy with a big bee

Brown—brownie

Bruce—bruise

Bryan—Brie (cheese) and ant, brine

Bryant—buy an ant

Buchanan—blue cannon

Buckley—buckles

Burgess—bird chest, (ice)berg chess

Burke—(ice)berg

Burns—burns, sideburns

Burton—a burr ton, bird ton

Byron—a running bike

Cabot—cabinet, cab and butt

Cahill—cave hill

Caldwell—cold well

Calhoun—cow and home, cow and hound

Callahan—cow and van, cow and hand

Calvin—cow and van

Cameron—camera

Campbell—camp, camper, Campbell's soup

Carlson—curl in the sun

Carmichael—car and bicycle

Carmody—car moody

Carroll—Christmas carol

Carson—car sun

Carter—car tear, Carter's Little Liver Pills

Cassidy—Hopalong, cast of tea

Castro—Fidel Castro, cast of rose

Cates—catering service

Cavanaugh—cave in a hall

Chadwick—chat and wick, shadow wick

Chamberlain—chamber in a lane

Chambers—chamber

Chandler—chandelier

Channing—chaining

Chapman—chapped man, chop man

Charles—charred legs

Chester—chestnut, chest of drawers

Chilton—chilled ton

Chisholm—chisel a ham, chisel a home

Christenson—cross in the sun

Christopher—kissed fur

Clark—clock, cloak, Clark bar

Clement—cement, inclement (weather)

Clinton—clean tin

Cochran—cock (rooster) ran

Cohen—(ice cream) cone

Colby—Colby cheese, coal and bees

Coleman—coal man, cold man

Collier—collar

Collins—Tom Collins drink

Colon—coal in

Compton—camp tin

Connolly—con(vict) and leaves

Connor—con(vict) door, condor

Cook—cook

Cooper—copper

Cortes—cord on an (jack)ass

Cosgrove—cost a grove

Costello—cast made of Jell-O

Coughlin—coughing

Cowen—cow in

Craig—crack

Crandall—crane and doll

Crawford—crawfish

Crawley—crawl leaves, crow lay

Cunningham—cutting a ham

Curtis—Tony Curtis, Helene Curtis shampoo

Cushing—cushion

Custer—custard, Custer's Last Stand

Daley—daily

Dalton—doll that weighs a ton

Daniels—dam yells

Danzinger—dancing cigar

Davenport—dancing port, diving into a port

Davies—days of ease

Davidson—divot sun

Davis—divots

Dawes—dogs, doors

Dawson—dog sun, doors sun

Delaney—delay a knee

Denjam—den and jam

Denton—dent ton, dent tin

Dentweiler—dent whaler

Deutsch—touch, deuce, German

Devlin—devil inn

Diaz—dais (podium)

Dickerson—man named Dick in the sun

Dillon—Marshall Dillon (*Gunsmoke*), dill land

Dixon—man named Dick in the sun

Dolan—Dole banana with an ant on it

Donahue—don (Mafia) with a hoe

Donald—don (mafia) on a wall, Donald Duck

Donaldson—don (Mafia) on a wall in the sun, Donald Duck in the sun

Donnelly—Donald Duck on leaves

Donovan—Donald Duck on a van

Dooley—dues with leaves, Tom Dooley ("Hang Down Your Head")

Doran—door ran

Dougherty—dough in tea, door in tea

Douglas—dog glasses

Dowling—ring going down

Downing—down ink

Doyle—doily

Driscoll—dress in coal

Drummond—drummer

Dudley—dead leaves

Duffy—duffer (on a golf course) with a bee

Dugan—dew on a can

Duncan—dunking, Duncan Hines

Dunlap—down lip, dunk lip

Dunn—dunn (goose), well-done steak

Durant—door and ant

Durham—door and ham

Dutton—ton of dots

Dwyer—dryer

Eagan—eagle

Easley—easel with a bee on it

Eastland—yeast on land

Eastman—yeast on a man

Eaton—eat a ton

Eberhardt—ebony heart

Eckstein—egg and stein

Edelman—easel and man

Edelstein—a bell with a stein in it

Edwards—heard warts

Egan—egg in a can

Ehrlich—air lick

Eisenberg—eyes on (ice)berg

Eldridge—elf on a ridge, elk on a ridge

Elias—eel highest

Elliott—an L-shaped yacht or lot

Ellis—L-shaped (jack)ass

Ellsworth—elf's wart, elf's hearth

Emerson—every sun

Endicott—end of a cot

Engle—angle, ink gull

Epstein—epileptic stein

Ericson—earache in the sun, a ring in the sun

Esposito—S-shaped potato

Ettinger—a finger injured with tin

Evans—a van in an oven

Everett—evergreen in a net

Ewing—ewe and wing, chewing

Fagan—fake can, flake can

Fallon—felon, fall on the lawn

Farber—far bear, far bar

Farley—far leaves, far bee

Farrell—fall rail, barrel with a flea in it

Faulkner—fork near

Feinberg—(traffic) fine on (ice)berg

Feldman—felt man

Felix—feel legs
Ferguson—fur gust in the sun
Fernandez—fern and ant with legs
Feuer—foyer
Finch—finch (bird)
Findlay—finned hay, finned lei
Finney—fin on your knee
Fisk—fist, frisk
Fitzgerald—fist chair old
Fitzpatrick—fist pad brick
Fleming—flame ink
Fletcher—lecher with a big F,
  fetch chair
Floyd—flood
Flynn—flying, Errol Flynn
Foley—foal
Forbes—four bees
Forman—boss, four men
Forrester—forester, forest tear
Foster—frosting
Fowler—foul law
Franklin—frank (hot dog) playing
  a violin, Ben Franklin
Frazier—freezer
Frederick—fried brick, red brick
Freedman—freed man
Freund—friend
Fried—freed
Friedlander—freed land
Fuller—full barrel
Fulton—full ton
Galbraith—gull breath
Gallagher—galley of fur
Garcia—car cedar, gar (fish) cedar
Gardner—gardener
Garrison—chair in the sun, cherry
  sun
Gaynor—half gainer dive
Geller—gala
Gelman—kill man

Gerber—Gerber's (baby food)
Gibbons—green ribbons
Gibbs—green bibs
Gibson—green bibs in the sun
Gilbert—gills on a bird
Gillespie—gills on a pea
Gilligan—kill a can
Ginsberg—gin on (ice)berg
Giordano—gore a piano
Gladstone—GLAD (bag) on a stone
Gleason—grease and sun, Jackie
  Gleason
Gomez—comb and (jack)ass, comb
  and Jell-O
Gonzales—guns and Jell-O
Goodwin—gold twin
Gordon—garden, Gordon's gin
Gorman—gore a man, doorman
Gould—gold
Graham—gray ham, graham
  cracker
Granger—green ranger
Grant—granite
Gregory—gray quarry
Griffin—grip fin
Griffith—grip fish, grip a fifth
  (booze)
Grover—grow fur
Gulliver—gull over, giant (*Gulli-
  ver's Travels*)
Gunther—gun tore, gun fur
Haber—hay bear
Hagan—hay can
Haggerty—hay girl tea
Hahn—hand
Halpern—hall perm, hall fern
Hamilton—ham melting, ham and
  ton
Hammond—ham mound, Ham-
  mond organ

Hanrahan—hen ran

Hansen—hand in the sun

Harper—harp with R, harpoon

Harrington—hair ink ton, herring ton

Harris—hair S

Harrison—hairy sun

Hartley—heart and leaves

Hartman—heart and man

Harvey—heart shaped like a V, heart fee

Hastings—hay stinks

Hathaway—hat files away

Haupt—hopped

Hawkins—hawk inns

Hayden—hay and den

Haynes—hay and nose, Hanes hosiery

Healey—heat feet, Austin Healy

Hecht—hacked

Heller—hello, and raising hell

Hellman—man in hell, helm and man

Henderson—hen and doors in the sun

Hendricks—hen and bricks

Henry—hen read, Oh Henry! (candy bar)

Herbert—sherbet, her bird

Herman—hermit man

Hernandez—hen ant doze

Hess—hiss

Hicks—hiccups

Higgins—hug riggings

Hirsch—Hershey bar

Hirshfield—Hershey bar fell

Hobart—hobo art

Hobbs—hops

Hodges—hedges

Hoffman—half moon, cough man

Hogan—hole in a den, whole den

Hollis—holster, hollers

Holt—halter (top), hold a bolt

Hooper—Hula Hoop

Hopkins—hop and cans

Hornsby—horn with bees coming out

Horowitz—horror witch, harem witch

Horton—hair ton, hurting

Houlihan—hold a hand, hula hand (Hawaiian dance)

Houston—house and ton

Howard—hold a coward

Hoyle—hurl, oil with a big H

Hubbard—a hubcap with a beard

Hughes—hues (of color)

Humphrey—hump free, Hubert Humphrey

Hutchinson—hutch in the sun

Hutton—hut and ton

Hyatt—high hat, Hyatt hotels

Hyman—high man

Ingersoll—ingot and sole

Ingram—ink ram

Irving—iridescent ring

Isaacs—eye sacks, ice ax

Israel—ice rail, Star of David

Jackson—jack (car) in the sun, Reggie or Jesse Jackson

Jacobs—Jacob's ladder, jay(bird) with a cob (corn)

Jacobson—jays with cobs in the sun

Jacoby—jays with cobs in the sky

Jaffe—a bee on a giraffe

James—chains, cane

Jamison—chains in the sun

Jansen—jam sun

Jarrett—chair rat, jar and rat

Jeffers—chef hairs, chef furs

Jefferson—chef furs sun

Jeffries—chef fries, chef freeze

Jenkins—chain cans

Jennings—chain inks

Jerome—jar roam, chair roam

Jimenez—gym and (jack)ass

Johanson—giraffe's toe in the sun

Johnson—john (toilet) and sun,
    yawn sun

Jonas—show (jack)ass

Jones—bones shaped like a
    jay(bird)

Jordan—jaw dam

Joseph—hose off

Josephson—hose off sun

Joyce—juice

Kagan—case of cans, cake can

Kahn—con(vict), can

Kaiser—geyser

Kantor—can door, can tore

Kaplan—cap land

Kaufman—cough man

Kearns—kernals, coins

Keating—kiting, heat ink

Keegan—key can

Keith—keys, wreath shaped like a
    K

Kelleher—color fur

Keller—color, Helen Keller

Kelly—kelly green, kill E

Kemp—camp

Kennedy—can of tea, John F.
    Kennedy

Kenny—can knee

Kent—bent key

Keough—keyhole

Kern—kernal, coin

Kerr—car, curve

Kessler—a killing wrestler

Kimball—can ball, gamble

Kingsley—kings leaf, kings leaves

Kirby—curb bee, Kirby vacuum

Kirk—kick

Klein—climb, Calvin Klein

Knapp—nap, knap(sack)

Knowles—knolls, noels

Knox—knocks, Fort Knox

Koening—king, coin nick

Kolodny—clogged knee

Kornfeld—cornfield

Krakauer—crack hour

Kramer—creamer

Kraus—kraut (food)

Krieger—creeper, cry girl

Kroger—crow girl, Kroger
    supermarket

Krug—crook, rug with a big K

Kruger—Krugerrand (gold coin)

Lafferty—laughing area

Laird—layered, laid

Lambert—lamb bird

Landau—land dough

Lang—long

Langer—long girl

Larkin—lark inn, lark can

Larson—little arson

Latimore—ladder more

Lawrence—lower ants

Lawson—law sun

Lawton—law ton, law tin

Lazarus—laster S

Leary—Lear(jet) with a bee on it

Lederman—letter man

Lee—lee, leaf, Robert E. Lee
    (general)

Lefkowitz—left cow witch, laugh
    cow witch

Lehman—lei man, layman

Leiberman—labor man

Leibowitz—lea bow witch

Leonard—lean yard, Sugar Ray
  Leonard

Leopold—leap pole, Leo (lion) pole

Leslie—less lee, less leaves

Lester—little jester, Listerine
  (mouthwash)

Leventhal—loving thaw

Levin—L-shaped vine

Levine—lee vine

Levinson—lord of heaven and the
  sun

Levitt—level 'Vette (Corvette),
  love 'Vette

Levy—levee, Levi's

Lewis—loose witch, Jerry Lewis

Lindsey—lint sea

Lindstrom—lint strum (a banjo),
  lint strong

Livingston—living stone, living tin

Lloyd—lard, Chris Evert Lloyd

Logan—low can, log can

Loomis—loom mist, looms

Lopez—low pass, low pest

Loring—low ring, lowering

Loughram—laugh ram, lock ram

Lovell—low veil

Lovett—low 'Vette (Corvette)

Lowell—low well

Lowenthal—low ant thaw, low
  and tall

Lubin—loop bin, low bin

Lund—land

Lynch—lynching or noose

MacGregor—Mack (truck) or (Big)
  Mac crater

MacLeod—Big Mac cloud

McAllister—(Big) Mac holster

McCarthy—(Big) Mac cart tea

McClellan—(Big) Mac yellin'

McCormick—(Big) Mac core mike
  (microphone)

McCoy—decoy of a (Big) Mac

McDonald—Ronald McDonald,
  (Big) Mac with Donald Duck

McElroy—a (Big) Mac fell on a
  (Rolls) Royce

McGee—(Big) Mac key

McGrath—((Big) Mac rat

McKay—(Big) Mac hay

McLoughlin—(Big) Mac laughing

McMann—(Big) Mac man

Madison—medicine, mad at sun

Mahoney—ma (mother) honey

Malone—ma (mother) along

Maloney—ma (mother) loony

Manning—man ink

Marcus—mark kiss, mark S

Marlow—ma (mother) low

Marshall—marshal (sheriff)

Martin—Martian, Dean Martin

Martinez—mark a net, martinets

Martinson—ma (mother) tin sun

Mason—mason (jar), May sun

Matheson—mad at sun, mat in sun

Matthew(s)—mat ewe(s)

Maurer—more air, mower

Maxwell—mix well, Maxwell
  House (coffee)

Mayer—mayor

Maynard—mane yard

Mead—meat, meet (track)

Mercer—mercenary

Meredith—mare and dish

Merrill—mare ill, mare roll

Metcalf—meat calf

Meyer(s)—mirror(s), my ear(s)

Michaels—bicycles, mike (micro-phone) kills sun

Middleton—metal ton, middle ton

Miller—mill, miller, Miller High Life (beer)

Milton—melt ton, melt in

Mitchell—mitt shell

Monahan—man and hand

Monroe—man row, Marilyn Monroe

Montgomery—mound gum hairy

Moore—moor, mower (lawn)

Morales—moral less, mural

Moran—moor ran

Morgan—morgue can, moor can

Morris—more rice, Morris the Cat

Morrison—more rice in the sun, Morris in the sun

Morrow—marrow (bone), narrow

Morse—moss, Morse code

Morton—mutton (chops), moor ton

Moskowitz—mask on a witch

Moynihan—man and hand

Murphy—mercury, morphine

Murray—more (sun) rays

Nash—naked, but with a sash

Nathan—gnat tan, knot tan

Nathanson—gnat tan sun

Neill—kneel

Nelson—kneel sun

Newman—new man (wearing sales tags)

Nicholas—nickel (jack)ass

Nichols—nickels

Nicholson—nickels sun

Nixon—nicks and sun, Richard Nixon

Noonan—new nun (wearing sales tags)

Norman—north (pole) man

Norton—gnaw ton

Nugent—nugget (gold), new gent

Nussbaum—nose bomb

O'Brien—oak brain

O'Connell—oak con(vict) oar

O'Donnell—a donor fell

Ogden—egg den

O'Hara—oak-colored hair

Oliver—rotting olive

Olsen—old sun

O'Malley—home alley

O'Neal—kneel low

Oppenheim—open home

O'Reilly—oar oily

O'Rourke—oar rake

Ortiz—oar trees, orange tissue

Osborne—ostrich being born

Osgood—an old god

Oswald—a bald ostrich

Otis—oats, Otis (elevator)

Otto—a toe

Owen—owning a hen

Padgett—patch it

Paige—page

Paley—pail with a bee

Palmer—palm with a fur, Arnold Palmer

Papadopoulos—pap topple us, papa adopt us

Pappas—pa (father) pass

Parker—park with a fur, parking meter

Parkinton—parking a ton

Pastemak—paste her neck

Pastore—pastor, paste store

Patrick—pet trick

Patterson—pad in the sun

Paul—pole

Pawley—pulley

Paxton—pack tin

Peabody—pea body

Pearce—pierce

Pearson—pear or pier in the sun

Pendleton—petal ton, pedal tin

Perez—pear (jack)ass

Perkins—perking

Perlman—pearl man

Perlmutter—pearl mudder

Perry—pear with a bee, bury, Perrier

Peters—pea tears

Peterson—pea tears in the sun

Phelan—failing

Phelps—felts

Philby—fill bee, full bee

Phillips—full lips, Phillips screwdriver

Pincus—pink (jack)ass, pin cush(ion)

Platt—plate

Poindexter—point egg stir

Pollock—pole lock

Pomerantz—bomber ants

Powell—towel with a big bee, pa (father) will

Powers—power (tool) towers with a bee

Preston—pressed on

Pritchard—pitch yard

Proctor—doctor with a peg

Quinn—quinella (racetrack bet)

Rabinowitz—robin and witch

Rafferty—raft tree, raft tea

Raleigh—roll lee, raw leaves

Ramirez—ram ear (jack)ass

Rand—ran, rammed, Rand McNally (atlas)

Randall—ram doll, ran doll

Randolph—ram dolph(in)

Raphael—raffle

Rappaport—rap on port

Ratner—rat on knee

Raymond—ray mount, rain mound

Reagan—ray gun, Ronald Reagan

Reeves—far away leaves

Reinhart—rain hard, rain yard

Reiss—rice

Resnick—rest neck

Reynolds—rain knolls

Rhodes—roads, Rhodes (scholar)

Richards—rich yards

Richardson—rich yards in the sun

Richter—bricked tear, Richter scale (earthquakes)

Rigney—rig knee

Riley—rye leaf, rye leaves

Riordan—rear dam, rear down

Rivera—river, Riviera (Buick)

Roberts—rope birds, robbers

Robertson—robbers in the sun

Robeson—robe in the sun

Robinson—robin in the sun

Rogers—rod jars, Roy Rogers

Romero—room arrow, roam arrow

Rooney—ruin knee, Mickey Rooney

Rosen—rose sand, rose inn

Rosenberg—rose on (ice)berg

Rosenzweig—rose and wig

Ross—rose-colored rust

Rossiter—rose sitter

Roth—rat, wrath

Rothschild—rat child

Rubin—Reuben (sandwich), ruby bin

Rubinstein—Reuben (sandwich) and stein

Rudolph—red dolphin, Rudolph the 'Red-Nosed' Reindeer

Rupper—rose bird

Russell—rustler, rust cell
Rutledge—rat ledge
Ryan—rind
Samuels—sand mules
Samuelson—sand mule sun
Sanchez—sand chess, sand chest
Sanders—sanders
Sanford—sand Ford
Santiago—sand tea auto
Satenstein—satin stein
Saunders—sauna doors, sun doors
Sawyer—saw yard, Tom Sawyer
Saxon—sacks, sun saxophone
Sayres—Zayres (store), (sooth)sayers
Scanlon—scan line
Schechter—shack tear, shack tore
Scher—share (stock) chair
Schlesinger—sled singer
Schmidt—shy mitt
Schneider—shy bird
Schoenberg—shine (ice)berg
Schultz—shoots, shields
Schuster—shoe stir, shoe store
Schwartz—shy warts
Scott—Scott towels
Sears—Sears, Roebuck
Seaton—seat tin, seat ton
Sedgwick—sled wick, sledge wick
Seiden—sign den
Seward—steward
Saxton—sacks ton, sexy ton
Schaeffer—shaver, shave fur
Seymour—see moor
Shannon—chaining, shy cannon
Shapiro—shy pear with a piece of gold in it
Shaw—shawl, shore
Shay—shade
Sheehan—shoe ham
Sheldon—shelled on, shell down

Shelley—shell leaf, shell leaves
Shelton—shell ton, shell tin
Sheridan—share a den, Sheraton (hotels)
Sherman—shirt man, Sherman tank
Shulman—school man
Siegel—seagull
Silvera—silver
Simmons—summons, Simmons (mattress), cinnamon
Simms—seams, shins
Simon—sign man, Simon says
Simpson—shrimp in the sun
Sinclair—sun chair, Sinclair gas
Sitron—sit run, Citroën (car)
Skidmore—skid moor
Slade—slate, slayed
Slater—slate tear, slate tore
Sloan—silly loan (silly investment)
Slocum—slow comb
Smith—blacksmith, anvil
Snead—sneeze, Sam Snead
Snyder—shy door
Solomon—solo man, wise man
Sommers—summers
Spaulding—spoiled ink, scalding
Spector—spectator, (in)spector
Spencer—pen sore, pen store
Sperry—spare bee, spear a bee
Squire—square, school choir
Stacey—state with a bee in it
Stafford—staff Ford
Stanley—stand leaf, stand leaves
Stanton—stand tin, stand
Sterling—sterling silver, starling
Stern—stern (of a boat)
Stevens—stove fins
Stevenson—stove fins in the sun
Stewart—steward, stew art

Stoddard—stood in the yard

Strauss—straw house

Sullivan—sold a van

Sumner—summer

Sutherland—other land

Sutton—sudden, setting

Swanson—swan in the sun, Swanson (TV dinner)

Sweeney—sweet knee

Taft—taffy

Talmadge—tall midget, tall badge

Tannenbaum—tanning

Tate—tight, tea ate

Taub—tub

Taylor—tailor

Teitelbaum—title bomb

Terry—terry cloth (towel)

Thatcher—man who thatches roofs

Theodore—having tea near a door

Thomas—thumb (jack)ass

Thompson—tom-tom drum in the sun

Thorndyke—thorn dike

Thorpe—tore up

Tipton—tip ton, tip tin

Tobias—tow bias, toe buy us

Todd—toddle, toad

Tompkins—thumb cans

Torres—tore (jack)ass, Taurus

Tracy—trace E, tray sea

Travers—travel

Treadway—tread (tire) weigh

Trent—bent tree

Trowbridge—drawbridge

Trumbull—drum bull

Tucker—trucker

Tuttle—turtle

Tyler—tiler

Udall—U-shaped doll, yodel

Ullmann—old man

Under—under, an udder (cow)

Valdez—vault with a (jack)ass in it

Van Buren—van and bureau

Vance—a man dancing in a van

Vargas—far gas

Vaughan—a van with a john (toilet) in it

Victor—winner, victory, Viking with a torn muscle

Vincent—vintage costing a cent, fins costing a cent

Vogel—vocal cords

Wagner—wagon knee

Walker—baby walker

Wallace—wall lace, wall ice

Walsh—waltz

Walters—wall tears, waiters

Walton—wall ton, wall tin

Warner—war knee

Warren—war wren

Warrington—war ring ton

Washington—washing machine, George Washington

Wasserman—water man

Watkins—watt cans

Watson—watt in the sun, wet sun

Watts—watts, light bulb

Waverly—wave fur leaf

Wayne—walking through water with a cane

Weber—web bar

Webster—web stir, dictionary

Weeks—calendar week

Weiner—weiner (frank)

Weintraub—wine tub

Weiss—weasel

Welch—Welch (grape juice), wino's belch

Wellington—ton of ink in a well

Wesley—wet lee, wet leaves

West—waterproof vest

Wexler—wax law

Whalen—whale inn

Whetman—wet man

Whitman—witty man

Whitney—wet knee

Whittaker—wet a car

Wilkes—wilts, milks with a big W

Wilkinson—wild kin (son)

Williams—will yams

Williamson—will yams in the sun

Wilson—will in the sun

Winston—Winston Churchill

Winthrop—winter throb

Woolsey—wool sea

Worthington—work ink ton

Wright—write

Wrightson—write in the sun

York—yellow fork

Young—young, yellow sun

Zachary—sack hairy

Zeigler—sick law

Zimmer—simmer (cooking)

Zimmerman—a man simmering (cannibals' pot)

Zucker—sucker on a zebra

Zuckerman—suckered man on a zebra

For more information about tapes, workshops, and live appearances regarding Kevin Trudeau and "Mega Memory," please call or write:

American Memory Institute
"The World's Largest Memory Training School™"
2038 N. Clark, #354
Chicago, Illinois 60614
(312) 975-0455

Index